Answer Key

Learn To Read English With Directions In Spanish
Answer Key
Classwork
Color Edition

Classwork

ISBN 978-1-945738-16-6
© 2022 – Wendy A. Charles & Alexander J. Charles
All Rights Reserved
Baldwin, New York
www.intellastic.com

All rights reserved. No portion of this book may be reproduced, stored in a retrieval system, or transmitted in any form or by any means – electronic, mechanical, photocopy, recording, video presentation, private instruction, scanning or other – except for brief quotations in critical reviews or articles, without the prior written permission of the writers.

All Rights Reserved. Printed in the USA.

Answer Key

Table of Contents

Unit A

Lesson 1.1	Reading Words with the Letter A/a	1
Lesson 1.2	Reading Words with the Short Vowel "a" Sound	2
Lesson 1.2	Reading & Writing Words with the Short Vowel "a" Sound	3
Lesson 1.3	Reading Words with the Long Vowel "a" Sound	4
Lesson 1.3	Reading & Writing Words with the Long Vowel "a" Sound	5
Lessons 1.2 & 1.3	Reading Short Vowel and Long Vowel Words	6
Lesson 1.4	Reading Words with the "age" Letter Combination	7
Lesson 1.5	Reading Words with the "ai" Vowel Pair	8
Lesson 1.6	Reading Letter "a" Words with the Schwa Sound	9
Lesson 1.7	Reading Words with the "ar" Letter Combination	10
Lesson 1.7	Reading Words with the "ar" Letter Combination	11
Lesson 1.8	Reading Words with a Silent Letter "a"	12
Unit Review	Reading Words with Vowel "a" Sounds: /ă/, /ā/, /ə/ & Silent	13
Lesson 1.9	Reading Multisyllable Words	14
Lesson 1.9	Reading Multisyllable Words	15
Lesson 1.10	Proper and Common Nouns and Adjectives	16

Unit B

Lesson 2.1	Reading Words with the Letter B/b	17
Lesson 2.2	Reading Words with the "br" Letter Combination	18
Lesson 2.3	Reading Words with the "bl" Letter Combination	19
Lesson 2.3	Reading Words with the "ble" Letter Combination	20
Lesson 2.4	Reading Words with the "mb" Letter Combination	21
Lesson 2.4	Reading Words with the "bt" Letter Combination	22
Lesson 2.5	Reading Words with a Silent Letter "b"	23
Lesson 2.6	Reading Multisyllable Words	24
Lesson 2.6	Reading Multisyllable Words	25
Lesson 2.7	Proper and Common Nouns and Adjectives	26

iii

Classwork

Unit C

Lesson 3.1	Reading Words with the Letter C/c	27
Lesson 3.1	Reading Words with the Hard Letter "c"	28
Lesson 3.2	Reading Words with the Soft Letter "c"	29
Lessons 3.1 & 3.2	Reading Hard Letter "c" and Soft Letter "c" Words	30
Lesson 3.3	Reading Words with the "cr" Letter Combination	31
Lesson 3.4	Reading Words with the "cl" Letter Combination	32
Lesson 3.4	Reading Words with the "cle" Letter Combination	33
Lesson 3.5	Reading Words with the "ct" Letter Combination	34
Lesson 3.6	Reading Soft Letter "c" Words	35
Lesson 3.6	Reading Soft Letter "c" Words	36
Lesson 3.7	Reading Words with the "ch" Letter Combination	37
Lesson 3.8	Reading Words with the "cc" Letter Combination	38
Lesson 3.9	Reading Words with a Silent Letter "c"	39
Lesson 3.10	Reading Multisyllable Words	40
Lesson 3.10	Reading Multisyllable Words	41
Lesson 3.11	Proper and Common Nouns and Adjectives	42

Unit D

Lesson 4.1	Reading Words with the Letter D/d	43
Lesson 4.2	Reading Letter "d" Words with the /d/ Sound & /j/ Sound	44
Lesson 4.2	Reading Words with the "dr" Letter Combination	45
Lesson 4.3	Reading Words with the "ed" Suffix/Past Tense Verbs	46
Lesson 4.4	Reading Words with a Silent Letter "d"	47
Lesson 4.5	Reading Multisyllable Words	48
Lesson 4.5	Reading Multisyllable Words	49
Lesson 4.6	Proper and Common Nouns and Adjectives	50

Unit E

Lesson 5.1	Reading Words with the Letter E/e	51
Lesson 5.2	Reading Words with the Short Vowel "e" Sound	52
Lesson 5.2	Reading & Writing Words with the Short Vowel "e" Sound	53

Answer Key

Lesson 5.3	Reading Words with the Long Vowel "e" Sound	54
Lesson 5.3	Reading & Writing Words with the Long Vowel "e" Sound	55
Lessons 5.2 & 5.3	Reading Short Vowel and Long Vowel Words	56
Lesson 5.4	Reading Words with Letter "e" Vowel Pairs	57
Lesson 5.5	Reading Words with the Final Letter "e"	58
Lesson 5.6	Reading Letter "e" Words with the Schwa Vowel Sound	59
Lesson 5.7	Reading Words with the "er" Letter Combination	60
Lesson 5.8	Reading Words with the "eu" and "ew" Letter Combinations	61
Lesson 5.9	Reading Words with the "ey" Letter Combination	62
Lesson 5.10	Reading Words with a Silent Letter "e"	63
Unit Review	Reading Words with Vowel "e" Sounds: /ĕ/, /ē/, /ə/ & Silent	64
Lesson 5.11	Reading Multisyllable Words	65
Lesson 5.11	Reading Multisyllable Words	66
Lesson 5.12	Proper and Common Nouns and Adjectives	67

Unit F

Lesson 6.1	Reading Words with the Letter F/f	68
Lesson 6.2	Reading Words with the "fr" Letter Combination	69
Lesson 6.3	Reading Words with the "fl" Letter Combination	70
Lesson 6.3	Reading Words with the "fle" Letter Combination	71
Lesson 6.4	Reading Words with the "ft," "lf" and "ff" Letter Combinations	72
Lesson 6.5	Reading Words with a Silent Letter "f"	73
Lesson 6.6	Reading Singular and Plural forms of Words Ending in "-f" & "-fe"	74
Lesson 6.7	Reading Multisyllable Words	75
Lesson 6.7	Reading Multisyllable Words	76
Lesson 6.8	Proper and Common Nouns and Adjectives	77

Unit G

Lesson 7.1	Reading Words with the Letter G/g	78
Lesson 7.1	Reading Words with the Hard Letter "g"	79
Lesson 7.2	Reading Words with the Soft Letter G/g	80
Lessons 7.1 & 7.2	Reading Hard Letter "g" and Soft Letter "g" Words	81

Classwork

Lessons 7.1 & 7.2	Reading Hard Letter "g" and Soft Letter "g" Words	82
Lesson 7.3	Reading Words with the "gr" Letter Combination	83
Lesson 7.4	Reading Words with the "gl" Letter Combination	84
Lesson 7.4	Reading Words with the "gle" Letter Combination	85
Lesson 7.5	Reading Words with the "gh" Letter Combination	86
Lesson 7.6	Reading Words with the "gn" Letter Combination	87
Lesson 7.7	Reading Words with a Silent Letter "g"	88
Lesson 7.8	Reading Multisyllable Words	89
Lesson 7.8	Reading Multisyllable Words	90
Lesson 7.9	Proper and Common Nouns and Adjectives	91

Unit H

Lesson 8.1	Reading Words with the Letter H/h	92
Lesson 8.2	Reading Words with the Letter "h" Combinations: "sh," "wh," "ch," "th," "rh," "ph" and "gh"	93
Lesson 8.2	Reading Words with the Letter "h" Combinations: "sh," "wh," "ch," "th," "rh," "ph," "gh" and "sch"	94
Lesson 8.3	Reading Words with a Silent Letter "h"	95
Lesson 8.4	Reading Multisyllable Words	96
Lesson 8.4	Reading Multisyllable Words	97
Lesson 8.5	Proper and Common Nouns and Adjectives	98

Unit I

Lesson 9.1	Reading Words with the Letter I/i	99
Lesson 9.2	Reading Words with the Short Vowel "i" Sound	100
Lesson 9.2	Reading & Writing Words with the Short Vowel "i" Sound	101
Lesson 9.3	Reading Words with the Long Vowel "i" Sound	102
Lesson 9.3	Reading & Writing Words with the Long Vowel "i" Sound	103
Lessons 9.2 & 9.3	Reading Short Vowel and Long Vowel Words	104
Lesson 9.4	Reading Words with Letter "i" Vowel Pairs	105
Lesson 9.5	Reading Words with the Final Letter "i"	106
Lesson 9.6	Reading Letter "i" Words with the Schwa Vowel Sound	107

Answer Key

Lesson 9.7	Reading Words with the "ir" Letter Combination	108
Lesson 9.8	Reading Letter "i" Words with the Long Vowel "e" Sound	109
Lesson 9.9	Reading Words with a Silent Letter "i"	110
Unit Review	Reading Words with Vowel "i" Sounds: /ĭ/, /ī/, /ə/ & Silent	111
Lesson 9.10	Reading Multisyllable Words	112
Lesson 9.10	Reading Multisyllable Words	113
Lesson 9.11	Proper and Common Nouns and Adjectives	114

Unit J

Lesson 10.1	Reading Words with the Letter J/j	115
Lesson 10.2	Reading Multisyllable Words	116
Lesson 10.2	Reading Multisyllable Words	117
Lesson 10.3	Proper and Common Nouns and Adjectives	118

Unit K

Lesson 11.1	Reading Words with the Letter K/k	119
Lesson 11.2	Reading Words with the Letter "k" and "ck" Letter Combination	120
Lesson 11.3	Reading Words with the "kle" Letter Combination	121
Lesson 11.4	Reading Words with a Silent Letter "k"	122
Lesson 11.5	Reading Multisyllable Words	123
Lesson 11.5	Reading Multisyllable Words	124
Lesson 11.6	Proper and Common Nouns and Adjectives	125

Unit L

Lesson 12.1	Reading Words with the Letter L/l	126
Lesson 12.2	Reading Words with the Letter "l" Combinations: "fl," "pl" & "sl"	127
Lesson 12.3	Reading Words with a Silent Letter "l"	128
Lesson 12.4	Reading Multisyllable Words	129
Lesson 12.4	Reading Multisyllable Words	130
Lesson 12.5	Proper and Common Nouns and Adjectives	131

Classwork

Unit M

Lesson 13.1	Reading Words with the Letter M/m	132
Lesson 13.2	Reading Words with a Silent Letter "m"	133
Lesson 13.3	Reading Multisyllable Words	134
Lesson 13.3	Reading Multisyllable Words	135
Lesson 13.4	Proper and Common Nouns and Adjectives	136

Unit N

Lesson 14.1	Reading Words with the Letter N/n	137
Lesson 14.2	Reading Words with the "ng" Letter Combination	138
Lesson 14.3	Reading Words with a Silent Letter "n"	139
Lesson 14.4	Reading Multisyllable Words	140
Lesson 14.4	Reading Multisyllable Words	141
Lesson 14.5	Proper and Common Nouns and Adjectives	142

Unit O

Lesson 15.1	Reading Words with the Letter O/o	143
Lesson 15.2	Reading Words with the Short Vowel "o" Sound	144
Lesson 15.2	Reading & Writing Words with the Short Vowel "o" Sound	145
Lesson 15.3	Reading Words with the Long Vowel "o" Sound	146
Lesson 15.3	Reading & Writing Words with the Long Vowel "o" Sound	147
Lessons 15.2 & 15.3	Reading Short Vowel and Long Vowel Words	148
Lesson 15.4	Reading Words with Letter "o" Vowel Pairs	149
Lesson 15.5	Reading Words with the Final Letter "o"	150
Lesson 15.6	Reading Letter "o" Words with the Schwa Vowel Sound	151
Lesson 15.7	Reading Words with Vowel "o" Sounds: /ŏ/, /ō/ & /o͞o/	152
Lesson 15.8	Reading Words with the "or" Letter Combination	153
Lesson 15.8	Reading Words with the "or" Letter Combination	154
Lesson 15.9	Reading Words with a Silent Letter "o"	155
Unit Review	Reading Words with Vowel "o" Sounds: /ŏ/, /ō/, /ə/ & Silent	156
Lesson 15.10	Reading Multisyllable Words	157
Lesson 15.10	Reading Multisyllable Words	158

Answer Key

Lesson 15.11	Proper and Common Nouns and Adjectives	159
Unit P		
Lesson 16.1	Reading Words with the Letter P/p	160
Lesson 16.2	Reading Words with the "ph" Letter Combination	161
Lesson 16.3	Reading Words with the "pr" Letter Combination	162
Lesson 16.4	Reading Words with the "pl" Letter Combination	163
Lesson 16.4	Reading Words with the "ple" Letter Combination	164
Lesson 16.5	Reading Words with a Silent Letter "p"	165
Lesson 16.6	Reading Multisyllable Words	166
Lesson 16.6	Reading Multisyllable Words	167
Lesson 16.7	Proper and Common Nouns and Adjectives	168
Unit Q		
Lesson 17.1	Reading Words with the Letter Q/q	169
Lesson 17.2	Reading Words with the Letter "q" and "qu" Letter Combination	170
Lesson 17.2	Reading Words with the "qu" Letter Combination	171
Lesson 17.3	Reading Multisyllable Words	172
Lesson 17.3	Reading Multisyllable Words	173
Lesson 17.4	Proper and Common Nouns and Adjectives	174
Unit R		
Lesson 18.1	Reading Words with the Letter R/r	175
Lesson 18.2	Reading Words with the Letter "r" Combinations: "br," "cr," "dr," "fr," "gr," "pr" and "tr"	176
Lesson 18.3	Reading Multisyllable Words	177
Lesson 18.3	Reading Multisyllable Words	178
Lesson 18.4	Proper and Common Nouns and Adjectives	179
Unit S		
Lesson 19.1	Reading Words with the Letter S/s	180
Lesson 19.1	Reading Words with the Letter S/s	181

Classwork

Lesson 19.2	Reading Words with the "sion," "sial" & "scious" Suffixes	182
Lesson 19.3	Reading Words with the "sch" Letter Combination	183
Lesson 19.4	Reading Words with the "scr," "shr," "spr" & "str" Letter Combinations	184
Lesson 19.5	Reading Words with the "sl" & "sle" Letter Combinations	185
Lesson 19.5	Reading Words with the "sle" Letter Combination	186
Lesson 19.6	Reading Words with the "sm" Letter Combination	187
Lesson 19.7	Reading Words with the "ss" Letter Combination	188
Lesson 19.8	Reading Words with a Silent Letter "s"	189
Lesson 19.9	Reading Multisyllable Words	190
Lesson 19.9	Reading Multisyllable Words	191
Lesson 19.10	Proper and Common Nouns and Adjectives	192

Unit T

Lesson 20.1	Reading Words with the Letter T/t	193
Lesson 20.2	Reading Words with the "thm" Letter Combination	194
Lesson 20.3	Reading Words with the "tion," "tial" & "tious" Suffixes	195
Lesson 20.4	Reading Words with the "tr" Letter Combination	196
Lesson 20.5	Reading Words with the "tle" Letter Combination	197
Lesson 20.6	Reading Words with the Letter "t" Sounds	198
Lesson 20.7	Reading Words with a Silent Letter "t"	199
Lesson 20.8	Reading Multisyllable Words	200
Lesson 20.8	Reading Multisyllable Words	201
Lesson 20.9	Proper and Common Nouns and Adjectives	202

Unit U

Lesson 21.1	Reading Words with the Letter U/u	203
Lesson 21.2	Reading Words with the Short Vowel "u" Sound	204
Lesson 21.2	Reading & Writing Words with the Short Vowel "u" Sound	205
Lesson 21.3	Reading Words with the Long Vowel "u" Sound	206
Lesson 21.3	Reading & Writing Words with the Long Vowel "u" Sound	207
Lessons 21.2 & 21.3	Reading Short Vowel and Long Vowel Words	208
Lesson 21.4	Reading Words with Letter "u" Vowel Pairs	209

Answer Key

Lesson 21.5	Reading Words with the Final Letter "u"	210
Lesson 21.6	Reading Letter "u" Words with the Schwa Vowel Sound	211
Lesson 21.7	Reading Words with the "ur" Letter Combination	212
Lesson 21.8	Reading Words with a Silent Letter "u"	213
Unit Review	Reading Words with Vowel "u" Sounds: /ŭ/, /o͞o/, /ə/ & Silent	214
Lesson 21.9	Reading Multisyllable Words	215
Lesson 21.9	Reading Multisyllable Words	216
Lesson 21.10	Proper and Common Nouns and Adjectives	217

Unit V

Lesson 22.1	Reading Words with the Letter V/v	218
Lesson 22.2	Reading Multisyllable Words	219
Lesson 22.2	Reading Multisyllable Words	220
Lesson 22.3	Proper and Common Nouns and Adjectives	221

Unit W

Lesson 23.1	Reading Words with the Letter W/w	222
Lesson 23.2	Reading Words with a Vowel before the Letter "w"	223
Lesson 23.3	Reading Words with a Silent "w" and "wr" Letter Combination	224
Lesson 23.3	Reading Words with a Silent Letter "w"	225
Lesson 23.4	Reading Multisyllable Words	226
Lesson 23.4	Reading Multisyllable Words	227
Lesson 23.5	Proper and Common Nouns and Adjectives	228

Unit X

Lesson 24.1	Reading Words with the Letter X/x	229
Lesson 24.1	Reading Words with the Letter X/x	230
Lesson 24.2	Reading Multisyllable Words	231
Lesson 24.2	Reading Multisyllable Words	232
Lesson 24.3	Proper and Common Nouns and Adjectives	233

Classwork

Unit Y

Lesson 25.1	Reading Words with the Letter Y/y	234
Lesson 25.1	Reading Words with the Letter Y/y	235
Lesson 25.2	Reading Words with a Vowel before the Letter "y"	236
Lesson 25.3	Reading Words with the "cy" Letter Combination	237
Lesson 25.4	Reading Words with the Final Letter "y"	238
Lesson 25.5	Reading Words with the "yr" Letter Combination	239
Lesson 25.6	Reading Letter "y" Words with the Schwa Sound	240
Lesson 25.7	Reading Words with a Silent Letter "y"	241
Lesson 25.8	Reading Multisyllable Words	242
Lesson 25.8	Reading Multisyllable Words	243
Lesson 25.9	Proper and Common Nouns and Adjectives	244

Unit Z

Lesson 26.1	Reading Words with the Letter Z/z	245
Lesson 26.1	Reading Words with the Letter Z/z	246
Lesson 26.2	Reading Words with a Silent Letter "z"	247
Lesson 26.3	Reading Multisyllable Words	248
Lesson 26.3	Reading Multisyllable Words	249
Lesson 26.4	Proper and Common Nouns and Adjectives	250

Appendix

Appendix 1.0	Introduction of the Letter A/a	251
Appendix 2.0	Introduction of the Letter B/b	252
Appendix 2.0	Letter Recognition B/b	253
Appendix 3.0	Introduction of the Letter C/c	254
Appendix 3.0	Letter Recognition C/c	255
Appendix 4.0	Introduction of the Letter D/d	256
Appendix 4.0	Letter Recognition D/d	257
Appendix 5.0	Introduction of the Letter E/e	258
Appendix 6.0	Introduction of the Letter F/f	259
Appendix 6.0	Letter Recognition F/f	260

Appendix 7.0	Introduction of the Letter G/g	261
Appendix 7.0	Letter Recognition G/g	262
Appendix 8.0	Introduction of the Letter H/h	263
Appendix 8.0	Letter Recognition H/h	264
Appendix 9.0	Introduction of the Letter I/i	265
Appendix 10.0	Introduction of the Letter J/j	266
Appendix 10.0	Letter Recognition J/j	267
Appendix 11.0	Introduction of the Letter K/k	268
Appendix 11.0	Letter Recognition K/k	269
Appendix 12.0	Introduction of the Letter L/l	270
Appendix 12.0	Letter Recognition L/l	271
Appendix 13.0	Introduction of the Letter M/m	272
Appendix 13.0	Letter Recognition M/m	273
Appendix 14.0	Introduction of the Letter N/n	274
Appendix 14.0	Letter Recognition N/n	275
Appendix 15.0	Introduction of the Letter O/o	276
Appendix 16.0	Introduction of the Letter P/p	277
Appendix 16.0	Letter Recognition P/p	278
Appendix 17.0	Introduction of the Letter Q/q	279
Appendix 17.0	Letter Recognition Q/q	280
Appendix 18.0	Introduction of the Letter R/r	281
Appendix 18.0	Letter Recognition R/r	282
Appendix 19.0	Introduction of the Letter S/s	283
Appendix 19.0	Letter Recognition S/s	284
Appendix 20.0	Introduction of the Letter T/t	285
Appendix 20.0	Letter Recognition T/t	286
Appendix 21.0	Introduction of the Letter U/u	287
Appendix 22.0	Introduction of the Letter V/v	288
Appendix 22.0	Letter Recognition V/v	289
Appendix 23.0	Introduction of the Letter W/w	290
Appendix 23.0	Letter Recognition W/w	291

Classwork

Appendix 24.0	Introduction of the Letter X/x	292
Appendix 24.0	Letter Recognition X/x	293
Appendix 25.0	Introduction of the Letter Y/y	294
Appendix 25.0	Letter Recognition Y/y	295
Appendix 26.0	Introduction of the Letter Z/z	296
Appendix 26.0	Letter Recognition Z/z	297

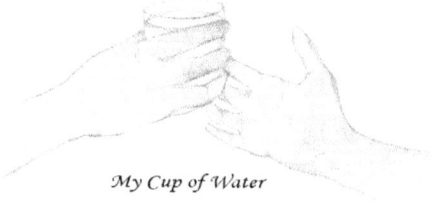

My Cup of Water

Answer Key

Name: _____ Date: ___/___/_____ Score: _____

Lesson 1.1

Reading Words with the Letter A/a

✓ Lesson Check Point

Directions: Read each target word. Find the letter "a" and put a check (✓) in the column that identifies its position: beginning, within or end.
Direcciones: Lee cada palabra objetivo. Encuentra la letra "a" y coloca un signo de verificación (✓) en la columna que identifique su posición: inicio, interior o final.

Target Words	Beginning (First Letter)	Within	End (Last Letter)
1. taxicab		✓	
2. black		✓	
3. anklet	✓		
4. opera			✓
5. above	✓		

Directions: Read each target word. Read the words in the row and circle the word that has a different vowel "a" sound.
Direcciones: Lee cada palabra objetivo. Lee las palabras en la fila y encierra la palabra que tenga un sonido vocal "a" diferente.

Target Words				
6. am	cat	sand	(pail)	bank
7. apple	cab	(sofa)	back	sad
8. happy	band	ant	sank	(cake)
9. pants	(zebra)	sat	cap	man
10. thanks	cash	(bake)	map	pan

Learn To Read English With Directions In Spanish

Classwork

 Name: _____ Date: ___/___/_____ Score: _____

Lesson 1.2

Reading Words with the Short Vowel "a" Sound

✓ **Lesson Check Point**

Directions: Read the words in the four boxes. Circle two words with the short vowel /ă/ sound. The anchor word for the short vowel /ă/ sound is <u>apple</u>.

Direcciones: Lee las palabras en las cuatro cajas. Encierra en un círculo dos palabras con el sonido vocal corto /ă/. La palabra ejemplo para el sonido vocal corto /ă/ es la palabra, <u>apple</u>.

day	(hat)	(grass)	(nap)	agree	(yam)
(cap)	sofa	tuna	lake	(sand)	paint

Asia	(pad)	walk	father	(flag)	(man)
ago	(back)	(flap)	(map)	grape	bake

Directions: Read the words in the four boxes. Circle two words that rhyme. Rhyming words have the same ending sound, such as <u>tap</u> and <u>map</u>.

Direcciones: Lee las palabras en las cuatro cajas. Encierra en un círculo dos que rimen. Las palabras que riman tienen el mismo sonido al final, como <u>tap</u> y <u>map</u>.

(had)	tax	(nap)	cake	(camp)	(lamp)
(dad)	zap	cape	(map)	spa	alike

away	plane	game	(cat)	take	(tan)
(ran)	(man)	(sat)	lane	ate	(ran)

Answer Key

 Name: _____ Date: ___/___/_____ Score: _____

Lesson 1.2

Reading & Writing Words with the Short Vowel "a" Sound

✓ Lesson Check Point

 Directions: Read each sentence and underline three words with the short vowel /ă/ sound. Then, write the underlined words on the lines below. The anchor word for the short vowel /ă/ sound is apple.

Direcciones: Lee cada oración y subraya tres palabras con el sonido vocal corto /ă/. Luego, escribe las palabras subrayadas en las líneas siguientes. La palabra ejemplo para el sonido vocal corto /ă/ es la palabra, apple.

Model

Ann raised her hand in class.

    Ann   hand   class

1. Pam's tan hat is faded.

    Pam's   tan   hat

2. My father asked for apples and grapes.

    asked   apples   and

3. Sam and Dan walked by the lake.

    Sam   and   Dan

4. David planted the flag in the sand.

    planted   flag   sand

5. My music teacher plays the sax in a large jazz band.

    sax   jazz   band

Learn To Read English With Directions In Spanish

Classwork

 Name: _____ Date:___/___/_____ Score: _____

Lesson 1.3

Reading Words with the Long Vowel "a" Sound

✓ Lesson Check Point

 Directions: Read the words in the four boxes. Circle two words with the long vowel /ā/ sound. The anchor word for the long vowel /ā/ sound is <u>ape</u>.

Direcciones: Lee las palabras en las cuatro cajas. Encierra en un círculo dos palabras con el sonido vocal largo /ā/. La palabra ejemplo para el sonido vocal largo /ā/ es la palabra, <u>ape</u>.

cap	(sale)
talk	(nail)

alike	cat
(gain)	(pace)

(ate)	sofa
(wave)	tap

rat	(lake)
(male)	ago

(page)	(mate)
pan	about

(stay)	above
alone	(sail)

 Directions: Read the words in the four boxes. Circle two words that rhyme. Rhyming words have the same ending sound, such as <u>wait</u> and <u>date</u>.

Direcciones: Lee las palabras en las cuatro cajas. Encierra en un círculo dos palabras que rimen. Las palabras que riman tienen el mismo sonido al final, como <u>wait</u> y <u>date</u>.

mama	(wake)
(take)	ban

tuna	(lane)
dad	(cane)

land	puma
(rate)	(late)

(came)	man
(same)	panda

(tale)	Asia
bran	(mail)

(pave)	(gave)
villa	have

Answer Key

Name: _____ Date:___/___/_____ Score:_____

Lesson 1.3

Reading & Writing Words with the Long Vowel "a" Sound

✓ **Lesson Check Point**

Directions: Read each sentence and underline three words with the long vowel /ā/ sound. Then, write the underlined words on the lines below. The anchor word for the long vowel /ā/ sound is <u>ape</u>.

Direcciones: Lee cada oración y subraya tres palabras con el sonido vocal largo /ā/. Luego, escribe las palabras subrayadas en las líneas siguientes. La palabra ejemplo para el sonido vocal largo /ā/ es la palabra, <u>ape</u>.

Model

Ann has <u>grapes</u> and <u>cake</u> on her <u>plate</u>.

| grapes | cake | plate |

1. <u>Dain</u> can't <u>wait</u> to <u>paint</u> the chair.

| Dain | wait | paint |

2. The <u>skates</u> and <u>sails</u> are packed in the <u>basement</u>.

| skates | sails | basement |

3. Alvin did not <u>take</u> the large slice of <u>cake</u> from the <u>plate</u>.

| take | cake | plate |

4. <u>Dale</u> Anderson said, "Beware of garter <u>snakes</u> by the <u>lake</u>."

| Dale | snakes | lake |

5. Jackson and Andrew sold chocolate <u>cupcakes</u> at Annie's <u>bake</u> <u>sale</u>.

| cupcakes | bake | sale |

Learn To Read English With Directions In Spanish

Classwork

Name: _____ Date: ___/___/_____ Score: _____

Review Lessons 1.2 & 1.3 / Reading Short Vowel and Long Vowel Words

Directions: Read the target words in the word box. In the first column, write the words that have the short vowel /ă/ sound, as in the word apple. In the second column, write the words that have the long vowel /ā/ sound, as in the word ape.

Direcciones: Lee las palabras objetivo en el cuadro de texto. En la primera columna, escribe las palabras que tengan el sonido vocal corto /ă/, como en la palabra inglés apple. En la segunda columna, escribe las palabras que tengan el sonido vocal largo /ā/, como en la palabra inglés ape.

Target Word Box				
bagel	grass	glad	clan	basic
trap	came	taken	grapes	hat
fame	maps	sand	stay	gain
slaps	bake	train	flag	brand

Letter "a" has the /ă/ sound as in the word apple

Letter "a" has the /ā/ sound as in the word ape

hat	gain
glad	stay
clan	came
trap	bake
flag	train
grass	fame
sand	basic
slaps	bagel
maps	taken
brand	grapes

Answer Key

 Name: _____ Date: ___/___/_____ Score: _____

Lesson 1.4

Reading Words with the "age" Letter Combination

✓ Lesson Check Point

 Directions: Read each target word. Find the "age" letter combination and put a check (✓) in the column that correctly identifies its sounds.
Direcciones: Lee cada palabra objetivo. Encuentra la combinación de letras "age" y coloca un signo de verificación (✓) en la columna que identifique correctamente su sonido.

Target Words	"age" has the /ā/ + /j/ sounds as in the word stage	"age" has the /ĭ/ + /j/ sounds as in the word package	"age" has the /ä/ + /j/ or /ä/ + /zh/ sounds as in the word massage
1. camouflage			✓
2. Anchorage		✓	
3. enrage	✓		
4. baggage		✓	
5. teenagers	✓		

 Directions: Read each sentence and underline the word that has an "age" letter combination that has the /ĭ/ + /j/ sounds, as in the word package.
Direcciones: Lee cada oración y subraya la palabra que tenga la combinación de letras "age" que tenga los sonidos /ĭ/ + /j/, como en la palabra inglés package.

6. The teenager's albums and books are in the cottage.

7. The teenager's luggage set was stolen from the airport.

8. My large boxes from Anchorage, Alaska are on the stage.

9. The backstage manager ate apple pie and drank lemonade.

10. Everyone in the entourage had massages after their long voyage.

Classwork

 Name: _____ Date:___/___/_____ Score:_____

Lesson 1.5

Reading Words with the "ai" Vowel Pair

✓ Lesson Check Point

 Directions: Read each target word. Circle the word in the column that has the same "ai" sound as the target word.
Direcciones: Lee cada palabra objetivo. Encierra en un círculo la palabra en la columna que tenga el mismo sonido "ai" que la palabra objetivo.

mail	a. said
	b. **male** (circled)

wait	**a. basic** (circled)
	b. land

paid	**a. change** (circled)
	b. salt

aim	a. plant
	b. page (circled)

 Directions: Read each target word. Put a check (✓) under the correct column heading.
Direcciones: Lee cada palabra objetivo. Coloca un signo de verificación (✓) bajo el encabezado de la columna correcta.

Target Words	Words have the long "a" sound as in the word <u>sail</u>	Words do not have the long "a" sound
1. tail	✓	
2. trait	✓	
3. plaid		✓
4. pain	✓	

Learn To Read English With Directions In Spanish

Answer Key

 Name: _____ Date: ___/___/_____ Score: _____

Lesson 1.6

Reading Letter "a" Words with the Schwa Vowel Sound

✓ Lesson Check Point

 Directions: Read each target word. Circle the word in the column that has the same "a" sound as the target word.
Direcciones: Lee cada palabra objetivo. Encierra en un círculo la palabra en la columna que tenga el mismo sonido "a" que la palabra objetivo.

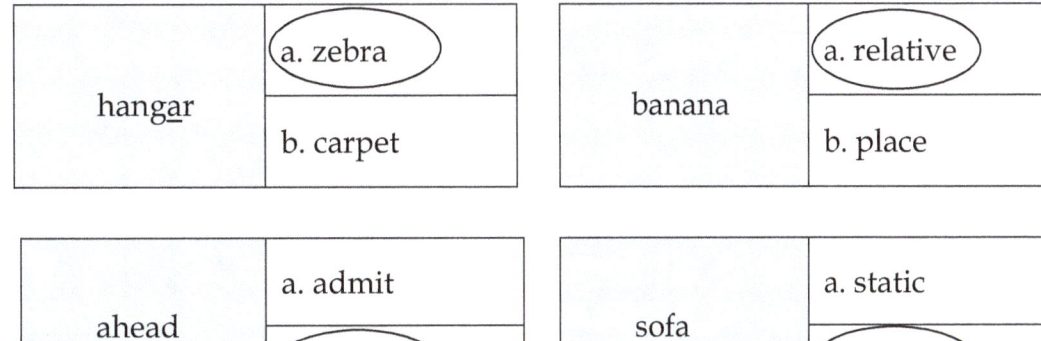

 Directions: Read each sentence and underline the letter "a" word that has the schwa vowel /ə/ sound. The anchor word for the letter "a" schwa vowel sound is sofa.
Direcciones: Lee cada oración y subraya la letra "a" en palabras que tengan el sonido schwa /ə/. La palabra ancla para el sonido de la vocal schwa de la letra "a" es sofa.

1. The class is going to the <u>opera</u>.

2. The Erie <u>Canal</u> is an awesome place.

3. On Saturday, Ann ate two large <u>bananas</u>.

4. This year, I have an <u>amazing</u> math teacher.

5. Dr. Anderson paid the cab driver three <u>dollars</u>.

6. Andrew ate whole wheat <u>spaghetti</u> with white sauce.

Classwork

 Name: _____ Date: ___/___/_____ Score: _____

Lesson 1.7

Reading Words with the "ar" Letter Combination

✓ Lesson Check Point

 Directions: Read each target word. Circle the word in the column that has the same "a" + "r" sounds as the target word.
Direcciones: Lee cada palabra objetivo. Encierra en un círculo la palabra en la columna que tenga los mismos sonidos "a" + "r" que la palabra objetivo.

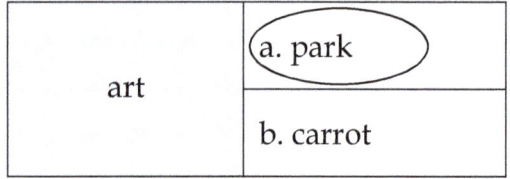
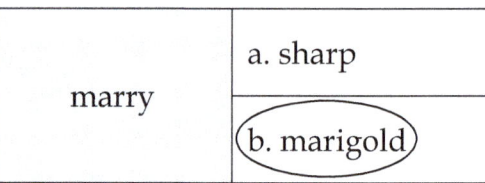
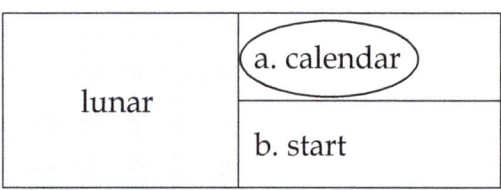
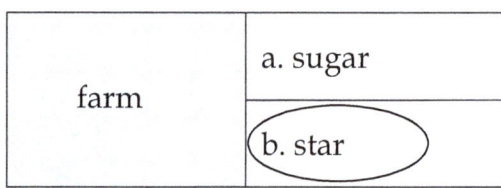

 Directions: Read each target word. Put a check (✓) under the correct column heading.
Direcciones: Lee cada palabra objetivo. Coloca un signo de verificación (✓) bajo el encabezado de la columna correcta.

Target Words	"ar" has the /ă/ + /r/ sounds as in the word baron	"ar" has the /ə/ + /r/ sounds as in the word dollar	"ar" has the /ä/ + /r/ sounds as in the word car	"ar" has the /ô/ + /r/ sounds as in the word war
1. art			✓	
2. marry	✓			
3. lunar		✓		
4. farm			✓	

Answer Key

Name: _____ Date: ___/___/_____ Score: _____

Lesson 1.7

Reading Words with the "ar" Letter Combination

Dictionary Skills/ Vocabulary

✓ Lesson Check Point

Directions: Read each target word and its definition. Write the target word on the line in front of its meaning. Use a dictionary or the Internet to check your answers.

Direcciones: Lee cada palabra objetivo y su definición. Escribe la palabra objetivo en la línea frente a su significado. Usa un diccionario o Internet para verificar tus respuestas.

Target Word Box				
Oscar	narrator	party	paramedics	garlic

1. _party_____   a fun gathering where people socialize
2. _paramedics_ medical professionals
3. _Oscar_____   a boy or man's name
4. _garlic____   an edible plant that looks like a bulb
5. _narrator___ a person who tells the events of the story

Directions: Read each sentence and write the target word that correctly completes the sentence.

Direcciones: Lee cada oración y escribe la palabra objetivo que complete la sentencia.

6. Baroness invited all her friends to the ____party____.

7. _Oscar__ registered for classes at the registrar's office.

8. The dynamic __narrator__ dramatically read the play's stage directions.

9. I enhanced the flavor of the soup by adding vinegar and ___garlic___.

10. The skilled ___paramedics___ saved Arty's life by administering CPR.

Classwork

Name: _____ Date: ___/___/_____ Score: _____

Lesson 1.8

Reading Words with a Silent Letter "a"

✓ **Lesson Check Point**

Directions: Read the target words in the word box. Write the words that have a silent letter "a" in the first column. Write the words that do not have a silent letter "a" in the second column.

Direcciones: Lee las palabras objetivo en el cuadro de texto. Escribe las palabras que tengan una letra muda "a" en la primera columna. Escribe las palabras que no tengan una letra muda "a" en la segunda columna.

Target Word Box				
floats	pain	dragon	aisle	goats
games	broad	oasis	sandy	anthills
beauty	oats	days	raining	crash
central	gloating	bread	bureau	boating

Letter "a" is silent

- oats
- aisle
- goats
- broad
- beauty
- floats
- bread
- bureau
- boating
- gloating

Letter "a" has a letter "a" sound

- pain
- crash
- days
- oasis
- sandy
- games
- anthills
- raining
- dragon
- central

Learn To Read English With Directions In Spanish

Answer Key

 Name: _____ Date:___/___/_____ Score:_____

Unit Review - A/a

Reading Words with Vowel "a" Sounds: /ă/, /ā/, /ə/ & Silent

✓ **Lesson Check Point**

 Directions: Read each target word. Circle the word in the column that has the same "a" sound as the target word.

Direcciones: Lee cada palabra objetivo. Encierra en un círculo la palabra en la columna que tenga el mismo sonido "a" que la palabra objetivo.

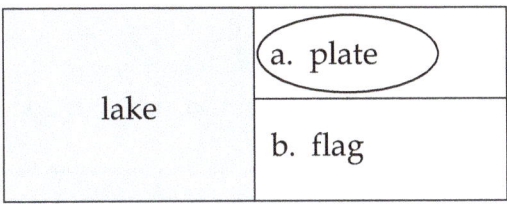

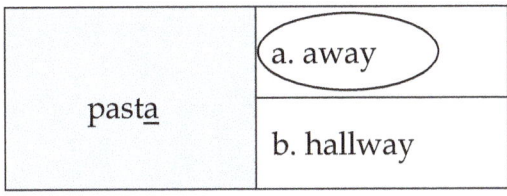
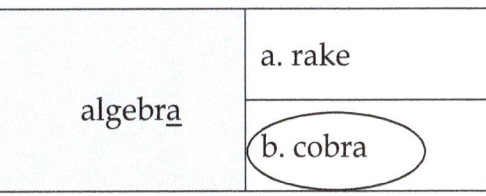

 Directions: Read each target word. Put a check (✓) under the correct column heading.

Direcciones: Lee cada palabra objetivo. Coloca un signo de verificación (✓) bajo el encabezado de la columna correcta.

Target Words	"a" has the /ă/ sound as in the word <u>apple</u>	"a" has the /ā/ sound as in the word <u>ate</u>	"a" has the /ə/ sound as in the word <u>sofa</u>	"a" is silent as in the word <u>boat</u>
1. lake		✓		
2. plant	✓			
3. past<u>a</u>			✓	
4. algebr<u>a</u>			✓	

Classwork

 Name: _____ Date:___/___/_____ Score:_____

The Reading Challenge

Lesson 1.9

Reading Multisyllable Words

✓ **Lesson Check Point**

 Directions: Read and divide each target word into syllables. Write each word and place a hyphen (-) between the syllables in the second column. Write the number of syllables in the third column. Use a dictionary or the Internet to check your answers.

Direcciones: Lee y separa en sílabas cada palabra objetivo. Escribe cada palabra y coloca un guión (-) entre las sílabas en la segunda columna. Escribe el número de sílabas en la tercera columna. Usa un diccionario o Internet para verificar tus respuestas.

Target Words	Words Divided into Syllables	Number of Syllables
1. payback	pay-back	2
2. slogan	slo-gan	2
3. turban	tur-ban	2
4. abdomen	ab-do-men	3
5. batman	bat-man	2
6. husband	hus-band	2
7. Alaskan	A-las-kan	3
8. Scotland	Scot-land	2
9. embanking	em-bank-ing	3
10. migrated	mi-grat-ed	3

Answer Key

 Name: _____ Date: ___/___/_____ Score: _____

The Reading Challenge

Lesson 1.9

Reading Multisyllable Words

✓ **Lesson Check Point**

 Directions: Read each target word. Circle the word in the row that is divided correctly into syllables. Use a dictionary or the Internet to check your answers.

Direcciones: Lee cada palabra objetivo. Encierra en un círculo la palabra en la fila que esté correctamente separada en sílabas. Usa un diccionario o Internet para verificar tus respuestas.

Model

| important | **a. im-por-tant** ⭕ | b. im-port-ant | c. im-porta-nt |

1. diploma	**a. di-plo-ma** ⭕	b. di-plom-a	c. dip-lom-a
2. absolute	a. a-bso-lute	b. a-bsol-ute	**c. ab-so-lute** ⭕
3. admonish	a. adm-o-nish	b. a-dmon-ish	**c. ad-mon-ish** ⭕
4. magistrate	**a. mag-is-trate** ⭕	b. mag-i-strate	c. ma-gis-trate
5. kilogram	a. ki-lo-gram	b. ki-log-ram	**c. kil-o-gram** ⭕
6. caravan	a. ca-rav-an	**b. car-a-van** ⭕	c. car-av-an
7. admiral	a. ad-mir-al	**b. ad-mi-ral** ⭕	c. a-dmir-al
8. monogram	a. mo-no-gram	b. mo-nog-ram	**c. mon-o-gram** ⭕

Learn To Read English With Directions In Spanish

Classwork

Name: _____ Date: ___/___/_____ Score: _____

Lesson 1.10

Reading and Writing

Proper and Common Nouns and Adjectives

Directions: Read the words in the word box. Put an (X) on the line next to each word that is written incorrectly. Remember that all proper nouns and proper adjectives are capitalized. Use a dictionary or the Internet to check your answers.

Direcciones: Lee las palabras en el cuadro de texto. Coloca una (X) en la línea próxima a las palabras que estén escritas de forma incorrecta. Recuerda que todos los nombres propios y adjetivos propios empiezan con mayúscula. Usa un diccionario o Internet para verificar tus respuestas.

Word Box					
__	August	__	Argentina	X	Author
X	Achievers	__	advanced	__	adventure
X	apollo	X	athens	__	America
__	airmail	X	alaska	X	ArubA

Directions: Read each unedited sentence and underline the word that is written incorrectly. Write each sentence correctly on the line.

Direcciones: Lee cada oración sin editar y subraya la palabra que está escrita de forma incorrecta. Escribe cada oración correctamente en la línea.

Model
Andrew has a view of the <u>atlantic</u> Ocean from his apartment.
Andrew has a view of the Atlantic Ocean from his apartment.

1. Anne and <u>alex</u> are from Australia.
Anne and Alex are from Australia.

2. The <u>Author's</u> article, "Awaken," is amazing.
The author's article, "Awaken," is amazing.

3. Mr. <u>aaron</u> got a lot of cash from the ATM.
Mr. Aaron got a lot of cash from the ATM.

4. In <u>august</u>, Ashley will attend Ace Academy.
In August, Ashley will attend Ace Academy.

Answer Key

 Name: _____ Date: ___/___/_____ Score: _____

Lesson 2.1

Reading Words with the Letter B/b

✓ **Lesson Check Point**

 Directions: Read each target word. Find the letter "b" and put a check (✓) in the column that identifies its position: beginning, within or end.

Direcciones: Lee cada palabra objetivo. Encuentra la letra "b" y coloca un signo de verificación (✓) en la columna que identifique su posición: inicio, interior o final.

Target Words	Beginning (First Letter)	Within	End (Last Letter)
1. cab			✓
2. bit	✓		
3. table		✓	
4. tab			✓
5. bottom	✓		

 Directions: Read each sentence and underline the words that begin with the letter "b." Write all the underlined words in alphabetical order on the lines below.

Direcciones: Lee cada oración y subraya las palabras que empiecen con la letra "b." Escribe todas las letras subrayadas en orden alfabético en las líneas que siguen.

6. Andy's <u>bat</u> is <u>black</u>.

7. He has a <u>belt</u> and a <u>billfold</u>.

8. There is a cat on the <u>baby's</u> <u>bib</u>.

9. Abe and Andy are in the <u>big</u> <u>band</u>.

10. Annie and Aaron have the <u>best</u> <u>books</u>.

baby's   band   bat
belt   best   bib
big   billfold   black
                books

Classwork

Name: _____ Date: ___/___/_____ Score: _____

Lesson 2.2

Reading Words with the "br" Letter Combination

Dictionary Skills/ Vocabulary

✓ **Lesson Check Point**

Directions: Read each target word and its definition. Write the letter of the definition on the line of each target word. Use a dictionary or the Internet to check your answers.

Direcciones: Lee cada palabra objetivo y su definición. Escribe la letra de la definición en la línea de cada palabra objetivo. Usa un diccionario o Internet para verificar tus respuestas.

Target Words	Definitions
1. _c_ brags	a. a large country on the South American continent
2. _a_ Brazil	b. a physical injury without an open cut
3. _d_ broccoli	c. to say something in a boastful way
4. _e_ bridal	d. a green vegetable with densely clustered flower buds
5. _b_ bruise	e. something or someone pertaining to a wedding

Directions: Read each sentence. Underline the word in the parentheses that correctly completes each sentence. Then, write the underlined word on the line.

Direcciones: Lee cada oración. Subraya la palabra entre paréntesis que completa correctamente cada oración. Luego, escribe la palabra subrayada en la línea.

6. The bride has a nice _____bridal_____ dress. (<u>bridal</u>, brags)

7. The _____bruise_____ on Betsy's back is black. (Brazil, <u>bruise</u>)

8. I ate ___broccoli___ and bread for breakfast. (bruise, <u>broccoli</u>)

9. Brenda ___brags___ about her brand new boat. (<u>brags</u>, broccoli)

10. Do you know that ___Brazil___ is a big country? (bruise, <u>Brazil</u>)

Answer Key

Name: _____ Date: ___/___/_____ Score: _____

Lesson 2.3

Reading Words with the "bl" Letter Combination

Dictionary Skills/ Vocabulary

✓ **Lesson Check Point**

Directions: Read each target word and its definition. Write the target word on the line in front of its meaning. Use a dictionary or the Internet to check your answers.

Direcciones: Lee cada palabra objetivo y su definición. Escribe la palabra objetivo en la línea frente a su significado. Usa un diccionario o Internet para verificar tus respuestas.

Target Word Box				
blanket	blasted	bleed	blender	blinks

1. <u>bleed</u>   the flow of blood out of a blood vessel
2. <u>blender</u>   a machine that mixes things together
3. <u>blinks</u>   the quick closing and opening movement of eyes
4. <u>blasted</u>   to have shot something out with great force
5. <u>blanket</u>   a large cloth covering used to cover a bed

Directions: Read each sentence. Underline the word in the parentheses that correctly completes each sentence. Then, write the underlined word on the line.

Direcciones: Lee cada oración. Subraya la palabra entre paréntesis que completa correctamente cada oración. Luego, escribe la palabra subrayada en la línea.

6. My big rocket <u>blasted</u> off. (blinks, <u>blasted</u>)

7. Bill blends bananas in his <u>blender</u>. (blanket, <u>blender</u>)

8. Bethany <u>blinks</u> her big, brown eyes. (bleed, <u>blinks</u>)

9. Betty puts a big, blue <u>blanket</u> on her bed. (<u>blanket</u>, blender)

10. The big blade cut Bill and made him <u>bleed</u>. (<u>bleed</u>, blasted)

Classwork

 Name: _____ Date: ___/___/_____ Score: _____

Lesson 2.3

Reading Words with the "ble" Letter Combination

✓ Lesson Check Point

 Directions: Read each target word. Find the "ble" letter combination and put a check (✓) in the column that identifies its position: beginning, within or end.

Direcciones: Lee cada palabra objetivo. Encuentra la combinación de letras "ble" y coloca un signo de verificación (✓) en la columna que identifique su posición: inicio, interior o final.

Target Words	Beginning (First 3 Letters)	Within	End (Last 3 Letters)
1. table			✓
2. problem		✓	
3. bleach	✓		
4. adorable			✓
5. scribbler		✓	

 Directions: Read each target word. Put a check (✓) in the "yes" column if the "ble" letter combination has the /b/ + /ə/ + /l/ sounds. Put a check (✓) in the "no" column if the "ble" letter combination does not have the /b/ + /ə/ + /l/ sounds.

Direcciones: Lee cada palabra objetivo. Coloca un signo de verificación (✓) en la columna del "sí" si la combinación de letras "ble" tiene el sonidos /b/ + /ə/ + /l/. Coloca un signo de verificación (✓) en la columna del "no" si la combinación de letras "ble" no tiene el sonidos /b/ + /ə/ + /l/.

Target Words	Yes	No
6. bleed		✓
7. bleach		✓
8. babble	✓	
9. agreeable	✓	
10. collectible	✓	

Answer Key

 Name: _____ Date: ___/___/_____ Score: _____

Lesson 2.4

Reading Words with the "mb" Letter Combination

✓ Lesson Check Point

 Directions: Read each target word. Circle the word in the column that has the same "mb" sound(s) as the target word.

Direcciones: Lee cada palabra objetivo. Encierra en un círculo la palabra en la columna que tenga el mismo sonido(s) "mb" que la palabra objetivo.

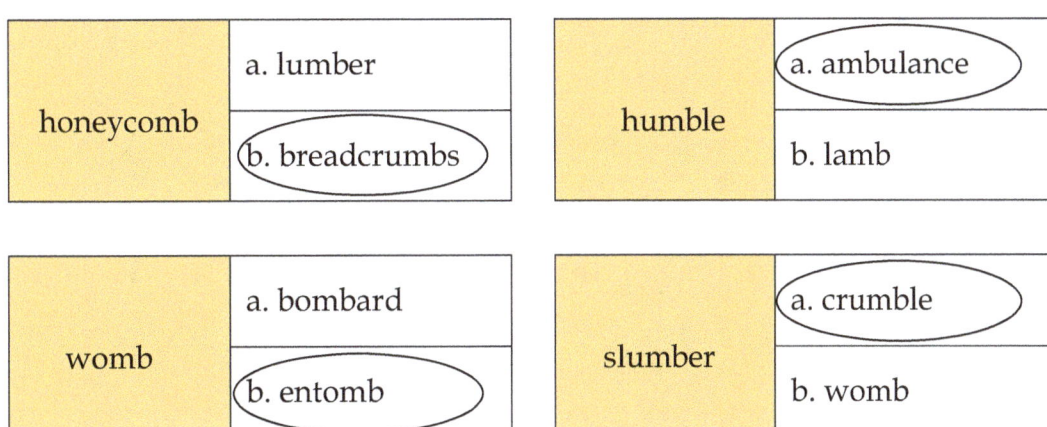

 Directions: Read each target word. In the second column, write the number of letters in the word. In the third column, write the number of letters heard in the word.

Direcciones: Lee cada palabra objetivo. En la segunda columna, escribe el número de letras en la palabra. En la tercera columna, escribe el número de letras que tienen sonido en la palabra.

Target Words	Number of letters in the word	Number of letters heard
1. combat	6	6
2. climber	7	6
3. limbs	5	4
4. lumber	6	6

Learn To Read English With Directions In Spanish

Classwork

 Name: _____ Date:___/___/_____ Score:_____

Lesson 2.4

Reading Words with the "bt" Letter Combination

✓ Lesson Check Point

  Directions: Read each target word. Circle the word in the column that has the same "bt" sound(s) as the target word.

Direcciones: Lee cada palabra objetivo. Encierra en un círculo la palabra en la columna que tenga el mismo sonido(s) "bt" que la palabra objetivo.

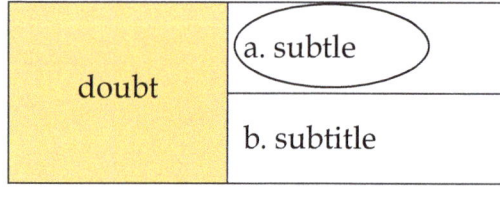
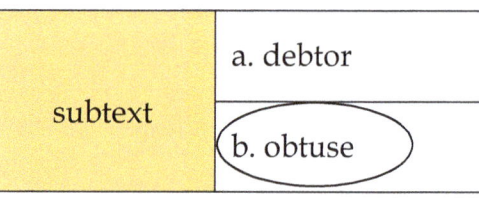
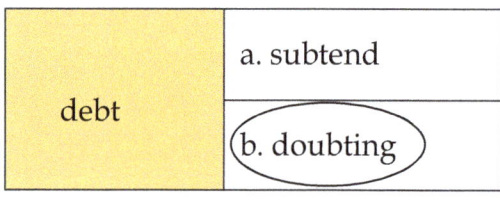
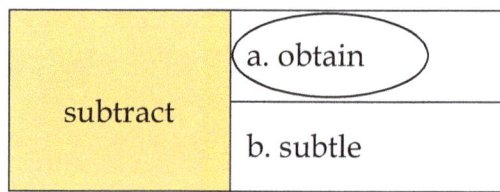

 Directions: Read each target word. In the second column, write the number of letters in the word. In the third column, write the number of letters heard in the word.

Direcciones: Lee cada palabra objetivo. En la segunda columna, escribe el número de letras en la palabra. En la tercera columna, escribe el número de letras que tienen sonido en la palabra.

Target Words	Number of letters in the word	Number of letters heard
1. doubt	5	4
2. subtext	7	7
3. debt	4	3
4. subtract	8	8

Answer Key

 Name: _____ Date: ___/___/_____ Score: _____

Lesson 2.5

Reading Words with a Silent "b"

✓ **Lesson Check Point**

 Directions: Read the target words in the word box. Write the words that have a silent letter "b" in the first column. Write the words that do not have a silent letter "b" in the second column.
Direcciones: Lee las palabras objetivo en el cuadro de texto. Escribe las palabras que tengan una letra muda "b" en la primera columna. Escribe las palabras que no tengan una letra muda "b" en la segunda columna.

Target Word Box				
labels	climbing	bread	zebra	subpoena
thumbs	bugs	debt	crumb	lamb
abandon	plumbers	basement	ability	bedroom
combs	brother	entomb	books	limbs

Letter "b" is silent

- debt
- crumb
- limbs
- lamb
- thumbs
- entomb
- combs
- climbing
- plumbers
- subpoena

Letter "b" has the /b/ sound

- labels
- books
- bugs
- ability
- bread
- zebra
- brother
- abandon
- basement
- bedroom

Classwork

 Name: _____ Date: ___/___/_____ Score: _____

The Reading Challenge

Lesson 2.6

Reading Multisyllable Words

✓ Lesson Check Point

 Directions: Read and divide each target word into syllables. Write each word and place a hyphen (-) between the syllables in the second column. Write the number of syllables in the third column. Use a dictionary or the Internet to check your answers.

Direcciones: Lee y separa en sílabas cada palabra objetivo. Escribe cada palabra y coloca un guión (-) entre las sílabas en la segunda columna. Escribe el número de sílabas en la tercera columna. Usa un diccionario o Internet para verificar tus respuestas.

Target Words	Words Divided into Syllables	Number of Syllables
1. balance	bal-ance	2
2. submit	sub-mit	2
3. sublet	sub-let	2
4. bigwig	big-wig	2
5. banana	ba-nan-a	3
6. obstacle	ob-sta-cle	3
7. biceps	bi-ceps	2
8. tablet	tab-let	2
9. beckon	beck-on	2
10. blanket	blan-ket	2

Answer Key

Name: _____ Date: ___/___/_____ Score: _____

The Reading Challenge

Lesson 2.6

Reading Multisyllable Words

✓ **Lesson Check Point**

Directions: Read each target word. Circle the word in the row that is divided correctly into syllables. Use a dictionary or the Internet to check your answers.

Direcciones: Lee cada palabra objetivo. Encierra en un círculo la palabra en la fila que esté correctamente separada en sílabas. Usa un diccionario o Internet para verificar tus respuestas.

Model

| because | (a. be-cause) | b. beca-use | c. b-ecause |

1. bachelor	a. bac-he-lor	(b. bach-e-lor)	c. ba-ch-elor
2. backpack	(a. back-pack)	b. ba-ckpa-ck	c. ba-ckp-ack
3. bellboy	a. be-llboy	b. bellb-oy	(c. bell-boy)
4. blackout	a. bla-ckout	(b. black-out)	c. bl-ackout
5. bicycle	a. bi-cycle	(b. bi-cy-cle)	c. bicy-cle
6. baritone	a. ba-ri-tone	b. ba-rit-one	(c. bar-i-tone)
7. bracelet	a. bracel-et	b. bra-celet	(c. brace-let)
8. bumblebee	(a. bum-ble-bee)	b. bumb-le-bee	c. bu-mbleb-ee

Unit B Lesson 2.6

Learn To Read English With Directions In Spanish   Copyrighted Material

Classwork

Name: _____ Date: ___/___/_____ Score: _____

Lesson 2.7

Reading and Writing

Proper and Common Nouns and Adjectives

Directions: Read the words in the word box. Put an (X) on the line next to each word that is written incorrectly. Remember that all proper nouns and proper adjectives are capitalized. Use a dictionary or the Internet to check your answers.

Direcciones: Lee las palabras en el cuadro de texto. Coloca una (X) en la línea próxima a las palabras que estén escritas de forma incorrecta. Recuerda que todos los nombres propios y adjetivos propios empiezan con mayúscula. Usa un diccionario o Internet para verificar tus respuestas.

Word Box						
__	Bolivia	X	BuBBle	__	absent
__	barber	__	bottom	X	BarBados
X	Bread	__	bread	__	bridges
X	buckingham	X	bulB	X	bahamas

Directions: Read each unedited sentence and underline the word that is written incorrectly. Write each sentence correctly on the line.

Direcciones: Lee cada oración sin editar y subraya la palabra que está escrita de forma incorrecta. Escribe cada oración correctamente en la línea.

Model
brandon's books are about big boats.
Brandon's books are about big boats.

1. The black Bat is really big.
The black bat is really big.

2. bob has a brown bag.
Bob has a brown bag.

3. The blue taBle is too big.
The blue table is too big.

4. benjamin's baked bread is in his bag.
Benjamin's baked bread is in his bag.

Answer Key

 Name: _____ Date: ___/___/_____ Score: _____

Lesson 3.1

Reading Words with the Letter C/c

✓ Lesson Check Point

 Directions: Read each target word. Find the letter "c" and put a check (✓) in the column that identifies its position: beginning, within or end.
Direcciones: Lee cada palabra objetivo. Encuentra la letra "c" y coloca un signo de verificación (✓) en la columna que identifique su posición: inicio, interior o final.

Target Words	Beginning (First Letter)	Within	End (Last Letter)
1. clog	✓		
2. toxic			✓
3. tackle		✓	
4. basic			✓
5. picture		✓	

 Directions: Read each sentence and underline the words that begin with the letter "c." Write all the underlined words in alphabetical order on the lines below.
Direcciones: Lee cada oración y subraya las palabras que empiecen con la letra "c." Escribe todas las letras subrayadas en orden alfabético en las líneas que siguen.

6. The big <u>cows</u> are <u>cute</u>.

7. The black <u>car</u> is very <u>clean</u>.

8. The <u>child</u> is in the blue <u>crib</u>.

9. Bobby has a <u>cap</u> and a big <u>coat</u>.

10. The boys are <u>chasing</u> the <u>chicken</u>.

cap _____   car _____   chasing _____
chicken _____   child _____   clean _____
coat _____   cows _____   crib _____
                      cute _____

Learn To Read English With Directions In Spanish

Classwork

Name: _____ Date:___/___/_____ Score:_____

Lesson 3.1

Reading Words with the Hard Letter "c"

✓ Lesson Check Point

Directions: Read each target word. Put a check (✓) under the correct column heading.

Direcciones: Lee cada palabra objetivo. Coloca un signo de verificación (✓) bajo el encabezado de la columna correcta.

Target Words	Hard "c" has the /k/ sound as in the word <u>cat</u>	Soft "c" has the /s/ sound as in the word <u>cell</u>
1. school	✓	
2. cleaning	✓	
3. cement		✓
4. civilized		✓
5. character	✓	

Directions: Read each sentence and underline the words that have the hard "c" sound, as in the word <u>cat</u>. Write all the underlined words in alphabetical order on the lines below.

Direcciones: Lee cada oración y subraya las palabras que tengan el sonido fuerte "c", como en la palabra inglés <u>cat</u>. Escribe todas las palabras subrayadas en orden alfabético en las líneas siguientes.

6. Ms. <u>Clarke's</u> big chips are <u>crunchy</u>.

7. The <u>cake</u> has a <u>caramel</u> apple center.

8. Andrew is chewing <u>cranberry</u> <u>candy</u>.

9. Cindy is <u>counting</u> the <u>crabs</u> in the bowl.

10. Everyone in my <u>class</u> had a bowl of ice <u>cream</u>.

<u>cake_____</u>   <u>candy_____</u>   <u>caramel_____</u>

<u>Clarke's____</u>   <u>class_____</u>   <u>counting_____</u>

<u>crabs_____</u>   <u>cranberry____</u>   <u>cream_____</u>

                       <u>crunchy_____</u>

Answer Key

 Name: _____ Date: ___/___/_____ Score: _____

Lesson 3.2

Reading Words with the Soft Letter "c"

✓ Lesson Check Point

 Directions: Read each target word. Put a check (✓) under the correct column heading.

Direcciones: Lee cada palabra objetivo. Coloca un signo de verificación (✓) bajo el encabezado de la columna correcta.

Target Words	Hard "c" has the /k/ sound as in the word cat	Soft "c" has the /s/ sound as in the word cell
1. face		✓
2. curl	✓	
3. cast	✓	
4. city		✓
5. clue	✓	

 Directions: Read each sentence and underline the words that have the soft "c" sound, as in the word cell. Write all the underlined words in alphabetical order on the lines below.

Direcciones: Lee cada oración y subraya las palabras que tengan el sonido suave "c", como en la palabra inglés cell. Escribe todas las palabras subrayadas en orden alfabético en las líneas siguientes.

6. City Hall is in the center of Clarkston.

7. Lucy said, "The comedian is a cynic."

8. Caleb said, "We live in a civilized society."

9. The baby in the crib ate cranberry and cinnamon cereal.

10. I stored my bicycles and ceramic casserole dishes in the den.

bicycles   center   ceramic
cereal   cinnamon   City
civilized   cynic   Lucy
                society

Classwork

Name: _____ Date: ___/___/_____ Score: _____

Review Lessons 3.1 & 3.2

Reading Hard Letter "c" and Soft Letter "c" Words

Directions: Read the target words in the word box. In the first column, write the words with the letter "c" that have the /k/ sound, as in the word <u>cat</u>. In the second column, write the words with the letter "c" that have the /s/ sound, as in the word <u>cell</u>.

Direcciones: Lee las palabras objetivo en el cuadro de texto. En la primera columna, escribe las palabras con la letra "c" que tengan el sonido /k/, como en la palabra inglés <u>cat</u>. En la segunda columna, escribe las palabras con la letra "c" que tengan el sonido /s/, como en la palabra inglés <u>cell</u>.

Target Word Box				
cause	cook	citizen	city	curb
curve	mice	cute	code	citrus
cedar	cube	cake	call	spicy
coil	cysts	place	cease	cent

Hard letter "c" has the /k/ sound as in the word <u>cat</u>	Soft letter "c" has the /s/ sound as in the word <u>cell</u>
call	cent
coil	city
code	mice
cook	cysts
cube	cedar
cute	place
curb	cease
cake	citrus
curve	spicy
cause	citizen

Answer Key

 Name: _____ Date: ___/___/_____ Score: _____

Lesson 3.3

Reading Words with the "cr" Letter Combination

Dictionary Skills/ Vocabulary

✓ Lesson Check Point

 Directions: Read each target word and its definition. Write the letter of the definition on the line of each target word. Use a dictionary or the Internet to check your answers.

Direcciones: Lee cada palabra objetivo y su definición. Escribe la letra de la definición en la línea de cada palabra objetivo. Usa un diccionario o Internet para verificar tus respuestas.

Target Words	Definitions
1. _d_ cranberry	a. to really want something, such as food
2. _a_ craving	b. to move along the ground on hands and knees
3. _b_ crawls	c. a thick dairy product made from milk
4. _c_ cream	d. a small, tart, red berry-like fruit
5. _e_ crumbs	e. small pieces of bread or other baked goods

 Directions: Read each sentence. Underline the word in the parentheses that correctly completes each sentence. Then, write the underlined word on the line.

Direcciones: Lee cada oración. Subraya la palabra entre paréntesis que completa correctamente cada oración. Luego, escribe la palabra subrayada en la línea.

6. The cats ate the cookie __crumbs__. (crawls, <u>crumbs</u>)

7. Cindy's ice __cream__ is very cold. (<u>cream</u>, craving)

8. The baby __crawls__ on the carpet. (<u>crawls</u>, cream)

9. I have a __craving__ for cotton candy. (<u>craving</u>, cranberry)

10. Chad likes to drink __cranberry__ juice. (crumbs, <u>cranberry</u>)

Classwork

Name: _____ Date: ___/___/_____ Score: _____

Lesson 3.4

Reading Words with the "cl" Letter Combination

Dictionary Skills/ Vocabulary

✓ Lesson Check Point

Directions: Read each target word and its definition. Write the target word on the line in front of its meaning. Use a dictionary or the Internet to check your answers.

Direcciones: Lee cada palabra objetivo y su definición. Escribe la palabra objetivo en la línea frente a su significado. Usa un diccionario o Internet para verificar tus respuestas.

Target Word Box				
cleared	cliff	clipped	clock	closet

1. cliff_____ the overhanging of a mountain
2. clock_____ a device used to display time
3. closet_____ a small inner room used for clothing and storage
4. cleared_____ to have moved something out of the way
5. clipped_____ to fasten or grip with a firm metal or plastic clamp

Directions: Read each sentence. Underline the word in the parentheses that correctly completes each sentence. Then, write the underlined word on the line.

Direcciones: Lee cada oración. Subraya la palabra entre paréntesis que completa correctamente cada oración. Luego, escribe la palabra subrayada en la línea.

6. Chad cleaned out his bedroom ____closet____. (closet, cliff)

7. Charles ____cleared____ the clogged drain. (cleared, closet)

8. Yesterday, we climbed up the steep ___cliff___. (clipped, cliff)

9. I ____clipped____ my index cards on the clipboard. (clipped, clock)

10. This morning, my alarm ___clock___ woke me up. (clock, cleared)

Answer Key

 Name: _____ Date:___/___/_____ Score:_____

Lesson 3.4

Reading Words with the "cle" Letter Combination

✓ Lesson Check Point

Directions: Read each target word. Find the "cle" letter combination and put a check (✓) in the column that identifies its position: beginning, within or end.

Direcciones: Lee cada palabra objetivo. Encuentra la combinación de letras "cle" y coloca un signo de verificación (✓) en la columna que identifique su posición: inicio, interior o final.

Target Words	Beginning (First 3 Letters)	Within	End (Last 3 Letters)
1. article			✓
2. cleaning	✓		
3. inclement		✓	
4. particle			✓
5. cleverly	✓		

Directions: Read each target word. Put a check (✓) in the "yes" column if the "cle" letter combination has the /k/ + /ə/ + /l/ sounds. Put a check (✓) in the "no" column if the "cle" letter combination does not have the /k/ + /ə/ + /l/ sounds.

Direcciones: Lee cada palabra objetivo. Coloca un signo de verificación (✓) en la columna del "sí" si la combinación de letras "cle" tiene el sonidos /k/ + /ə/ + /l/. Coloca un signo de verificación (✓) en la columna del "no" si la combinación de letras "cle" no tiene el sonidos /k/ + /ə/ + /l/.

Target Words	Yes	No
6. article	✓	
7. cleaning		✓
8. inclement		✓
9. particle	✓	
10. cleverly		✓

Classwork

 Name: _____ Date: ___/___/_____ Score: _____

Lesson 3.5

Reading Words with the "ct" Letter Combination

✓ **Lesson Check Point**

 Directions: Read each target word. Circle the word in the column that has the same "ct" sound(s) as the target word.

Direcciones: Lee cada palabra objetivo. Encierra en un círculo la palabra en la columna que tenga el mismo sonido(s) "ct" que la palabra objetivo.

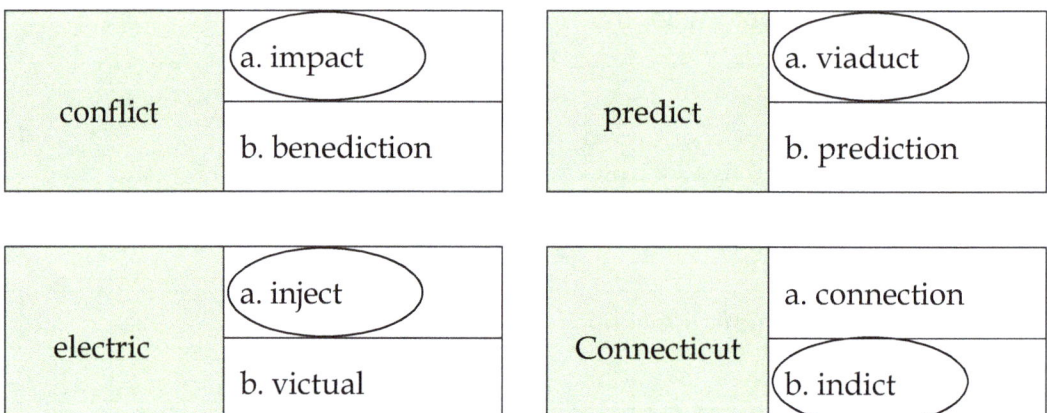

 Directions: Read each target word. Put a check (✓) under the correct column heading.

Direcciones: Lee cada palabra objetivo. Coloca un signo de verificación (✓) bajo el encabezado de la columna correcta.

Target Words	"ct" has the /k/ + /t/ sounds as in the word <u>fact</u>	"ct" has the silent "c" + /t/ sound as in the word <u>indict</u>
1. conflict	✓	
2. predict	✓	
3. electric	✓	
4. Connecticut		✓

Answer Key

 Name: _____ Date: ___/___/_____ Score: _____

Lesson 3.6

Reading Soft Letter "c" Words

✓ **Lesson Check Point**

 Directions: Read each target word. Circle the word in the column that has the same "cean," "cian," "cial," "cious," or "cient" sound as the target word.

Direcciones: Lee cada palabra objetivo. Encierra en un círculo la palabra en la columna que tenga el mismo sonido "cean," "cian," "cial," "cious," o "cient" que la palabra objetivo.

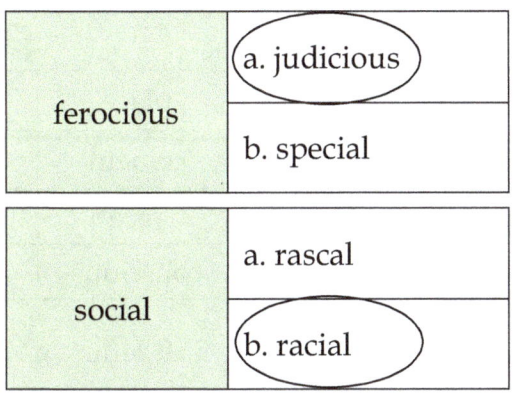
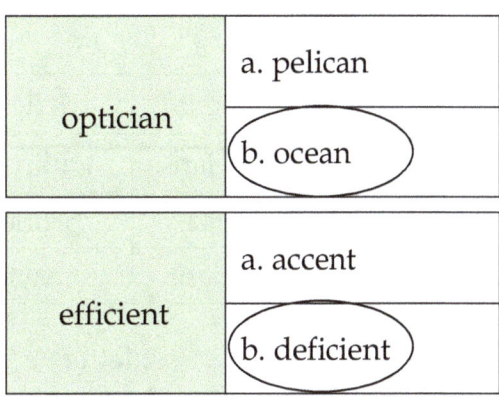

 Directions: Read each target word. Put a check (✓) in the column that identifies the same "cean," "cian," "cial," "cious," or "cient" sound within the target word.

Direcciones: Lee cada palabra objetivo. Coloca un signo de verificación (✓) que identifique los mismos sonidos "cean," "cian," "cial," "cious," o "cient" de la palabra objetivo.

Target Words	"cean" has the /sh/+/ə/+/n/ sounds as in the word <u>ocean</u>	"cial" has the /sh/+/ə/+/l/ sounds as in the word <u>special</u>	"cious" has the /sh/+/ə/+/s/ sounds as in the word <u>delicious</u>	"cient" has the /sh/+/ə/+/n/+/t/ sounds as in the word <u>ancient</u>
1. ferocious			✓	
2. optician	✓			
3. social		✓		
4. efficient				✓

Learn To Read English With Directions In Spanish

Classwork

Name: _____ Date: ___/___/_____ Score: _____

Lesson 3.6

Reading Soft Letter "c" Words

Directions: Read the target words in the word box. In the first column, write the words with the letter "c" that have the /s/ sound, as in the word <u>cell</u>. In the second column, write the words with the letter "c" that have the /sh/ sound, as in the word <u>ocean</u>.

Direcciones: Lee las palabras objetivo en el cuadro de texto. En la primera columna, escribe las palabras con la letra "c" que tengan el sonido /s/, como en la palabra inglés <u>cell</u>. En la segunda columna, escribe las palabras con la letra "c" que tengan el sonido /sh/, como en la palabra inglés <u>ocean</u>.

Target Word Box				
commercial	delicious	office	place	lacy
technician	gallinacean	spices	cement	artificial
circus	proficient	prince	race	decided
omniscient	twice	optician	conscious	socialize

Soft letter "c" has the /s/ sound as in the word <u>cell</u>

- lacy
- race
- place
- twice
- circus
- office
- spices
- prince
- cement
- decided

Soft letter "c" has the /sh/ sound as in the word <u>ocean</u>

- socialize
- optician
- artificial
- delicious
- conscious
- proficient
- omniscient
- gallinacean
- technician
- commercial

Answer Key

 Name: _____ Date: ___/___/_____ Score: _____

Lesson 3.7

Reading Words with the "ch" Letter Combination

✓ Lesson Check Point

 Directions: Read each target word. Circle the word in the column that has the same "ch" sound as the target word.
Direcciones: Lee cada palabra objetivo. Encierra en un círculo la palabra en la columna que tenga el mismo sonido "ch" que la palabra objetivo.

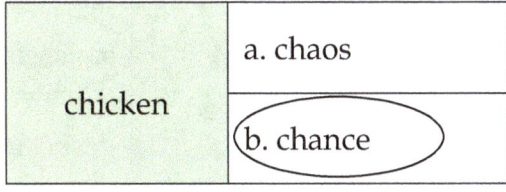

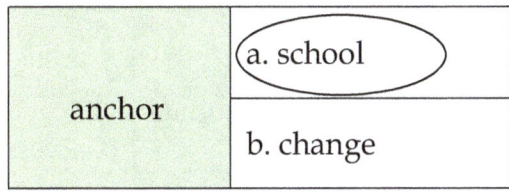

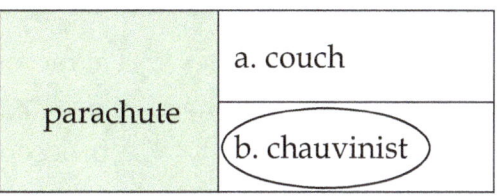

 Directions: Read each target word. Put a check (✓) under the correct column heading.
Direcciones: Lee cada palabra objetivo. Coloca un signo de verificación (✓) bajo el encabezado de la columna correcta.

Target Words	"ch" has the /ch/ sound as in the word **chain**	"ch" has the /sh/ sound as in the word **chef**	"ch" has the /k/ sound as in the word **chaos**	"ch" is silent as in the word **yacht**
1. chicken	✓			
2. fuchsia				✓
3. anchor			✓	
4. parachute		✓		

Learn To Read English With Directions In Spanish

Classwork

 Name: _____ Date: ___/___/_____ Score: _____

Lesson 3.8

Reading Words with the "cc" Letter Combination

✓ **Lesson Check Point**

 Directions: Read each target word. Circle the word in the column that has the same "cc" sound(s) as the target word.

Direcciones: Lee cada palabra objetivo. Encierra en un círculo la palabra en la columna que tenga los mismos sonidos "cc" que la palabra objetivo.

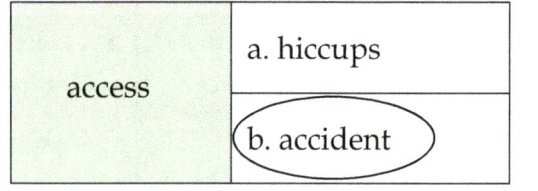

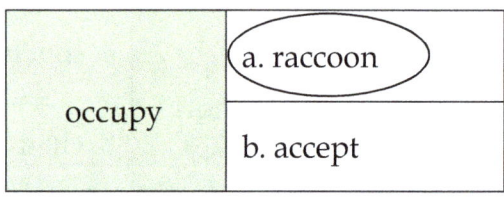 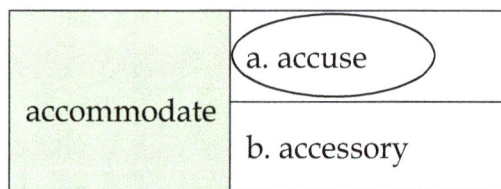

 Directions: Read each target word. Put a check (✓) under the correct column heading.

Direcciones: Lee cada palabra objetivo. Coloca un signo de verificación (✓) bajo el encabezado de la columna correcta.

Target Words	"cc" has the /k/ sound as in the word <u>soccer</u>	"cc" has the /k/ + /s/ sounds as in the word <u>accept</u>
1. access		✓
2. succeed		✓
3. occupy	✓	
4. accommodate	✓	

Answer Key

 Name: _____ Date:___/___/_____ Score:_____

Lesson 3.9

Reading Words with a Silent Letter "c"

✓ Lesson Check Point

 Directions: Read the target words in the word box. Write the words that have a silent letter "c" in the first column. Write the words that do not have a silent letter "c" in the second column.

Direcciones: Lee las palabras objetivo en el cuadro de texto. Escribe las palabras que tengan una letra muda "c" en la primera columna. Escribe las palabras que no tengan una letra muda "c" en la segunda columna.

Target Word Box				
czar	scent	scalp	cake	acquit
occupy	corpuscle	muscle	excited	scissors
citizens	produce	congress	scenery	ascend
classic	yacht	increase	court	scale

Letter "c" is silent

- czar
- scent
- yacht
- acquit
- ascend
- occupy
- scissors
- muscle
- scenery
- corpuscle

Letter "c" has the /k/, /s/ or /sh/ sound

- cake
- court
- scale
- scalp
- classic
- citizens
- excited
- produce
- increase
- congress

Unit C
Lesson 3.9

Classwork

Name: _____ Date: ___/___/_____ Score: _____

The Reading Challenge

Lesson 3.10

Reading Multisyllable Words

✓ Lesson Check Point

Directions: Read and divide each target word into syllables. Write each word and place a hyphen (-) between the syllables in the second column. Write the number of syllables in the third column. Use a dictionary or the Internet to check your answers.

Direcciones: Lee y separa en sílabas cada palabra objetivo. Escribe cada palabra y coloca un guión (-) entre las sílabas en la segunda columna. Escribe el número de sílabas en la tercera columna. Usa un diccionario o Internet para verificar tus respuestas.

Target Words	Words Divided into Syllables	Number of Syllables
1. climber	climb-er	2
2. cleaner	clean-er	2
3. climbing	climb-ing	2
4. crayons	cray-ons	2
5. construction	con-struc-tion	3
6. cereal	ce-re-al	3
7. crocodile	croc-o-dile	3
8. creditors	cred-i-tors	3
9. crackers	crack-ers	2
10. camping	camp-ing	2

Answer Key

Name: _____ Date: ___/___/_____ Score: _____

The Reading Challenge

Lesson 3.10

Reading Multisyllable Words

✓ **Lesson Check Point**

Directions: Read each target word. Circle the word in the row that is divided correctly into syllables. Use a dictionary or the Internet to check your answers.

Direcciones: Lee cada palabra objetivo. Encierra en un círculo la palabra en la fila que esté correctamente separada en sílabas. Usa un diccionario o Internet para verificar tus respuestas.

Model

| calculus | a. calcu-lus | (b. cal-cu-lus) | c. cal-culus |

1. chipmunk	(a. chip-munk)	b. chip-mu-nk	c. ch-ipmu-nk
2. calendar	a. ca-lend-ar	(b. cal-en-dar)	c. ca-le-ndar
3. circuit	a. cir-cu-it	b. circu-it	(c. cir-cuit)
4. compound	(a. com-pound)	b. co-mpou-nd	c. com-po-und
5. cereal	(a. ce-re-al)	b. cer-e-al	c. c-ere-al
6. charisma	a. char-isma	b. cha-rism-a	(c. cha-ris-ma)
7. cinema	(a. cin-e-ma)	b. cine-ma	c. ci-ne-ma
8. cylinder	a. cy-lin-der	(b. cyl-in-der)	c. cylin-der

Learn To Read English With Directions In Spanish

Classwork

Name: _____ Date: ___/___/_____ Score: _____

Lesson 3.11

Reading and Writing

Proper and Common Nouns and Adjectives

Directions: Read the words in the word box. Put an (X) on the line next to each word that is written incorrectly. Remember that all proper nouns and proper adjectives are capitalized. Use a dictionary or the Internet to check your answers.

Direcciones: Lee las palabras en el cuadro de texto. Coloca una (X) en la línea próxima a las palabras que estén escritas de forma incorrecta. Recuerda que todos los nombres propios y adjetivos propios empiezan con mayúscula. Usa un diccionario o Internet para verificar tus respuestas.

Word Box					
__	China	X	cliniC	__	camp
X	cleveland	X	College	__	Colombia
__	cities	__	castle	X	charles
X	chicago	X	chinese	__	cherry

Directions: Read each unedited sentence and underline the word that is written incorrectly. Write each sentence correctly on the line.

Direcciones: Lee cada oración sin editar y subraya la palabra que está escrita de forma incorrecta. Escribe cada oración correctamente en la línea.

Model
The <u>Camp</u> in Cleveland is closed.
<u>The camp in Cleveland is closed.</u>

1. The crickets chirp loudly on <u>clement</u> Cliff.
<u>The crickets chirp loudly on Clement Cliff.</u>

2. Do you like <u>cindy's</u> corn and chili?
<u>Do you like Cindy's corn and chili?</u>

3. The City of Chicago is cold and <u>Chilly</u>.
<u>The City of Chicago is cold and chilly.</u>

4. The <u>coyotes</u> is the name of our chess team.
<u>The Coyotes is the name of our chess team.</u>

Answer Key

 Name: _____ Date: ___/___/_____ Score: _____

Lesson 4.1

Reading Words with the Letter D/d

✓ Lesson Check Point

 Directions: Read each target word. Find the letter "d" and put a check (✓) in the column that identifies its position: beginning, within or end.
Direcciones: Lee cada palabra objetivo. Encuentra la letra "d" y coloca un signo de verificación (✓) en la columna que identifique su posición: inicio, interior o final.

Target Words	Beginning (First Letter)	Within	End (Last Letter)
1. calendar		✓	
2. dusting	✓		
3. garden		✓	
4. hard			✓
5. dictionary	✓		

 Directions: Read each sentence and underline the words that begin with the letter "d." Write all the underlined words in alphabetical order on the lines below.
Direcciones: Lee cada oración y subraya las palabras que empiecen con la letra "d." Escribe todas las letras subrayadas en orden alfabético en las líneas que siguen.

6. Brandon has a <u>dark</u> blue <u>drum</u>.

7. The barking <u>dogs</u> are on the <u>deck</u>.

8. The <u>driver</u> is <u>driving</u> a big blue bus.

9. My <u>daughter</u> ate the biggest <u>drumstick</u>.

10. Candice <u>designed</u> a beautiful black <u>dress</u>.

dark_____   daughter_____   deck_____
designed_____   dogs_____   dress_____
driver_____   driving_____   drum_____
                       drumstick_____

Classwork

 Name: _____ Date: ___/___/_____ Score: _____

Lesson 4.2

Reading Letter "d" Words with the /d/ Sound & /j/ Sound

✓ **Lesson Check Point**

 Directions: Read each target word. Circle the word in the column that has the same "d" sound as the target word.
Direcciones: Lee cada palabra objetivo. Encierra en un círculo la palabra en la columna que tenga el mismo sonido "d" que la palabra objetivo.

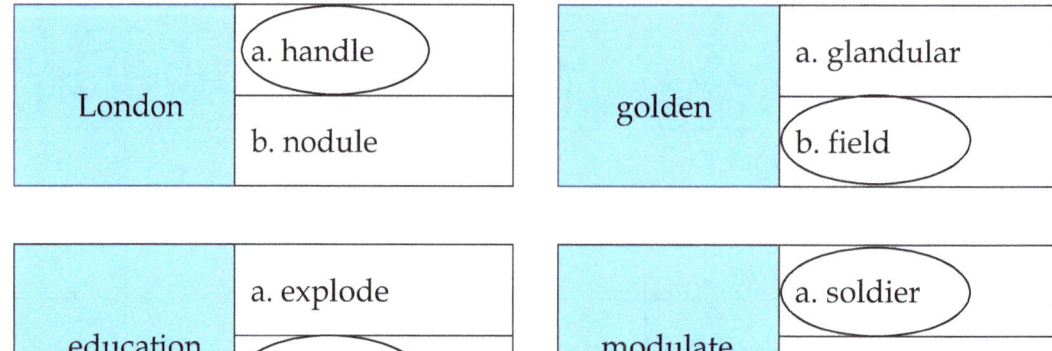

 Directions: Read each target word. Put a check (✓) under the correct column heading.
Direcciones: Lee cada palabra objetivo. Coloca un signo de verificación (✓) bajo el encabezado de la columna correcta.

Target Words	"d" has the /d/ sound as in the word doctor	"d" has the /j/ sound as in the word educate
1. London	✓	
2. golden	✓	
3. education		✓
4. modulate		✓

Unit D
Lesson 4.2

Learn To Read English With Directions In Spanish

Answer Key

 Name: _____ Date: ___/___/_____ Score: _____

Lesson 4.2

Reading Words with the "dr" Letter Combination

Dictionary Skills/ Vocabulary

✓ **Lesson Check Point**

 Directions: Read each target word and its definition. Write the letter of the definition on the line of each target word. Use a dictionary or the Internet to check your answers.

Direcciones: Lee cada palabra objetivo y su definición. Escribe la letra de la definición en la línea de cada palabra objetivo. Usa un diccionario o Internet para verificar tus respuestas.

Target Words	Definitions
1. _c_ dreams	a. to have fallen unintentionally
2. _d_ driveway	b. the cooked leg of a chicken, duck or turkey
3. _e_ driving	c. visualizing events that happen during sleep
4. _a_ dropped	d. a short path that leads to a house or garage
5. _b_ drumstick	e. the process of operating a vehicle

 Directions: Read each sentence. Underline the word in the parentheses that correctly completes each sentence. Then, write the underlined word on the line.

Direcciones: Lee cada oración. Subraya la palabra entre paréntesis que completa correctamente cada oración. Luego, escribe la palabra subrayada en la línea.

6. I drove the blue car into the _____driveway_____. (dreams, <u>driveway</u>)

7. The boy _____dropped_____ his big chocolate donut. (<u>dropped</u>, driving)

8. At night, Dan _____dreams_____ about big animals. (<u>dreams</u>, driveway)

9. I am _____driving_____ my car to Denver, Colorado. (<u>driving</u>, drumstick)

10. At dinner, David ate a delicious _____drumstick_____. (dropped, <u>drumstick</u>)

Classwork

 Name: _____ Date: ___/__/_____ Score: _____

Lesson 4.3

Reading Words with the "ed" Suffix/ Past Tense Verbs

✓ **Lesson Check Point**

 Directions: Read each target word. Circle the word in the column that has the same "ed" sound(s) as the target word.

Direcciones: Lee cada palabra objetivo. Encierra en un círculo la palabra en la columna que tenga el mismo sonido "ed" que la palabra objetivo.

| missed | a. ended |
| | b. (trapped) |

| burned | a. (grabbed) |
| | b. planted |

| named | a. snapped |
| | b. (pulled) |

| ended | a. signed |
| | b. (traded) |

 Directions: Read each target word. Put a check (✓) under the correct column heading.

Direcciones: Lee cada palabra objetivo. Coloca un signo de verificación (✓) bajo el encabezado de la columna correcta.

Target Words	"ed" has the /ĭ/ + /d/ sounds as in the word <u>rested</u>	"ed" has the /d/ sound as in the word <u>hugged</u>	"ed" has the /t/ sound as in the word <u>tipped</u>
1. missed			✓
2. burned		✓	
3. named		✓	
4. ended	✓		

Answer Key

 Name: _____ Date: ___/___/_____ Score: _____

Lesson 4.4

Reading Words with a Silent Letter "d"

✓ **Lesson Check Point**

 Directions: Read the target words in the word box. Write the words that have a silent letter "d" in the first column. Write the words that do not have a silent letter "d" in the second column.

Direcciones: Lee las palabras objetivo en el cuadro de texto. Escribe las palabras que tengan una letra muda "d" en la primera columna. Escribe las palabras que no tengan una letra muda "d" en la segunda columna.

Target Word Box				
handicap	Cambridge	dock	Windsor	elder
does	conduct	handsome	adjourn	adjustment
judge	adjacent	director	handkerchief	discuss
padlock	doctor	footbridge	Wednesday	depend

Letter "d" is silent	Letter "d" has the /d/ sound
judge	does
adjacent	dock
adjourn	doctor
Windsor	elder
footbridge	discuss
handsome	padlock
Wednesday	conduct
Cambridge	depend
adjustment	director
handkerchief	handicap

Learn To Read English With Directions In Spanish

Classwork

 Name: _____ Date:___/___/_____ Score:_____

The Reading Challenge

Lesson 4.5

Reading Multisyllable Words

✓ Lesson Check Point

Directions: Read and divide each target word into syllables. Write each word and place a hyphen (-) between the syllables in the second column. Write the number of syllables in the third column. Use a dictionary or the Internet to check your answers.

Direcciones: Lee y separa en sílabas cada palabra objetivo. Escribe cada palabra y coloca un guión (-) entre las sílabas en la segunda columna. Escribe el número de sílabas en la tercera columna. Usa un diccionario o Internet para verificar tus respuestas.

Target Words	Words Divided into Syllables	Number of Syllables
1. demonstrate	dem-on-strate	3
2. duplicate	du-pli-cate	3
3. diagram	di-a-gram	3
4. decimal	dec-i-mal	3
5. descendent	de-scen-dent	3
6. digital	dig-i-tal	3
7. disengaged	dis-en-gaged	3
8. doormat	door-mat	2
9. discomfort	dis-com-fort	3
10. driver	driv-er	2

Answer Key

 Name: _____ Date: ___/___/_____ Score: _____

The Reading Challenge

Lesson 4.5

Reading Multisyllable Words

✓ Lesson Check Point

 Directions: Read each target word. Circle the word in the row that is divided correctly into syllables. Use a dictionary or the Internet to check your answers.

Direcciones: Lee cada palabra objetivo. Encierra en un círculo la palabra en la fila que esté correctamente separada en sílabas. Usa un diccionario o Internet para verificar tus respuestas.

Model

| dictionary | a. di-ction-ary | b. dic-tion-ar-y (circled) | c. dic-tiona-ry |

1. disciple	a. di-sci-ple	b. dis-cip-le	c. dis-ci-ple (circled)
2. deceptive	a. de-cep-tive (circled)	b. dec-ep-tive	c. de-cept-ive
3. Dakota	a. Dako-ta	b. Da-kot-a	c. Da-ko-ta (circled)
4. disgruntle	a. dis-grun-tle (circled)	b. di-sgrun-tle	c. dis-grunt-le
5. dimension	a. dim-e-nsion	b. dim-en-sion	c. di-men-sion (circled)
6. domino	a. dom-i-no (circled)	b. do-min-o	c. dom-in-o
7. decelerate	a. decel-er-ate	b. dec-el-er-ate	c. de-cel-er-ate (circled)
8. distribute	a. dist-rib-ute	b. dis-tri-bute	c. dis-trib-ute (circled)

Classwork

Name: _____ Date: ___/___/_____ Score: _____

Lesson 4.6

Reading and Writing

Proper and Common Nouns and Adjectives

Directions: Read the words in the word box. Put an (X) on the line next to each word that is written incorrectly. Remember that all proper nouns and proper adjectives are capitalized. Use a dictionary or the Internet to check your answers.

Direcciones: Lee las palabras en el cuadro de texto. Coloca una (X) en la línea próxima a las palabras que estén escritas de forma incorrecta. Recuerda que todos los nombres propios y adjetivos propios empiezan con mayúscula. Usa un diccionario o Internet para verificar tus respuestas.

Word Box					
X	Daughter	X	denmark	__	Dutch
__	Dana	X	detroit	__	director
__	Denver	__	diner	X	danish
X	dakota	__	door	X	Detective

Directions: Read each unedited sentence and underline the word that is written incorrectly. Write each sentence correctly on the line.

Direcciones: Lee cada oración sin editar y subraya la palabra que está escrita de forma incorrecta. Escribe cada oración correctamente en la línea.

Model
Dan said, "My daughter's name is donna."
Dan said, "My daughter's name is Donna."

1. Drake's Dictionary is not on his desk.
   Drake's dictionary is not on his desk.

2. The dark blue Doormat has one big dot.
   The dark blue doormat has one big dot.

3. The diploma belongs to doctor Davis.
   The diploma belongs to Doctor Davis.

4. The danish pastries, pancakes, and donuts cost five dollars.
   The Danish pastries, pancakes, and donuts cost five dollars.

Answer Key

 Name: _____ Date:___/___/_____ Score:_____

Lesson 5.1

Reading Words with the Letter E/e

✓ **Lesson Check Point**

 Directions: Read each target word. Find the letter "e" and put a check (✓) in the column that identifies its position: beginning, within or end.
Direcciones: Lee cada palabra objetivo. Encuentra la letra "e" y coloca un signo de verificación (✓) en la columna que identifique su posición: inicio, interior o final.

Target Words	Beginning (First Letter)	Within	End (Last Letter)
1. eating	✓		
2. belong		✓	
3. cake			✓
4. father		✓	
5. embark	✓		

 Directions: Read each target word. Read the words in the row and circle the word that has a different vowel "e" sound.
Direcciones: Lee cada palabra objetivo. Lee las palabras en la fila y encierra la palabra que tenga un sonido vocal "e" diferente.

Target Words				
6. beds	leg	(she)	check	pet
7. men	(be)	ten	vet	hen
8. decks	yet	pen	(we)	set
9. stem	hem	(me)	net	fled
10. them	(he)	send	less	test

Learn To Read English With Directions In Spanish

Classwork

 Name: _____ Date:___/___/_____ Score:_____

Lesson 5.2

Reading Words with the Short Vowel "e" Sound

✓ Lesson Check Point

 Directions: Read the words in the four boxes. Circle two words with the short vowel /ĕ/ sound. The anchor word for the short vowel /ĕ/ sound is <u>egg</u>.

Direcciones: Lee las palabras en las cuatro cajas. Encierra en un círculo dos palabras con el sonido vocal corto /ĕ/. La palabra ejemplo para el sonido vocal corto /ĕ/ es la palabra, <u>egg</u>.

cake	(web)	bead	(speck)	ease	choose
(check)	theme	bee	(fed)	(dwelt)	(hem)

(Fred)	mean	(well)	(them)	(sped)	beat
eat	(hedge)	Pete	free	(yell)	mate

 Directions: Read the words in the four boxes. Circle two words that rhyme. Rhyming words have the same ending sound, such as <u>set</u> and <u>wet</u>.

Direcciones: Lee las palabras en las cuatro cajas. Encierra en un círculo dos que rimen. Las palabras que riman tienen el mismo sonido al final, como <u>set</u> y <u>wet</u>.

bean	(neck)	(gem)	(stem)	(bell)	each
wise	(deck)	deal	pie	true	(spell)

shoe	meat	toe	(bed)	(edge)	zeal
(men)	(ten)	(red)	heal	(pledge)	they

Answer Key

Name: _____ Date: ___/___/_____ Score: _____

Lesson 5.2

Reading & Writing Words with the Short Vowel "e" Sound

✓ **Lesson Check Point**

Directions: Read each sentence and underline three words with the short vowel /ĕ/ sound. Then, write the underlined words on the lines below. The anchor word for the short vowel /ĕ/ sound is <u>egg</u>.

Direcciones: Lee cada oración y subraya tres palabras con el sonido vocal corto /ĕ/. Luego, escribe las palabras subrayadas en las líneas siguientes. La palabra ejemplo para el sonido vocal corto /ĕ/ es la palabra, <u>egg</u>.

Model

She placed her <u>legs</u> on the <u>wet</u> <u>deck</u>.

legs   wet   deck

1. She will not <u>let</u> us <u>get</u> a <u>pet</u>.

   let   get   pet

2. We <u>smell</u> the three <u>wet</u> <u>hens</u>.

   smell   wet   hens

3. Andre <u>bent</u> his <u>leg</u> and <u>fell</u>.

   bent   leg   fell

4. Eve <u>went</u> to <u>Ed's</u> summer <u>wedding</u>.

   went   Ed's   wedding

5. We have to go to <u>bed</u> by <u>ten</u> o'clock for a <u>restful</u> night's sleep.

   bed   ten   restful

Learn To Read English With Directions In Spanish

Classwork

 Name: _____   Date: ___/___/_____   Score: _____

Lesson 5.3

Reading Words with the Long Vowel "e" Sound

✓ **Lesson Check Point**

 Directions: Read the words in the four boxes. Circle two words with the long vowel /ē/ sound. The anchor word for the long vowel /ē/ sound is <u>me</u>.

Direcciones: Lee las palabras en las cuatro cajas. Encierra en un círculo dos palabras con el sonido vocal largo /ē/. La palabra ejemplo para el sonido vocal largo /ē/ es la palabra, <u>me</u>.

break	(east)		(cease)	scene		chest	(these)
(pea)	spell		clever	here		cakes	(zebra)

(zero)	scent		(east)	next		(heal)	trend
(believe)	come		(eating)	beard		where	(react)

 Directions: Read the words in the four boxes. Circle two words that rhyme. Rhyming words have the same ending sound, such as <u>beep</u> and <u>reap</u>.

Direcciones: Lee las palabras en las cuatro cajas. Encierra en un círculo dos que rimen. Las palabras que riman tienen el mismo sonido al final, como <u>beep</u> y <u>reap</u>.

(speed)	(read)		lead	(eat)		(see)	were
bread	felt		when	(heat)		held	(tea)

(tease)	fence		head	(theme)		realm	temp
(lease)	there		(scheme)	deck		(leave)	(weave)

Answer Key

Name: _____ Date: ___/___/_____ Score: _____

Lesson 5.3

Reading & Writing Words with the Long Vowel "e" Sound

✓ **Lesson Check Point**

Directions: Read each sentence and underline three words with the long vowel /ē/ sound. Then, write the underlined words on the lines below. The anchor word for the long vowel /ē/ sound is <u>me</u>.

Direcciones: Lee cada oración y subraya tres palabras con el sonido vocal largo /ē/. Luego, escribe las palabras subrayadas en las líneas siguientes. La palabra ejemplo para el sonido vocal largo /ē/ es la palabra, <u>me</u>.

Model

<u>We</u> are <u>reading</u> an article entitled, "<u>Eagles</u> Bird of Prey."

　　　We　　　　　　　reading　　　　　　Eagles
　　─────　　　　　　─────　　　　　　─────

1. <u>Irene</u> and <u>Lee</u> are relaxing under the <u>tree</u> with their pets.

　　　Irene　　　　　　　Lee　　　　　　　tree
　　─────　　　　　　─────　　　　　　─────

2. The ten <u>Guyanese</u> <u>teams</u> are <u>extremely</u> talented.

　　Guyanese　　　　　　teams　　　　　　extremely
　　─────　　　　　　─────　　　　　　─────

3. This <u>evening</u>, Esther <u>received</u> a <u>speeding</u> ticket.

　　evening　　　　　　received　　　　　　speeding
　　─────　　　　　　─────　　　　　　─────

4. The <u>speaker</u> said, "<u>Lean</u> <u>meats</u> have relatively low-fat content."

　　speaker　　　　　　　Lean　　　　　　　meats
　　─────　　　　　　─────　　　　　　─────

5. The students will <u>speak</u> to the <u>dean</u> about the new <u>teachers</u>.

　　speak　　　　　　　dean　　　　　　teachers
　　─────　　　　　　─────　　　　　　─────

Learn To Read English With Directions In Spanish　　　Copyrighted Material

Classwork

Name: _____ Date: ___/___/_____ Score: _____

Review Lessons 5.2 & 5.3

Reading Short Vowel and Long Vowel Words

Directions: Read the target words in the word box. In the first column, write the words that have the short vowel /ĕ/ sound, as in the word <u>egg</u>. In the second column, write the words that have the long vowel /ē/ sound, as in the word <u>me</u>.

Direcciones: Lee las palabras objetivo en el cuadro de texto. En la primera columna, escribe las palabras que tengan el sonido vocal corto /ĕ/, como en la palabra inglés <u>egg</u>. En la segunda columna, escribe las palabras que tengan el sonido vocal largo /ē/, como en la palabra inglés <u>me</u>.

Target Word Box				
fled	theme	left	temp	went
these	step	scene	seeing	speed
held	athlete	complete	then	increase
extreme	self	west	free	test

Letter "e" has the /ĕ/ sound as in the word <u>egg</u>

- fled
- left
- test
- step
- held
- then
- self
- west
- went
- temp

Letter "e" has the /ē/ sound as in the word <u>me</u>

- free
- these
- theme
- scene
- seeing
- speed
- athlete
- complete
- increase
- extreme

Learn To Read English With Directions In Spanish

Answer Key

 Name: _____   Date: ___/___/_____   Score: _____

Lesson 5.4

Reading Words with Letter "e" Vowel Pairs

✓ Lesson Check Point

 Directions: Read each target word. Circle the word in the column that has the same vowel "ea," "ee," "ei," "eo" or "eu" sound as the target word.
Direcciones: Lee cada palabra objetivo. Encierra en un círculo la palabra en la columna que tenga el mismo sonido vocal "ea," "ee," "ei," "eo" o "eu" que la palabra objetivo.

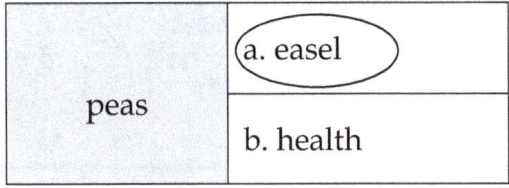

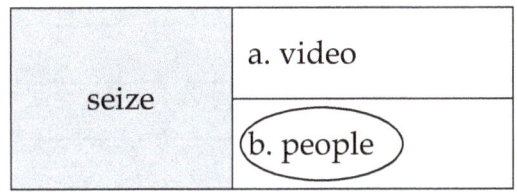

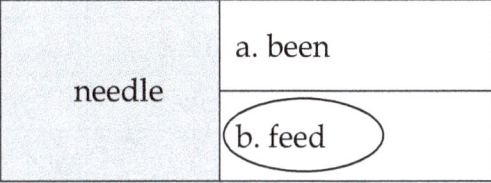

 Directions: Read each target word. Put a check (✓) under the correct column heading.
Direcciones: Lee cada palabra objetivo. Coloca un signo de verificación (✓) bajo el encabezado de la columna correcta.

Target Words	Words have the long "e" sound as in the word <u>tea</u>	Words do not have the long "e" sound
1. peas	✓	
2. veil		✓
3. seize	✓	
4. needle	✓	

Learn To Read English With Directions In Spanish

Classwork

 Name: _____ Date: ___/___/_____ Score: _____

Lesson 5.5

Reading Words with the Final Letter "e"

✓ **Lesson Check Point**

 Directions: Read each target word. Find the letter "e" and put a check (✓) in the column that identifies its position within the syllable.
Direcciones: Lee cada palabra objetivo. Encuentra la letra "e" y coloca un signo de verificación (✓) en la columna que identifique su posición dentro de la sílaba.

Target Words	"e" is at the end of a one syllable word	"e" is at the end of the first syllable	"e" is at the end of a multi-syllable word
1. becoming		✓	
2. he	✓		
3. recording		✓	
4. multiple			✓
5. we	✓		

 Directions: Read each target word. Put a check (✓) under the correct column heading.
Direcciones: Lee cada palabra objetivo. Coloca un signo de verificación (✓) bajo el encabezado de la columna correcta.

Target Words	"e" has the /ĕ/ sound as in the word egg	"e" has the /ē/ sound as in the word me	"e" has the /ə/ sound as in the word item	"e" is silent as in the word great
6. prefix		✓		
7. made				✓
8. marvel			✓	
9. season		✓		
10. travel			✓	

Answer Key

 Name: _____ Date:__/___/_____ Score:_____

Lesson 5.6

Reading Letter "e" Words with the Schwa Vowel Sound

✓ **Lesson Check Point**

 Directions: Read each target word. Circle the word in the column that has the same "e" sound as the target word.

Direcciones: Lee cada palabra objetivo. Encierra en un círculo la palabra en la columna que tenga el mismo sonido "e" que la palabra objetivo.

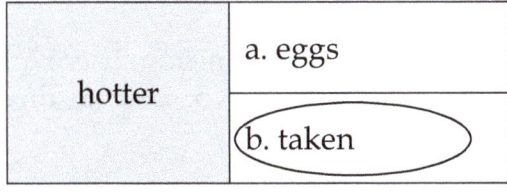

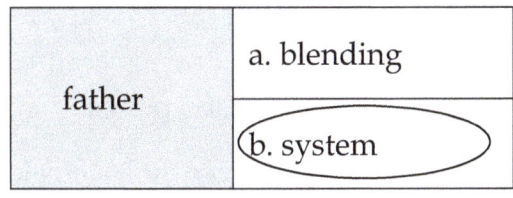
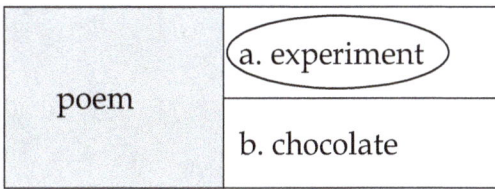

 Directions: Read each sentence and underline the letter "e" word that has the schwa vowel /ə/ sound. The anchor word for the letter "e" schwa vowel sound is <u>item</u>.

Direcciones: Lee cada oración y subraya la letra "e" en palabras que tengan el sonido schwa /ə/. La palabra ejemplo para el sonido schwa de la letra "e" es la palabra, <u>ítem</u>.

1. At <u>dinner</u>, I ate a slice of roast beef.

2. Five <u>movers</u> organized my bedroom set.

3. Every year, we <u>celebrated</u> Andrew's birthday.

4. Three large <u>barrels</u> are located next to cabinets.

5. Our <u>fishermen</u> sailed their ships twenty miles from shore.

6. Large animal populations are <u>scattered</u> throughout Africa.

Classwork

Name: _____ Date:___/___/_____ Score:_____

Lesson 5.7

Reading Words with the "er" Letter Combination

Dictionary Skills/ Vocabulary

✓ Lesson Check Point

Directions: Read each target word and its definition. Write the letter of the definition on the line of each target word. Use a dictionary or the Internet to check your answers.

Direcciones: Lee cada palabra objetivo y su definición. Escribe la letra de la definición en la línea de cada palabra objetivo. Usa un diccionario o Internet para verificar tus respuestas.

Target Words	Definitions
1. _b_ river	a. something very bad or unacceptable
2. _e_ sister	b. a body of water that is larger than a creek
3. _a_ terrible	c. a small fruit that has red or purple drupelets
4. _c_ raspberry	d. a verbal or written response to a question
5. _d_ answer	e. a female who has the same parent(s) as another

Directions: Read each sentence and write the target word that correctly completes the sentence.
Direcciones: Lee cada oración y escribe la palabra objetivo que complete la oración.

6. My younger _____sister_____ eats berries and cherries.

7. Jerry did not _____answer_____ Sherry's difficult questions.

8. Have you ever eaten a sweet, juicy _____raspberry_____?

9. Sherry's baked herring tasted _____terrible_____.

10. We are going to take a ferry ride along the _____river_____.

Answer Key

 Name: _____ Date: ___/___/_____ Score: _____

Lesson 5.8

Reading Words with the "eu" and "ew" Letter Combinations

✓ Lesson Check Point

 Directions: Read each sentence and underline the word that has a silent letter "e."

Direcciones: Lee cada oración y subraya la palabra que tenga una letra muda "e."

Model
My father said, "The apricot <u>streusel</u> is very tasty."

1. In Germany, I bought many elegant gifts with <u>euros</u>.

2. Jennifer and Cathy painted the ceiling a <u>neutral</u> color.

3. The <u>European</u> bound flight will depart at eleven o'clock.

4. The bridal party was <u>euphoric</u> during the wonderful wedding.

 Directions: Read each sentence and underline the word with an "eu" or "ew" letter combination that has the long vowel /y$\overline{oo}$/ or /$\overline{oo}$/ sound, as in the words <u>feud</u> and <u>flew</u>.

Direcciones: Lee cada oración y subraya la palabra con la combinación de letras "eu" o "ew" que tenga el sonido vocal largo /y$\overline{oo}$/ o /$\overline{oo}$/ como en las palabras inglés <u>feud</u> y <u>flew</u>.

5. Mom's apple <u>streusel</u> is delicious.

6. <u>Lieutenant</u> Edwards is a strong leader.

7. The engineering students ate grapes and <u>cashews</u>.

8. Eddie learned a lot of interesting information about <u>Zeus</u>.

9. The Elton family is <u>feuding</u> over Grandmother's possessions.

10. The shower was extremely clean after Jane used <u>mildew</u> remover.

Classwork

 Name: _____ Date:___/ ___/ _____ Score: _____

Lesson 5.9

Reading Words with the "ey" Letter Combination

✓ Lesson Check Point

 Directions: Read each target word. Put a check (✓) under the correct column heading.

Direcciones: Lee cada palabra objetivo. Coloca un signo de verificación (✓) bajo el encabezado de la columna correcta.

Target Words	"ey" has the long /ē/ sound as in the word <u>honey</u>	"ey" has the long /ā/ sound as in the word <u>hey</u>
1. monkey	✓	
2. survey		✓
3. convey		✓
4. kidney	✓	

 Directions: Read each sentence and underline the word with the "ey" letter combination. Put a check (✓) under the correct column heading.

Direcciones: Lee cada oración y subraya la palabra con la combinación de letras "ey". Coloca un signo de verificación (✓) bajo el encabezado de la columna correcta.

	"ey" has the long /ē/ sound as in the word <u>honey</u>	"ey" has the long /ā/ sound as in the word <u>hey</u>
5. The <u>survey</u> has ten questions.		✓
6. Lee received a new team <u>jersey</u>.	✓	
7. Today, <u>they</u> will have a yard sale.		✓
8. I did not <u>obey</u> my teachers' rules.		✓
9. Ethan enjoys playing <u>volleyball</u>.	✓	
10. The <u>jockey's</u> horse is on the track.	✓	

Answer Key

 Name: _____ Date: ___/___/_____ Score: _____

Lesson 5.10

Reading Words with a Silent Letter "e"

✓ **Lesson Check Point**

 Directions: Read the target words in the word box. Write the words that have a silent letter "e" in the first column. Write the words that do not have a silent letter "e" in the second column.

Direcciones: Lee las palabras objetivo en el cuadro de texto. Escribe las palabras que tengan una letra muda "e" en la primera columna. Escribe las palabras que no tengan una letra muda "e" en la segunda columna.

Target Word Box				
eating	cells	friends	game	vote
seat	base	depend	effect	fresh
tone	size	tube	beds	came
face	zebras	clue	drive	meal

Letter "e" is silent	Letter "e" has a letter "e" sound
clue	beds
vote	cells
base	seat
tone	meal
size	effect
tube	fresh
came	eating
face	zebras
drive	friends
game	depend

Unit E
Lesson 5.10

Classwork

Name: _____ Date:___/___/_____ Score:_____

Unit Review – E/e

Reading Words with Vowel "e" Sounds: /ĕ/, /ē/, /ə/ & Silent

✓ **Lesson Check Point**

Directions: Read each target word. Circle the word in the column that has the same "e" sound as the target word.

Direcciones: Lee cada palabra objetivo. Encierra en un círculo la palabra en la columna que tenga el mismo sonido "e" que la palabra objetivo.

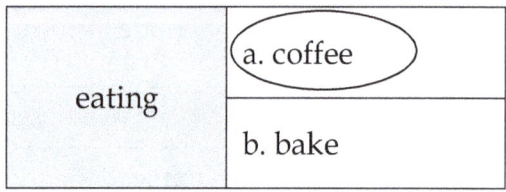

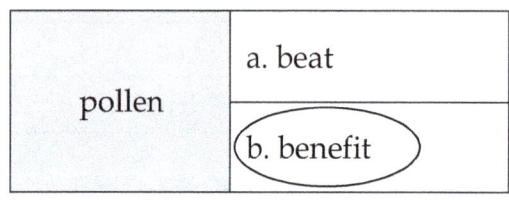
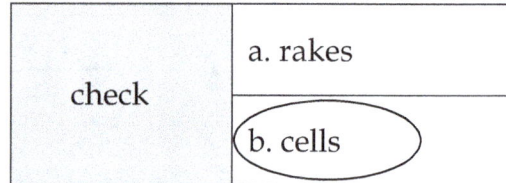

Directions: Read each target word. Put a check (✓) under the correct column heading.

Direcciones: Lee cada palabra objetivo. Coloca un signo de verificación (✓) bajo el encabezado de la columna correcta.

Target Words	"e" has the /ĕ/ sound as in the word <u>egg</u>	"e" has the /ē/ sound as in the word <u>me</u>	"e" has the /ə/ sound as in the word <u>item</u>	"e" is silent as in the word <u>great</u>
1. eating		✓		
2. barrel			✓	
3. pollen			✓	
4. check	✓			

Learn To Read English With Directions In Spanish

Answer Key

 Name: _____   Date: ___/___/_____   Score: _____

The Reading Challenge

Lesson 5.11

Reading Multisyllable Words

✓ **Lesson Check Point**

Directions: Read and divide each target word into syllables. Write each word and place a hyphen (-) between the syllables in the second column. Write the number of syllables in the third column. Use a dictionary or the Internet to check your answers.

Direcciones: Lee y separa en sílabas cada palabra objetivo. Escribe cada palabra y coloca un guión (-) entre las sílabas en la segunda columna. Escribe el número de sílabas en la tercera columna. Usa un diccionario o Internet para verificar tus respuestas.

Target Words	Words Divided into Syllables	Number of Syllables
1. decreasing	de-creas-ing	3
2. between	be-tween	2
3. peanut	pea-nut	2
4. shipwreck	ship-wreck	2
5. nutmeg	nut-meg	2
6. leghorn	leg-horn	2
7. farewell	fare-well	2
8. anthem	an-them	2
9. modem	mo-dem	2
10. itemize	i-tem-ize	3

Unit E
Lesson 5.11

Classwork

 Name: _____ Date:___/___/_____ Score:_____

The Reading Challenge

Lesson 5.11

Reading Multisyllable Words

✓ **Lesson Check Point**

 Directions: Read each target word. Circle the word in the row that is divided correctly into syllables. Use a dictionary or the Internet to check your answers.

Direcciones: Lee cada palabra objetivo. Encierra en un círculo la palabra en la fila que esté correctamente separada en sílabas. Usa un diccionario o Internet para verificar tus respuestas.

Model

| megabyte | a. me-ga-byte | **b. meg-a-byte** (circled) | c. me-gaby-te |

| 1. awaken | a. aw-a-ken | **b. a-wak-en** (circled) | c. a-wa-ken |

| 2. legacy | a. le-ga-cy | **b. leg-a-cy** (circled) | c. leg-ac-y |

| 3. forgiven | **a. for-giv-en** (circled) | b. for-gi-ven | c. fo-rgi-ven |

| 4. acknowledge | a. ack-now-ledge | b. ac-know-ledge | **c. ac-knowl-edge** (circled) |

| 5. turtleneck | **a. tur-tle-neck** (circled) | b. turt-len-eck | c. turt-le-neck |

| 6. celebrate | a. cel-eb-rate | **b. cel-e-brate** (circled) | c. ce-le-brate |

| 7. federal | a. fe-de-ral | b. fed-e-ral | **c. fed-er-al** (circled) |

| 8. ascending | **a. as-cend-ing** (circled) | b. asc-end-ing | c. as-cen-ding |

Answer Key

Name: _____ Date: ___/___/_____ Score: _____

Lesson 5.12

Reading and Writing

Proper and Common Nouns and Adjectives

Directions: Read the words in the word box. Put an (X) on the line next to each word that is written incorrectly. Remember that all proper nouns and proper adjectives are capitalized. Use a dictionary or the Internet to check your answers.

Direcciones: Lee las palabras en el cuadro de texto. Coloca una (X) en la línea próxima a las palabras que estén escritas de forma incorrecta. Recuerda que todos los nombres propios y adjetivos propios empiezan con mayúscula. Usa un diccionario o Internet para verificar tus respuestas.

Word Box					
X	eiffel Tower	X	Educator	X	east Asia
__	England	X	egyptian	X	el Dorado
__	egocentric	__	Estonia	__	editor
X	Envelope	__	European	__	environment

Directions: Read each unedited sentence and underline the word that is written incorrectly. Write each sentence correctly on the line.

Direcciones: Lee cada oración sin editar y subraya la palabra que está escrita de forma incorrecta. Escribe cada oración correctamente en la línea.

Model
All my friends are <u>Excited</u> about the class trip to Europe.
All my friends are excited about the class trip to Europe.

1. I will meet my friend, <u>eileen</u>, at five o'clock EST.
   I will meet my friend, Eileen, at five o'clock EST.

2. <u>evan</u> said, "Many of the citizens of Ethiopia speak English."
   Evan said, "Many of the citizens of Ethiopia speak English."

3. The address on the envelope indicates that the letter is from <u>egypt</u>.
   The address on the envelope indicates that the letter is from Egypt.

4. On Earth Day, Mr. <u>eglon's</u> class will discuss environmental issues.
   On Earth Day, Mr. Eglon's class will discuss environmental issues.

Classwork

Name: _____ Date: ___/___/_____ Score: _____

Lesson 6.1

Reading Words with the Letter F/f

✓ Lesson Check Point

Directions: Read each target word. Find the letter "f" and put a check (✓) in the column that identifies its position: beginning, within or end.
Direcciones: Lee cada palabra objetivo. Encuentra la letra "f" y coloca un signo de verificación (✓) en la columna que identifique su posición: inicio, interior o final.

Target Words	Beginning (First Letter)	Within	End (Last Letter)
1. flip	✓		
2. fresh	✓		
3. leaf			✓
4. defrost		✓	
5. comfort		✓	

Directions: Read each sentence and underline the words that begin with the letter "f." Write all the underlined words in alphabetical order on the lines below.
Direcciones: Lee cada oración y subraya las palabras que empiecen con la letra "f." Escribe todas las letras subrayadas en orden alfabético en las líneas que siguen.

6. Ashley and <u>Fred</u> are citizens of <u>France</u>.

7. Brad and Alex are <u>fabulous</u> <u>flute</u> players.

8. The <u>fence</u> in <u>front</u> of the house is dark blue.

9. The <u>flowers</u> in the <u>field</u> are extremely beautiful.

10. The <u>flag</u> of Belgium is <u>flying</u> high over the building.

fabulous   fence   field
flag   flowers   flute
flying   France   Fred
                  front

Answer Key

Name: _____ Date: ___/___/_____ Score: _____

Lesson 6.2

Reading Words with the "fr" Letter Combination

Dictionary Skills/ Vocabulary

✓ Lesson Check Point

Directions: Read each target word and its definition. Write the letter of the definition on the line of each target word. Use a dictionary or the Internet to check your answers.

Direcciones: Lee cada palabra objetivo y su definición. Escribe la letra de la definición en la línea de cada palabra objetivo. Usa un diccionario o Internet para verificar tus respuestas.

Target Words		Definitions
1. _d_	frog	a. to have broken or cracked something
2. _e_	framed	b. a branch of a business chain
3. _b_	franchise	c. to be ahead of someone or something
4. _a_	fractured	d. a small, smooth, tailless and wet-skinned animal
5. _c_	front	e. evidence or testimony presented to falsely incriminate

Directions: Read each sentence. Underline the word in the parentheses that correctly completes each sentence. Then, write the underlined word on the line.

Direcciones: Lee cada oración. Subraya la palabra entre paréntesis que completa correctamente cada oración. Luego, escribe la palabra subrayada en la línea.

6. The ____frog____ is croaking by the water. (<u>frog</u>, framed)

7. On the bus, Freda sat in ____front____ of Frankie. (<u>front</u>, franchise)

8. At the game, Flo fell and ____fractured____ her ankle. (frog, <u>fractured</u>)

9. Frank was ____framed____ for a crime he didn't commit. (front, <u>framed</u>)

10. Flossy purchased a fast food ____franchise____. (<u>franchise</u>, framed)

Classwork

Name: _____ Date: ___/___/_____ Score: _____

Lesson 6.3

Reading Words with the "fl" Letter Combination

Dictionary Skills/ Vocabulary

✓ Lesson Check Point

Directions: Read each target word and its definition. Write the target word on the line in front of its meaning. Use a dictionary or the Internet to check your answers.

Direcciones: Lee cada palabra objetivo y su definición. Escribe la palabra objetivo en la línea frente a su significado. Usa un diccionario o Internet para verificar tus respuestas.

Target Word Box				
fleet	flash	flower	fluently	fly

1. _fly_____   to travel through the air with wings
2. _flower____   the colorful part of a plant that contains seeds
3. _fleet_____   a number of vehicles owned as a unit
4. _flash_____   a device that provides light to brighten a picture
5. _fluently___   the ability to speak a language correctly

Directions: Read each sentence. Underline the word in the parentheses that correctly completes each sentence. Then, write the underlined word on the line.

Direcciones: Lee cada oración. Subraya la palabra entre paréntesis que completa correctamente cada oración. Luego, escribe la palabra subrayada en la línea.

6. Fred's camera has a built-in ____flash_____. (flash, flower)

7. Flamingos can ____fly____ up to 40 mph in the air. (flash, fly)

8. My friend speaks French and Finnish ____fluently____. (fluently, flash)

9. The florist made a beautiful ___flower___ arrangement. (fluently, flower)

10. After the funeral, a ___fleet__ of cars drove down the avenue. (fly, fleet)

Answer Key

 Name: _____ Date: ___/___/_____ Score: _____

Lesson 6.3

Reading Words with the "fle" Letter Combination

✓ Lesson Check Point

 Directions: Read each target word. Find the "fle" letter combination and put a check (✓) in the column that identifies its position: beginning, within or end.

Direcciones: Lee cada palabra objetivo. Encuentra la combinación de letras "fle" y coloca un signo de verificación (✓) en la columna que identifique su posición: inicio, interior o final.

Target Words	Beginning (First 3 Letters)	Within	End (Last 3 Letters)
1. waffle			✓
2. flesh	✓		
3. fleet	✓		
4. reflect		✓	
5. duffle			✓

 Directions: Read each target word. Put a check (✓) in the "yes" column if the "fle" letter combination has the /f/ + /ə/ + /l/ sounds. Put a check (✓) in the "no" column if the "fle" letter combination does not have the /f/ + /ə/ + /l/ sounds.

Direcciones: Lee cada palabra objetivo. Coloca un signo de verificación (✓) en la columna del "sí" si la combinación de letras "fle" tiene el sonidos /f/ + /ə/ + /l/. Coloca un signo de verificación (✓) en la columna del "no" si la combinación de letras "fle" no tiene el sonidos /f/ + /ə/ + /l/.

Target Words	Yes	No
6. waffle	✓	
7. flesh		✓
8. fleet		✓
9. reflect		✓
10. duffle	✓	

Classwork

Name: _____ Date:___/___/_____ Score:_____

Lesson 6.4

Reading Words with the "ft," "lf" and "ff" Letter Combinations

Dictionary Skills/ Vocabulary

✓ Lesson Check Point

Directions: Read each target word and its definition. Write the letter of the definition on the line of each target word. Use a dictionary or the Internet to check your answers.

Direcciones: Lee cada palabra objetivo y su definición. Escribe la letra de la definición en la línea de cada palabra objetivo. Usa un diccionario o Internet para verificar tus respuestas.

Target Words	Definitions
1. _d_ giraffe	a. a piece of writing that is not finalized
2. _e_ Gulf	b. to move along by wind or water
3. _a_ draft	c. a vehicle that can fly in the air
4. _c_ aircraft	d. the tallest land animal with dark spots
5. _b_ drift	e. a large body of water partially enclosed by land

Directions: Read each sentence and write the target word that correctly completes the sentence.
Direcciones: Lee cada oración y escribe la palabra objetivo que complete la oración.

6. I will write the first _____draft_____ of the report in class.

7. The _____aircraft_____ flew from New York City to Atlantic City.

8. At sunset, the boats and rafts will _____drift_____ along the lake.

9. The hurricane damaged the houses along the _____Gulf_____ Coast.

10. The guide said, "The _____giraffe_____ is the tallest African animal."

Answer Key

 Name: _____ Date: ___/___/_____ Score: _____

Lesson 6.5

Reading Words with a Silent Letter "f"

✓ **Lesson Check Point**

 Directions: Read the target words in the word box. Write the words that have a silent letter "f" in the first column. Write the words that do not have a silent letter "f" in the second column.

Direcciones: Lee las palabras objetivo en el cuadro de texto. Escribe las palabras que tengan una letra muda "f" en la primera columna. Escribe las palabras que no tengan una letra muda "f" en la segunda columna.

Target Word Box				
muffin	buffalo	infancy	faces	suffocate
wife	after	afresh	afford	flying
defect	effect	cliff	caffeine	officially
fitness	coffee	bullfrog	fast	taffy

Letter "f" is silent

- cliff
- taffy
- effect
- afford
- muffin
- coffee
- caffeine
- buffalo
- suffocate
- officially

Letter "f" has the /f/ sound

- wife
- fast
- defect
- after
- afresh
- faces
- flying
- fitness
- infancy
- bullfrog

Unit F
Lesson 6.5

Classwork

 Name: _____ Date:___/___/_____ Score:_____

Lesson 6.6

Reading Singular and Plural forms of Words Ending in "-f" & "-fe"

✓ **Lesson Check Point**

 Directions: Read each target word. Put a check (✓) in the second column if the plural form of the target word ends with "-ves." Put a check (✓) in the third column if the plural form of the target word ends with "-s" or "-es."

Direcciones: Lee cada palabra objetivo. Coloca un signo de verificación (✓) en la segunda columna si la forma plural de la palabra objetivo termina con "-ves". Coloca un signo de verificación (✓) en la tercera columna si la forma plural de la palabra objetivo termina con "-s" o "-es."

Target Words	The plural form of the target word ends with "-ves"	The plural form of the target word ends with "-s" or "-es"
1. roof		✓
2. half	✓	
3. life	✓	
4. thief	✓	
5. chef		✓

 Directions: Read each sentence. Complete each sentence by writing the plural form of the word on the line.

Direcciones: Lee cada oración. Completa cada oración escribiendo la forma correcta del plural de la palabra en la línea.

6. Doctors save _____lives_____ every day. (life)

7. The men gave flowers to their ____wives____. (wife)

8. Frank built five _____shelves_____ by himself. (shelf)

9. The girls filmed the events by ____themselves____. (herself)

10. Many ____wolves____ attacked the farmer's chicken. (wolf)

Answer Key

 Name: _____ Date:___/___/_____ Score:_____

The Reading Challenge

Lesson 6.7

Reading Multisyllable Words

✓ Lesson Check Point

 Directions: Read and divide each target word into syllables. Write each word and place a hyphen (-) between the syllables in the second column. Write the number of syllables in the third column. Use a dictionary or the Internet to check your answers.

Direcciones: Lee y separa en sílabas cada palabra objetivo. Escribe cada palabra y coloca un guión (-) entre las sílabas en la segunda columna. Escribe el número de sílabas en la tercera columna. Usa un diccionario o Internet para verificar tus respuestas.

Target Words	Words Divided into Syllables	Number of Syllables
1. fencing	fenc-ing	2
2. fabulous	fab-u-lous	3
3. friendship	friend-ship	2
4. facial	fa-cial	2
5. flawless	flaw-less	2
6. franchising	fran-chis-ing	3
7. falcon	fal-con	2
8. finalist	fi-nal-ist	3
9. florist	flo-rist	2
10. football	foot-ball	2

Classwork

 Name: _____ Date:___/___/_____ Score:_____

The Reading Challenge

Lesson 6.7

Reading Multisyllable Words

✓ **Lesson Check Point**

 Directions: Read each target word. Circle the word in the row that is divided correctly into syllables. Use a dictionary or the Internet to check your answers.

Direcciones: Lee cada palabra objetivo. Encierra en un círculo la palabra en la fila que esté correctamente separada en sílabas. Usa un diccionario o Internet para verificar tus respuestas.

Model

factory	a. fac-tor-y	b. fac-to-ry ⬭	c. fa-cto-ry

1. flexible	b. fle-x-ible	b. fle-xi-ble	c. flex-i-ble ⬭
2. festival	a. fest-i-val	b. fe-stiv-al	c. fes-ti-val ⬭
3. fabricate	a. fab-ri-cate ⬭	b. fa-bri-cate	c. fabr-ic-ate
4. finale	a. fin-al-e	b. fi-nal-e ⬭	c. fina-le
5. forensic	a. for-e-nsic	b. for-en-sic	c. fo-ren-sic ⬭
6. fortify	a. fort-i-fy	b. for-ti-fy ⬭	c. for-tif-y
7. familiar	a. fa-mil-iar ⬭	b. fam-i-liar	c. fam-il-iar
8. flavoring	a. fla-vor-ing ⬭	b. flav-or-ing	c. flav-o-ring

Answer Key

Name: _____ Date: ___/___/_____ Score: _____

Lesson 6.8

Reading and Writing

Proper and Common Nouns and Adjectives

Directions: Read the words in the word box. Put an (X) on the line next to each word that is written incorrectly. Remember that all proper nouns and proper adjectives are capitalized. Use a dictionary or the Internet to check your answers.

Direcciones: Lee las palabras en el cuadro de texto. Coloca una (X) en la línea próxima a las palabras que estén escritas de forma incorrecta. Recuerda que todos los nombres propios y adjetivos propios empiezan con mayúscula. Usa un diccionario o Internet para verificar tus respuestas.

	Word Box				
__	flower	__	Florida	X	far East
X	franklin	__	flock	X	france
X	french	X	Finalist	__	fashion
__	flamingo	X	frankfort	__	florist

Directions: Read each unedited sentence and underline the word that is written incorrectly. Write each sentence correctly on the line.

Direcciones: Lee cada oración sin editar y subraya la palabra que está escrita de forma incorrecta. Escribe cada oración correctamente en la línea.

Model
Fiji is my <u>Florist's</u> favorite holiday destination.
<u>Fiji is my florist's favorite holiday destination.</u>

1. Flossy and Frank were born in <u>france</u>.
<u>Flossy and Frank were born in France.</u>

2. <u>francis</u> speaks English and French fluently.
<u>Francis speaks English and French fluently.</u>

3. Freda works by <u>fort</u> Hamilton Parkway.
<u>Freda works by Fort Hamilton Parkway.</u>

4. Fred's baseball game is at <u>frankfurt</u> Field.
<u>Fred's baseball game is at Frankfurt Field.</u>

Classwork

Name: _____ Date: ___/___/_____ Score: _____

Lesson 7.1

Reading Words with the Letter G/g

✓ **Lesson Check Point**

Directions: Read each target word. Find the letter "g" and put a check (✓) in the column that identifies its position: beginning, within or end.
Direcciones: Lee cada palabra objetivo. Encuentra la letra "g" y coloca un signo de verificación (✓) en la columna que identifique su posición: inicio, interior o final.

Target Words	Beginning (First Letter)	Within	End (Last Letter)
1. glossary	✓		
2. hexagon		✓	
3. landing			✓
4. oblong			✓
5. government	✓		

Directions: Read each sentence and underline the words that begin with the letter "g." Write all the underlined words in alphabetical order on the lines below.
Direcciones: Lee cada oración y subraya las palabras que empiecen con la letra "g." Escribe todas las letras subrayadas en orden alfabético en las líneas que siguen.

6. Billy and Fran ate green grapes.

7. All the boys earned good grades.

8. My guests are going to the airport.

9. The girls forgot to put gas in the car.

10. The golfers play a challenging game.

game _____   gas _____   girls _____
going _____   golfers _____ good _____
grades _____   grapes _____   green _____
                   guests _____

Learn To Read English With Directions In Spanish

Answer Key

 Name: _____ Date: ___/___/_____ Score: _____

Lesson 7.1

Reading Words with the Hard Letter "g"

✓ **Lesson Check Point**

 Directions: Read each target word. Put a check (✓) under the correct column heading.

Direcciones: Lee cada palabra objetivo. Coloca un signo de verificación (✓) bajo el encabezado de la columna correcta.

Target Words	Hard "g" has the /g/ sound as in the word <u>gum</u>	Soft "g" has the /j/ sound as in the word <u>gem</u>
1. gills	✓	
2. golden	✓	
3. gentle		✓
4. geese	✓	
5. gallops	✓	

 Directions: Read each sentence and underline the words that have the hard "g" sound. The anchor word for the hard "g" sound is <u>gum</u>. Write all the underlined words in alphabetical order on the lines below.

Direcciones: Lee cada oración y subraya las palabras que tengan el sonido fuerte "g", como en la palabra <u>gum</u>. Escribe todas las palabras subrayadas en orden alfabético en las líneas siguientes.

6. <u>Gloria</u> and Gina have beautiful blue <u>glasses</u>.

7. Today, Georgette saw a cow, a <u>goat</u> and a <u>gazelle</u>.

8. Jennifer is <u>growing</u> geraniums in her <u>greenhouse</u>.

9. The children in Ms. George's class have <u>good</u> <u>grades</u>.

10. My <u>grandfather</u> has ginger chicken and corn on the <u>grill</u>.

gazelle   glasses   Gloria
goat   good   grades
grandfather   greenhouse   grill
                  growing

Classwork

Name: _____ Date: ___/___/_____ Score: _____

Lesson 7.2

Reading Words with the Soft Letter "g"

✓ **Lesson Check Point**

Directions: Read each target word. Put a check (✓) under the correct column heading.

Direcciones: Lee cada palabra objetivo. Coloca un signo de verificación (✓) bajo el encabezado de la columna correcta.

Target Words	Soft "g" has the /j/ or /zh/ sound as in the words gem & massage	Hard "g" has the /g/ sound as in the word gum	Both soft "g" and hard "g" sounds as in the word gauge
1. garage			✓
2. gear		✓	
3. intelligent	✓		
4. progress		✓	
5. grammar		✓	

Directions: Read each sentence and underline the words that have the soft "g" sound. The anchor word for the soft "g" sound is gem. Write all the underlined words in alphabetical order on the lines below.

Direcciones: Lee cada oración y subraya las palabras que tengan el sonido suave "g", como en la palabra gem. Escribe todas las palabras subrayadas en orden alfabético en las líneas siguientes.

6. Gloria's <u>giant</u> <u>gem</u> glistens in the sun.

7. <u>Gianna</u> is chewing gum in the <u>gymnasium</u>.

8. <u>Ginny</u> got a great grade in her <u>biology</u> class.

9. For graduation, I received a <u>gigantic</u> <u>package</u>.

10. The <u>teenagers</u> felt guilty because they did not go to the <u>gym</u>.

<u>biology</u>   <u>gem</u>   <u>Gianna</u>
<u>giant</u>   <u>gigantic</u>   <u>Ginny</u>
<u>gym</u>   <u>gymnasium</u>   <u>package</u>
                 <u>teenagers</u>

Answer Key

Name: _____ Date: ___/___/_____ Score: _____

Review Lessons 7.1 & 7.2

Reading Hard Letter "g" and Soft Letter "g" Words

✓ **Lesson Check Point**

Directions: Read each target word. Put a check (✓) under the correct column heading.

Direcciones: Lee cada palabra objetivo. Coloca un signo de verificación (✓) bajo el encabezado de la columna correcta.

Target Words	Soft "g" has the /j/ or /zh/ sound as in the words gem & massage	Hard "g" has the /g/ sound as in the word gum	Both soft "g" and hard "g" sounds as in the word gauge
1. get		✓	
2. biology	✓		
3. ground		✓	
4. ingested	✓		
5. fragrant		✓	

Directions: Read each sentence and underline the words that have the hard "g" sound. The anchor word for the hard "g" sound is gum. Write all the underlined words in alphabetical order on the lines below.

Direcciones: Lee cada oración y subraya las palabras que tengan el sonido fuerte "g", como en la palabra gum. Escribe todas las palabras subrayadas en orden alfabético en las líneas siguientes.

6. Georgette has good grades.

7. Greg enjoys going to the gym.

8. Gina's eyeglasses are glamorous.

9. Ben gave me a bronze chain as a gift.

10. My friend, Gio, graduated and traveled to Guyana.

eyeglasses	gave	gift
glamorous	going	good
grades	graduated	Greg
	Guyana	

Classwork

Name: _____ Date: ___/___/_____ Score: _____

Review Lessons 7.1 & 7.2

Reading Hard Letter "g" and Soft Letter "g" Words

Directions: Read the target words in the word box. In the first column, write the words with the letter "g" that have the /g/ sound, as in the word <u>gum</u>. In the second column, write the words with the letter "g" that have the /j/ sound, as in the word <u>gem</u>.

Direcciones: Lee las palabras objetivo en el cuadro de texto. En la primera columna, escribe las palabras con la letra "g" que tengan el sonido /g/, como en la palabra inglés <u>gum</u>. En la segunda columna, escribe las palabras con la letra "g" que tengan el sonido /j/, como en la palabra inglés <u>gem</u>.

Target Word Box				
digital	green	geese	ginger	page
germs	greet	gems	organ	gulf
grandson	glasses	large	sugar	engine
gate	gifts	gym	stage	orange

Hard letter "g" has the /g/ sound as in the word <u>gum</u>

- gifts
- gate
- green
- greet
- sugar
- gulf
- geese
- organ
- glasses
- grandson

Soft letter "g" has the /j/ sound as in the word <u>gem</u>

- gym
- page
- gems
- stage
- large
- germs
- orange
- digital
- engine
- ginger

Answer Key

Name: _____ Date: ___/___/_____ Score: _____

Lesson 7.3

Reading Words with the "gr" Letter Combination

Dictionary Skills/ Vocabulary

✓ **Lesson Check Point**

Directions: Read each target word and its definition. Write the letter of the definition on the line of each target word. Use a dictionary or the Internet to check your answers.

Direcciones: Lee cada palabra objetivo y su definición. Escribe la letra de la definición en la línea de cada palabra objetivo. Usa un diccionario o Internet para verificar tus respuestas.

Target Words	Definitions
1. _b_ grabs	a. to make a big, positive impression
2. _a_ grand	b. to take something quickly with one's hand(s)
3. _e_ gravel	c. something that contains or is covered with oil
4. _c_ greasy	d. to hold something firmly with one's hand(s)
5. _d_ grip	e. a mixture of very small rocks and pebbles

Directions: Read each sentence. Underline the word in the parentheses that correctly completes each sentence. Then, write the underlined word on the line.

Direcciones: Lee cada oración. Subraya la palabra entre paréntesis que completa correctamente cada oración. Luego, escribe la palabra subrayada en la línea.

6. Grandpa's driveway is made of _____gravel_____. (greasy, <u>gravel</u>)

7. I can't eat the burger because it is too ___greasy___. (grabs, <u>greasy</u>)

8. The gloves give me a better ___grip___ on the bars. (<u>grip</u>, grabbed)

9. Greg _____grabs_____ the books with both hands. (<u>grabs</u>, gravel)

10. At the dance, the girls made a ___grand___ entrance. (<u>grand</u>, greasy)

Classwork

Name: _____ Date: ___/___/_____ Score: _____

Lesson 7.4

Reading Words with the "gl" Letter Combination

Dictionary Skills/ Vocabulary

✓ Lesson Check Point

Directions: Read each target word and its definition. Write the target word on the line in front of its meaning. Use a dictionary or the Internet to check your answers.

Direcciones: Lee cada palabra objetivo y su definición. Escribe la palabra objetivo en la línea frente a su significado. Usa un diccionario o Internet para verificar tus respuestas.

Target Word Box				
glaze	globe	gloom	glossary	glowing

1. __glowing__ to shine brightly like a light or the sun
2. __gloom__ a state of sadness, hopelessness and/or depression
3. __glaze__ to spread a thin layer of something on a surface
4. __globe__ a three-dimensional, sphere shaped model of the earth
5. __glossary__ an alphabetical list of text-related words with definitions

Directions: Read each sentence. Underline the word in the parentheses that correctly completes each sentence. Then, write the underlined word on the line.

Direcciones: Lee cada oración. Subraya la palabra entre paréntesis que completa correctamente cada oración. Luego, escribe la palabra subrayada en la línea.

6. The beautiful, blushing bride is __glowing__. (gloom, <u>glowing</u>)

7. Gerald plans to travel around the __globe__. (<u>globe</u>, glowing)

8. Gloria __glazed__ the chicken with barbecue sauce. (<u>glazed</u>, globe)

9. The bad report brought deep __gloom__ to the family. (glossary, <u>gloom</u>)

10. The book's __glossary__ helps me define difficult words. (<u>glossary</u>, glowing)

Answer Key

 Name: _____ Date: ___/___/_____ Score: _____

Lesson 7.4

Reading Words with the "gle" Letter Combination

✓ Lesson Check Point

 Directions: Read each target word. Find the "gle" letter combination and put a check (✓) in the column that identifies its position: beginning, within or end.

Direcciones: Lee cada palabra objetivo. Encuentra la combinación de letras "gle" y coloca un signo de verificación (✓) en la columna que identifique su posición: inicio, interior o final.

Target Words	Beginning (First 3 Letters)	Within	End (Last 3 Letters)
1. glee	✓		
2. angle			✓
3. mangled		✓	
4. gleaming	✓		
5. triangle			✓

 Directions: Read each target word. Put a check (✓) in the "yes" column if the "gle" letter combination has the /g/ + /ə/ + /l/ sounds. Put a check (✓) in the "no" column if the "gle" letter combination does not have the /g/ + /ə/ + /l/ sounds.

Direcciones: Lee cada palabra objetivo. Coloca un signo de verificación (✓) en la columna del "sí" si la combinación de letras "gle" tiene el sonidos /g/ + /ə/ + /l/. Coloca un signo de verificación (✓) en la columna del "no" si la combinación de letras "gle" no tiene el sonidos /g/ + /ə/ + /l/.

Target Words	Yes	No
6. glee		✓
7. angle	✓	
8. mangled	✓	
9. gleaming		✓
10. triangle	✓	

Classwork

 Name: _____ Date: ___/___/_____ Score: _____

Lesson 7.5

Reading Words with the "gh" Letter Combination

✓ Lesson Check Point

 Directions: Read each target word. Circle the word in the column that has the same "gh" sound as the target word.

Direcciones: Lee cada palabra objetivo. Encierra en un círculo la palabra en la columna que tenga el mismo sonido "gh" que la palabra objetivo.

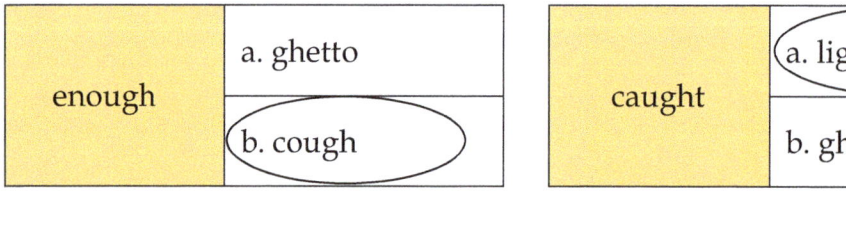

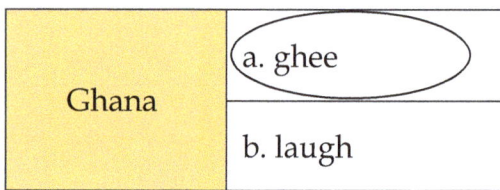

 Directions: Read each target word. Put a check (✓) under the correct column heading.

Direcciones: Lee cada palabra objetivo. Coloca un signo de verificación (✓) bajo el encabezado de la columna correcta.

Target Words	"gh" has the /g/ sound as in the word <u>ghetto</u>	"gh" has the /f/ sound as in the word <u>laugh</u>	"gh" is silent as in the word <u>light</u>
1. enough		✓	
2. caught			✓
3. bright			✓
4. Ghana	✓		

Answer Key

 Name: _____ Date: ___/___/_____ Score: _____

Lesson 7.6

Reading Words with the "gn" Letter Combination

✓ Lesson Check Point

 Directions: Read each target word. Circle the word in the column that has the same "gn" sound(s) as the target word.

Direcciones: Lee cada palabra objetivo. Encierra en un círculo la palabra en la columna que tenga el mismo sonido "gn" que la palabra objetivo.

| ignorance | a. resigned |
| | (b. cognition) ⭕ |

| designed | (a. alignment) ⭕ |
| | b. magnifying |

| signature | a. champagne |
| | (b. recognizable) ⭕ |

| benign | (a. foreigner) ⭕ |
| | b. pregnant |

 Directions: Read each target word. Put a check (✓) under the correct column heading.

Direcciones: Lee cada palabra objetivo. Coloca un signo de verificación (✓) bajo el encabezado de la columna correcta.

Target Words	"gn" has the /g/ + /n/ sounds as in the word **ignite**	"gn" has the silent "g" + /n/ sound as in the word **sign**
1. ignorance	✓	
2. designed		✓
3. signature	✓	
4. benign		✓

Classwork

 Name: _____   Date: ___/___/_____   Score: _____

Lesson 7.7

Reading Words with a Silent Letter "g"

✓ Lesson Check Point

 Directions: Read the target words in the word box. Write the words that have a silent letter "g" in the first column. Write the words that do not have a silent letter "g" in the second column.

Direcciones: Lee las palabras objetivo en el cuadro de texto. Escribe las palabras que tengan una letra muda "g" en la primera columna. Escribe las palabras que no tengan una letra muda "g" en la segunda columna.

Target Word Box				
daughter	sleigh	image	hunger	signal
glance	fight	thought	campaign	dough
frog	dignify	sign	magnify	regent
elegant	neighbor	assign	grand	weigh

Letter "g" is silent

- sign
- fight
- dough
- assign
- weigh
- sleigh
- thought
- neighbor
- daughter
- campaign

Letter "g" has the /g/ or /j/ sound

- frog
- image
- glance
- dignify
- grand
- elegant
- signal
- regent
- hunger
- magnify

Answer Key

 Name: _____   Date: ___/___/_____   Score: _____

The Reading Challenge

Lesson 7.8

Reading Multisyllable Words

✓ **Lesson Check Point**

 Directions: Read and divide each target word into syllables. Write each word and place a hyphen (-) between the syllables in the second column. Write the number of syllables in the third column. Use a dictionary or the Internet to check your answers.

Direcciones: Lee y separa en sílabas cada palabra objetivo. Escribe cada palabra y coloca un guión (-) entre las sílabas en la segunda columna. Escribe el número de sílabas en la tercera columna. Usa un diccionario o Internet para verificar tus respuestas.

Target Words	Words Divided into Syllables	Number of Syllables
1. grocery	gro-cer-y	3
2. Guyana	Guy-a-na	3
3. gardening	gar-den-ing	3
4. general	gen-er-al	3
5. glamorize	glam-or-ize	3
6. grandfather	grand-fa-ther	3
7. girlfriend	girl-friend	2
8. generous	gen-er-ous	3
9. guardian	guard-i-an	3
10. genetic	ge-net-ic	3

Classwork

 Name: _____ Date: ___/___/_____ Score: _____

The Reading Challenge

Lesson 7.8

Reading Multisyllable Words

✓ **Lesson Check Point**

 Directions: Read each target word. Circle the word in the row that is divided correctly into syllables. Use a dictionary or the Internet to check your answers.

Direcciones: Lee cada palabra objetivo. Encierra en un círculo la palabra en la fila que esté correctamente separada en sílabas. Usa un diccionario o Internet para verificar tus respuestas.

Model

| galaxy | a. ga-lax-y | b. gal-ax-y ⭕ | c. gal-a-xy |

1. glycerol	a. glyc-er-ol ⭕	b. gly-cer-ol	c. glyc-e-rol
2. governess	a. go-ver-ness	b. gov-ern-ess	c. gov-er-ness ⭕
3. general	a. gen-er-al ⭕	b. ge-ner-al	c. gene-r-al
4. graduate	a. gra-du-ate	b. grad-u-ate ⭕	c. grad-uat-e
5. granola	a. gra-nol-a	b. gra-no-la ⭕	c. gran-ol-a
6. gestation	a. gest-a-tion	b. ge-sta-tion	c. ges-ta-tion ⭕
7. germinate	a. ger-mi-nate ⭕	b. germ-i-nate	c. ge-rmi-nate
8. gratify	a. grat-i-fy ⭕	b. gra-tif-y	c. gr-ati-fy

Answer Key

Name: _____ Date: ___/___/_____ Score: _____

Lesson 7.9

Reading and Writing

Proper and Common Nouns and Adjectives

Directions: Read the words in the word box. Put an (X) on the line next to each word that is written incorrectly. Remember that all proper nouns and proper adjectives are capitalized. Use a dictionary or the Internet to check your answers.

Direcciones: Lee las palabras en el cuadro de texto. Coloca una (X) en la línea próxima a las palabras que estén escritas de forma incorrecta. Recuerda que todos los nombres propios y adjetivos propios empiezan con mayúscula. Usa un diccionario o Internet para verificar tus respuestas.

Word Box					
X	Geology	X	gandhi	_	groom
X	Gym	X	Group	_	grammar
_	Greece	_	globe	X	georgetown
_	Guyana	X	germany	_	Ghana

Directions: Read each unedited sentence and underline the word that is written incorrectly. Write each sentence correctly on the line.

Direcciones: Lee cada oración sin editar y subraya la palabra que está escrita de forma incorrecta. Escribe cada oración correctamente en la línea.

Model
Ginger and <u>gene</u> are going to Georgetown, Guyana.
<u>Ginger and Gene are going to Georgetown, Guyana.</u>

1. The Gambia and <u>ghana</u> are amazing African countries.
<u>The Gambia and Ghana are amazing African countries.</u>

2. The bride and the <u>Groom</u> are getting married in Grenada.
<u>The bride and the groom are getting married in Grenada.</u>

3. Everyone says that Mr. Grant will be Georgia's <u>Governor</u>.
<u>Everyone says that Mr. Grant will be Georgia's governor.</u>

4. George and <u>gem</u> said, "Grandma has beautiful new glasses."
<u>George and Gem said, "Grandma has beautiful new glasses."</u>

Classwork

!! Name: _____ Date: ___/___/_____ Score: _____

Lesson 8.1

Reading Words with the Letter H/h

✓ Lesson Check Point

Directions: Read each target word. Find the letter "h" and put a check (✓) in the column that identifies its position: beginning, within or end.
Direcciones: Lee cada palabra objetivo. Encuentra la letra "h" y coloca un signo de verificación (✓) en la columna que identifique su posición: inicio, interior o final.

Target Words	Beginning (First Letter)	Within	End (Last Letter)
1. inch			✓
2. cheeta<u>h</u>			✓
3. hallway	✓		
4. Fahrenheit		✓	
5. Savannah			✓

Directions: Read each sentence and underline the words that begin with the letter "h." Write all the underlined words in alphabetical order on the lines below.
Direcciones: Lee cada oración y subraya las palabras que empiecen con la letra "h." Escribe todas las letras subrayadas en orden alfabético en las líneas que siguen.

6. Barry's <u>home</u> is on top of the <u>hill</u>.

7. <u>Henry</u> lives in the center of <u>Houston</u>.

8. The <u>hummingbirds'</u> eggs are <u>hatching</u>.

9. The cats and <u>hamsters</u> are very <u>hungry</u>.

10. <u>Heather</u> Carrington is an <u>honest</u> person.

<u>hamster</u>   <u>hatching</u>   <u>Heather</u>
<u>Henry</u>   <u>hill</u>   <u>home</u>
<u>honest</u>   <u>Houston</u>   <u>hummingbirds'</u>
                      <u>hungry</u>

 Name: _____ Date:___/___/_____ Score:_____

Answer Key

Lesson 8.2

Reading Words with the Letter "h" Combinations: "sh," "wh," "ch," "th," "rh," "ph" and "gh"

✓ **Lesson Check Point**

 Directions: Read the target words in the word box. Identify the words with the following letter combinations: "sh," "wh," "ch," "th," "rh," "ph" and "gh." Write the word on the line that shows the position of the letter combination: beginning, within or end.

Direcciones: Lee las palabras objetivo en el cuadro de texto. Identifica las palabras con las siguientes combinaciones de letras: "sh," "wh," "ch," "th," "rh," "ph" y "gh." Escribe la palabra en la línea que muestre la posición de la combinación de letras: inicio, interior o final.

Target Word Box				
wheel	thanks	rhino	kitchen	sheep
dishes	paragraph	anywhere	phone	laugh
overheard	ghost	myrrh	nephew	brother
chocolate	south	goldfish	reach	caught

	Beginning	Within	End
sh	1. sheep	2. dishes	3. goldfish
wh	4. wheel	5. anywhere	
ch	6. chocolate	7. kitchen	8. reach
th	9. thanks	10. brother	11. south
rh	12. rhino	13. overheard	14. myrrh
ph	15. phone	16. nephew	17. paragraph
gh	18. ghost	19. caught	20. laugh

Classwork

 Name: _____ Date:___/___/_____ Score:_____

Lesson 8.2

Reading Words with the Letter "h" Combinations:
"sh," "wh," "ch," "th," "rh," "ph," "gh" and "sch"

✓ Lesson Check Point

 Directions: Read the target words in the word box. Identify the words with the following letter combinations: "sh," "wh," "ch," "th," "rh," "ph," "gh" and "sch." Write the target word that correctly completes each sentence on the line.

Direcciones: Lee las palabras objetivo en el cuadro de texto. Identifica las palabras con las siguientes combinaciones de letras: "sh," "wh," "ch," "th," "rh," "ph," "gh" y "sch." Escribe la palabra objetivo que complete correctamente la oración en la línea.

Target Word Box		
shower	Ghana	Children
Whales	theater	through
phones		Chemicals
school		rhombus

1. I am learning to read and write in _____school_____.

2. We are not allowed to have cellular ____phones____ in school.

3. The sun was shining brightly ____through____ the window.

4. Yesterday, Trevor used liquid soap during his ____shower____.

5. Brenda used her ruler to draw the shape of a ____rhombus____.

6. Children_____ should obey their parents and teachers.

7. Whales_____ are the largest mammals that live in the ocean.

8. The people from ____Ghana_____ speak many languages.

9. Thelma is hosting her birthday party at the movie ___theater___.

10. Chemicals____ found in processed foods may harm your health.

Answer Key

 Name: _____ Date: ___/___/_____ Score: _____

Lesson 8.3

Reading Words with a Silent Letter "h"

✓ Lesson Check Point

 Directions: Read the target words in the word box. Write the words that have a silent letter "h" in the first column. Write the words that do not have a silent letter "h" in the second column.

Direcciones: Lee las palabras objetivo en el cuadro de texto. Escribe las palabras que tengan una letra muda "h" en la primera columna. Escribe las palabras que no tengan una letra muda "h" en la segunda columna.

Target Word Box				
inherent	beehive	unhappy	myrrh	dehydrate
exhibit	white	fright	hundred	holding
silhouette	behind	exhaust	honor	Fahrenheit
heirloom	house	comprehend	perhaps	whales

Letter "h" is silent

- fright
- white
- exhaust
- whales
- myrrh
- exhibit
- honor
- heirloom
- silhouette
- Fahrenheit

Letter "h" has the /h/ sound

- house
- behind
- holding
- hundred
- beehive
- inherent
- unhappy
- perhaps
- dehydrate
- comprehend

Classwork

 Name: _____ Date: ___/___/_____ Score: _____

The Reading Challenge

Lesson 8.4

Reading Multisyllable Words

✓ Lesson Check Point

 Directions: Read and divide each target word into syllables. Write each word and place a hyphen (-) between the syllables in the second column. Write the number of syllables in the third column. Use a dictionary or the Internet to check your answers.

Direcciones: Lee y separa en sílabas cada palabra objetivo. Escribe cada palabra y coloca un guión (-) entre las sílabas en la segunda columna. Escribe el número de sílabas en la tercera columna. Usa un diccionario o Internet para verificar tus respuestas.

Target Words	Words Divided into Syllables	Number of Syllables
1. hallway	hall-way	2
2. heartache	heart-ache	2
3. honeycomb	hon-ey-comb	3
4. hyperlink	hy-per-link	3
5. headlights	head-lights	2
6. harmonize	har-mo-nize	3
7. homonym	hom-o-nym	3
8. hardware	hard-ware	2
9. hesitant	hes-i-tant	3
10. hazelnut	ha-zel-nut	3

Answer Key

Name: _____ Date: ___/___/_____ Score: _____

The Reading Challenge

Lesson 8.4

Reading Multisyllable Words

✓ Lesson Check Point

Directions: Read each target word. Circle the word in the row that is divided correctly into syllables. Use a dictionary or the Internet to check your answers.

Direcciones: Lee cada palabra objetivo. Encierra en un círculo la palabra en la fila que esté correctamente separada en sílabas. Usa un diccionario o Internet para verificar tus respuestas.

Model

| heroic | a. he-roi-c | b. her-o-ic | **c. he-ro-ic** ⭕ |

1. hatchet	**a. hatch-et** ⭕	b. ha-tch-et	c. hatc-het
2. hazelnut	a. haz-e-lnut	b. haz-el-nut	**c. ha-zel-nut** ⭕
3. hexagon	a. he-xa-gon	**b. hex-a-gon** ⭕	c. hex-ag-on
4. historic	a. hi-stor-ic	**b. his-tor-ic** ⭕	c. hist-or-ic
5. halogen	a. hal-og-en	**b. hal-o-gen** ⭕	c. ha-lo-gen
6. hairdresser	**a. hair-dress-er** ⭕	b. ha-ir-dresser	c. hair-dresse-r
7. harvesting	a. harv-est-ing	b. har-ves-ting	**c. har-vest-ing** ⭕
8. handicap	**a. hand-i-cap** ⭕	b. han-dic-ap	c. hand-ic-ap

Learn To Read English With Directions In Spanish

Classwork

Name: _____ Date: ___/___/_____ Score: _____

Lesson 8.5

Reading and Writing

Proper and Common Nouns and Adjectives

Directions: Read the words in the word box. Put an (X) on the line next to each word that is written incorrectly. Remember that all proper nouns and proper adjectives are capitalized. Use a dictionary or the Internet to check your answers.

Direcciones: Lee las palabras en el cuadro de texto. Coloca una (X) en la línea próxima a las palabras que estén escritas de forma incorrecta. Recuerda que todos los nombres propios y adjetivos propios empiezan con mayúscula. Usa un diccionario o Internet para verificar tus respuestas.

Word Box					
__	Haiti	X	House	X	halifax
X	hebrew	X	Hexagon	__	Hawaii
__	horses	X	Haiku	__	hiccup
__	home	__	Hindu	X	hispanic

Directions: Read each unedited sentence and underline the word that is written incorrectly. Write each sentence correctly on the line.

Direcciones: Lee cada oración sin editar y subraya la palabra que está escrita de forma incorrecta. Escribe cada oración correctamente en la línea.

Model
Mr. Hitt has a big house on <u>hope</u> Avenue.
<u>Mr. Hitt has a big house on Hope Avenue.</u>

1. Henry is studying <u>haitian</u> history at Hunter College.
<u>Henry is studying Haitian history at Hunter College.</u>

2. The local historian lives in <u>hartford's</u> Historic District.
<u>The local historian lives in Hartford's Historic District.</u>

3. The thoroughbred <u>Horses</u> are galloping along Houston Harbor.
<u>The thoroughbred horses are galloping along Houston Harbor.</u>

4. <u>heather</u> is a hard working housekeeper at the Hilton Garden Hotel.
<u>Heather is a hard working housekeeper at the Hilton Garden Hotel.</u>

Answer Key

Name: _____   Date: ___/___/_____   Score: _____

Lesson 9.1

Reading Words with the Letter I/i

✓ Lesson Check Point

Directions: Read each target word. Find the letter "i" and put a check (✓) in the column that identifies its position: beginning, within or end.
Direcciones: Lee cada palabra objetivo. Encuentra la letra "h" y coloca un signo de verificación (✓) en la columna que identifique su posición: inicio, interior o final.

Target Words	Beginning (First Letter)	Within	End (Last Letter)
1. incapable	✓		
2. Fuji			✓
3. alive		✓	
4. broccoli			✓
5. Ireland	✓		

Directions: Read each target word. Read the words in the row and circle the word that has a different vowel "i" sound.
Direcciones: Lee cada palabra objetivo. Lee las palabras en la fila y encierra la palabra que tenga un sonido vocal "i" diferente.

Target Words				
6. blimp	(child)	this	grim	lid
7. spin	fix	pin	dip	(bike)
8. trip	hip	(nine)	fin	pit
9. crib	big	dim	(mild)	six
10. king	hill	(kite)	grin	ship

Learn To Read English With Directions In Spanish   99   Copyrighted Material

Classwork

 Name: _____ Date:___/___/_____ Score:_____

Lesson 9.2

Reading Words with the Short Vowel "i" Sound

✓ **Lesson Check Point**

 Directions: Read the words in the four boxes. Circle two words with the short vowel /ĭ/ sound. The anchor word for the short vowel /ĭ/ sound is insect.

Direcciones: Lee las palabras en las cuatro cajas. Encierra en un círculo dos palabras con el sonido vocal corto /ĭ/. La palabra ejemplo para el sonido vocal corto /ĭ/ es la palabra, insect.

(bin)	(sip)	bike	(big)	(dig)	(slim)
child	mile	(hid)	fine	bite	pike

line	kite	(tint)	(will)	(twin)	pint
(crib)	(blip)	like	nine	taxi	(list)

 Directions: Read the words in the four boxes. Circle two words that rhyme. Rhyming words have the same ending sound, such as hip and dip.

Direcciones: Lee las palabras en las cuatro cajas. Encierra en un círculo dos que rimen. Las palabras que riman tienen el mismo sonido al final, como hip y dip.

pine	(bib)	(clip)	wife	(fit)	(sit)
hike	(rib)	rice	(slip)	life	nice

mile	lime	hide	(him)	(win)	pipe
(six)	(mix)	(dim)	mice	(tin)	side

Answer Key

Name: _____ Date: ___/___/_____ Score: _____

Lesson 9.2

Reading & Writing Words with the Short Vowel "i" Sound

✓ **Lesson Check Point**

Directions: Read each sentence and underline three words with the short vowel /ĭ/ sound. Then, write the underlined words on the lines below. The anchor word for the short vowel /ĭ/ sound is <u>insect</u>.

Direcciones: Lee cada oración y subraya tres palabras con el sonido vocal corto /ĭ/. Luego, escribe las palabras subrayadas en las líneas siguientes. La palabra ejemplo para el sonido vocal corto /ĭ/ es la palabra, <u>insect</u>.

Model

<u>Jim</u> placed a <u>big</u> cup of ice on the <u>windowsill</u>.

    Jim   big   windowsill

1. Irene gave <u>Jill</u> a <u>big</u> <u>wig</u>.

    Jill   big   wig

2. The <u>kids</u> <u>did</u> not <u>kick</u> the ball on the field.

    kids   did   kick

3. <u>Billy</u> said, "<u>Tim</u> <u>licked</u> the ice pop."

    Billy   Tim   licked

4. <u>Milly</u> <u>sipped</u> the medium-sized <u>drink</u>.

    Milly   sipped   drink

5. The <u>big</u> <u>dishes</u> used to serve the pizza are by the <u>sink</u>.

    big   dishes   sink

Classwork

Name: _____ Date: ___/___/_____ Score: _____

Lesson 9.3

Reading Words with the Long Vowel "ī" Sound

✓ **Lesson Check Point**

Directions: Read the words in the four boxes. Circle two words with the long vowel /ī/ sound. The anchor word for the long vowel /ī/ sound is <u>ice</u>.

Direcciones: Lee las palabras en las cuatro cajas. Encierra en un círculo dos palabras con el sonido vocal largo /ī/. La palabra ejemplo para el sonido vocal largo /ī/ es la palabra, <u>ice</u>.

brain	(wild)	bill	(bike)	(hike)	taxi
kick	(fine)	(lime)	mini	sick	(dice)

(mine)	pink	chili	sing	pain	(vile)
train	(tile)	(mime)	(tide)	miss	(side)

Directions: Read the words in the four boxes. Circle two words that rhyme. Rhyming words have the same ending sound, such as <u>rice</u> and <u>nice</u>.

Direcciones: Lee las palabras en las cuatro cajas. Encierra en un círculo dos que rimen. Las palabras que riman tienen el mismo sonido al final, como <u>rice</u> y <u>nice</u>.

lift	(dime)	(nine)	link	(bite)	fill
pick	(time)	kids	(pine)	(kite)	crib

(line)	skill	(like)	(pike)	(life)	rib
(vine)	Mali	drill	dim	lick	(wife)

Answer Key

Name: _____ Date: ___/___/_____ Score: _____

Lesson 9.3

Reading & Writing Words with the Long Vowel "i" Sound

✓ **Lesson Check Point**

Directions: Read each sentence and underline three words with the long vowel /ī/ sound. Then, write the underlined words on the lines below. The anchor word for the long vowel /ī/ sound is <u>ice</u>.

Direcciones: Lee cada oración y subraya tres palabras con el sonido vocal largo /ī/. Luego, escribe las palabras subrayadas en las líneas siguientes. La palabra ejemplo para el sonido vocal largo /ī/ es la palabra, <u>ice</u>.

Model

David and <u>I</u> flew our big, <u>white</u> <u>kite</u> along the riverbank.

I	white	kite

1. <u>Brian</u> has to fix his mountain <u>bike's</u> <u>tire</u>.

Brian	bike's	tire

2. <u>Mike</u> went <u>outside</u> to <u>climb</u> the steep hill.

Mike	outside	climb

3. Jill said, "The <u>bride</u> has a <u>nice</u>, <u>white</u> dress."

bride	nice	white

4. <u>Irene's</u> husband <u>retired</u> from working as a <u>firefighter</u>.

Irene's	retired	firefighter

5. The principal <u>invited</u> the <u>entire</u> class to his <u>tiny</u> office.

invited	entire	tiny

Learn To Read English With Directions In Spanish

Classwork

Name: _____ Date: ___/___/_____ Score: _____

Review Lessons 9.2 & 9.3

Reading Short Vowel and Long Vowel Words

Directions: Read the target words in the word box. In the first column, write the words that have the short vowel /ĭ/ sound, as in the word <u>insect</u>. In the second column, write the words that have the long vowel /ī/ sound, as in the word <u>ice</u>.

Direcciones: Lee las palabras objetivo en el cuadro de texto. En la primera columna, escribe las palabras que tengan el sonido vocal corto /ĭ/, como en la palabra inglés <u>insect</u>. En la segunda columna, escribe las palabras que tengan el sonido vocal largo /ī/, como en la palabra inglés <u>ice</u>.

Target Word Box				
child	dinner	trip	bill	gift
tie	hint	I	pink	diner
hi	bike	diet	skim	client
inward	pie	lint	ripe	disk

Letter "i" has the /ĭ/ sound as in the word <u>insect</u>

- lint
- trip
- bill
- gift
- disk
- hint
- pink
- skim
- inward
- dinner

Letter "i" has the /ī/ sound as in the word <u>ice</u>

- I
- hi
- pie
- tie
- bike
- diet
- ripe
- child
- client
- diner

Learn To Read English With Directions In Spanish

Answer Key

Name: _____ Date: ___/___/_____ Score: _____

Lesson 9.4

Reading Words with Letter "i" Vowel Pairs

✓ **Lesson Check Point**

Directions: Read each target word. Circle the word in the column that has the same vowel "ia," "ie," "io" or "iu" sound(s) as the target word.

Direcciones: Lee cada palabra objetivo. Encierra en un círculo la palabra en la columna que tenga el mismo sonido vocal "ia," "ie," "io," o "iu" que la palabra objetivo.

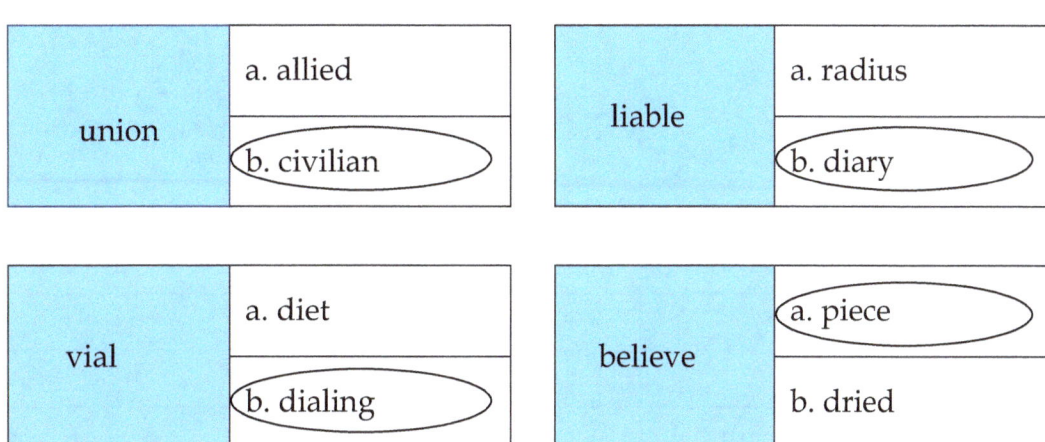

Directions: Read each target word. Put a check (✓) under the correct column heading.

Direcciones: Lee cada palabra objetivo. Coloca un signo de verificación (✓) bajo el encabezado de la columna correcta.

Target Words	Words have the long "i" sound as in the word <u>dial</u>	Words do not have the long "i" sound
1. union		✓
2. liable	✓	
3. vial	✓	
4. believe		✓

Learn To Read English With Directions In Spanish

Classwork

 Name: _____ Date: ___/___/_____ Score: _____

Lesson 9.5

Reading Words with the Final Letter "i"

✓ **Lesson Check Point**

 Directions: Read each target word. Find the letter "i" and put a check (✓) in the column that identifies its position within the syllable.
Direcciones: Lee cada palabra objetivo. Encuentra la letra "i" y coloca un signo de verificación (✓) en la columna que identifique su posición dentro de la sílaba.

Target Words	"i" is at the end of a one syllable word	"i" is at the end of the first syllable	"i" is at the end of a multi-syllable word
1. hi	✓		
2. final		✓	
3. alib<u>i</u>			✓
4. iron		✓	
5. dinosaur		✓	

 Directions: Read each target word. Put a check (✓) under the correct column heading.
Direcciones: Lee cada palabra objetivo. Coloca un signo de verificación (✓) bajo el encabezado de la columna correcta.

Target Words	"i" has the /ĭ/ sound as in the word <u>insect</u>	"i" has the /ī/ sound as in the word <u>bike</u>	"i" has the /ə/ sound as in the word <u>pencil</u>	"i" is silent as in the word <u>maid</u>
6. kite		✓		
7. pilgr<u>i</u>m			✓	
8. himself	✓			
9. business				✓
10. utensil			✓	

 Name: _____ Date: ___/___/_____ Score: _____

Answer Key

Lesson 9.6

Reading Letter "i" Words with the Schwa Vowel Sound

✓ **Lesson Check Point**

 Directions: Read each target word. Circle the word in the column that has the same "i" sound as the target word.

Direcciones: Lee cada palabra objetivo. Encierra en un círculo la palabra en la columna que tenga el mismo sonido "i" que la palabra objetivo.

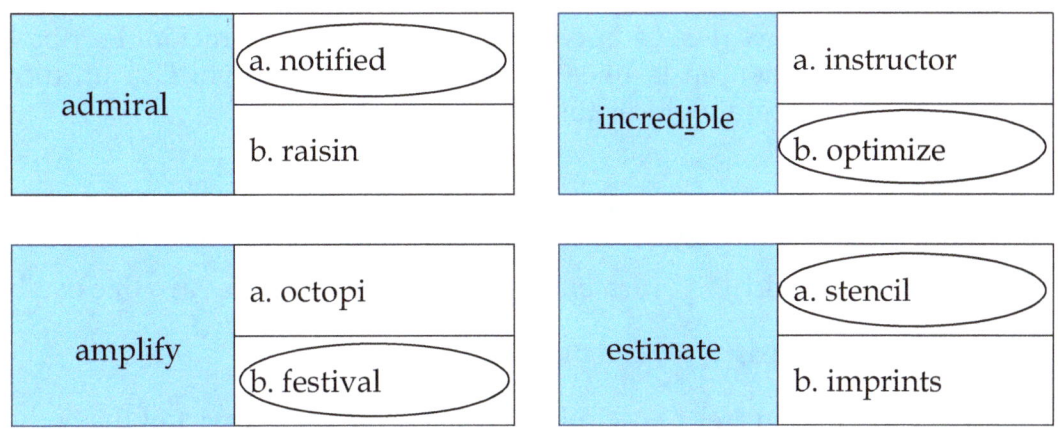

admiral	(a. notified)
	b. raisin

incredible	a. instructor
	(b. optimize)

amplify	a. octopi
	(b. festival)

estimate	(a. stencil)
	b. imprints

 Directions: Read each sentence and underline the letter "i" word that has the schwa vowel /ə/ sound. The anchor word for the letter "i" schwa vowel sound is <u>pencil</u>.

Direcciones: Lee cada oración y subraya la letra "i" en palabras que tengan el sonido schwa /ə/. La palabra ejemplo para el sonido schwa de la letra "i" es la palabra, <u>pencil</u>.

1. I will <u>notify</u> the girls about the field trip.

2. The child is experiencing pain in his <u>nostrils</u>.

3. Trinidad's <u>carnival</u> is a major cultural event.

4. The <u>binoculars</u> are inside my white briefcase.

5. I bought vanilla ice cream at the <u>convenience</u> store.

6. The president encouraged every <u>individual</u> to vote.

Classwork

 Name: _____ Date:___/___/_____ Score:_____

Lesson 9.7

Reading Words with the "ir" Letter Combination

Dictionary Skills/ Vocabulary

✓ **Lesson Check Point**

 Directions: Read each target word and its definition. Write the letter of the definition on the line of each target word. Use a dictionary or the Internet to check your answers.

Direcciones: Lee cada palabra objetivo y su definición. Escribe la letra de la definición en la línea de cada palabra objetivo. Usa un diccionario o Internet para verificar tus respuestas.

Target Words	Definitions
1. _c_ shirt	a. a bushy-tailed rodent that lives in a tree or a burrow
2. _e_ birds	b. females
3. _a_ squirrel	c. clothing worn on the upper part of the body
4. _d_ twirl	d. to spin or turn something around with one's fingers
5. _b_ girls	e. egg-laying animals that have wings

 Directions: Read each sentence and write the target word that completes the sentence.

Direcciones: Lee cada oración y escribe la palabra objetivo que complete la oración.

6. My white ____shirt____ has a clean collar.

7. The cheerleaders ____twirl____ their batons.

8. The ____girls____ like to eat ice cream cones.

9. Millions of ____birds____ migrate along the flyway.

10. The ____squirrel____ climbed up the tree quickly.

Answer Key

 Name: _____ Date: ___/___/_____ Score: _____

Lesson 9.8

Reading Letter "i" Words with the Long Vowel "e" Sound

✓ **Lesson Check Point**

 Directions: Read each target word. Circle the word in the column that has the same "i" sound as the target word.

Direcciones: Lee cada palabra objetivo. Encierra en un círculo la palabra en la columna que tenga el mismo sonido "i" que la palabra objetivo.

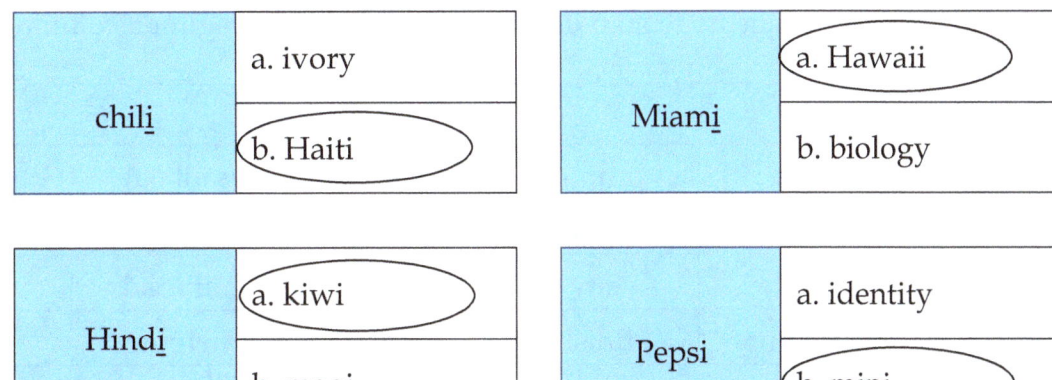

| chil<u>i</u> | a. ivory |
| | (b. Haiti) |

| Miam<u>i</u> | (a. Hawaii) |
| | b. biology |

| Hind<u>i</u> | (a. kiwi) |
| | b. magi |

| Pepsi | a. identity |
| | (b. mini) |

 Directions: Read each sentence and underline the letter "i" word that has the long vowel /ē/ sound. Then, write the word on the line. The anchor word, <u>taxi</u> has a letter "i" that represents the long vowel /ē/ sound.

Direcciones: Lee cada oración y subraya la palabra con la letra "i" que tenga el sonido vocal largo /ē/. Luego, escribe la palabra en la línea. La palabra ejemplo, <u>taxi</u> tiene una letra "i" que tiene el sonido largo /ē/.

1. It is not wise to go <u>skiing</u> at night.   skiing

2. Jim and Mike enjoy eating <u>pita</u> bread.   pita

3. The children admire the <u>police</u> officers.   police

4. My family likes to eat dinner on the <u>patio</u>.   patio

5. I will use the sewing <u>machine</u> to sew a pillow.   machine

6. Baked <u>ziti</u> is a classic Italian-American dish.   ziti

Classwork

 Name: _____ Date: ___/___/_____ Score: _____

Lesson 9.9

Reading Words with a Silent Letter "i"

✓ **Lesson Check Point**

 Directions: Read the target words in the word box. Write the words that have a silent letter "i" in the first column. Write the words that do not have a silent letter "i" in the second column.

Direcciones: Lee las palabras objetivo en el cuadro de texto. Escribe las palabras que tengan una letra muda "i" en la primera columna. Escribe las palabras que no tengan una letra muda "i" en la segunda columna.

Target Word Box				
aside	camping	Jamaica	sailboat	stained
waist	afraid	giggles	bail	fifteen
bigger	city	hiking	railroad	distinct
attaining	finish	suit	helping	again

Letter "i" is silent	Letter "i" has a letter "i" sound
suit	city
bail	aside
again	finish
waist	hiking
afraid	bigger
stained	giggles
railroad	helping
Jamaica	distinct
sailboat	fifteen
attaining	camping

Answer Key

 Name: _____ Date:___/___/_____ Score:_____

Unit Review - I/i

Reading Words with Vowel "i" Sounds: /ĭ/, /ī/, /ə/ & Silent

✓ Lesson Check Point

 Directions: Read each target word. Circle the word in the column that has the same "i" sound as the target word.

Direcciones: Lee cada palabra objetivo. Encierra en un círculo la palabra en la columna que tenga el mismo sonido "i" que la palabra objetivo.

fire	a. trip
	(b. dine)

testify	a. wish
	(b. Russia)

brick	a. file
	(b. fill)

milk	(a. pinch)
	b. time

 Directions: Read each target word. Put a check (✓) under the correct column heading.

Direcciones: Lee cada palabra objetivo. Coloca un signo de verificación (✓) bajo el encabezado de la columna correcta.

Target Words	"i" has the /ĭ/ sound as in the word <u>insect</u>	"i" has the /ī/ sound as in the word <u>bike</u>	"i" has the /ə/ sound as in the word <u>pencil</u>	"i" is silent as in the word <u>maid</u>
1. fire		✓		
2. testify			✓	
3. brick	✓			
4. milk	✓			

Classwork

 Name: _____ Date:___/___/_____ Score:_____

The Reading Challenge

Lesson 9.10

Reading Multisyllable Words

✓ Lesson Check Point

 Directions: Read and divide each target word into syllables. Write each word and place a hyphen (-) between the syllables in the second column. Write the number of syllables in the third column. Use a dictionary or the Internet to check your answers.

Direcciones: Lee y separa en sílabas cada palabra objetivo. Escribe cada palabra y coloca un guión (-) entre las sílabas en la segunda columna. Escribe el número de sílabas en la tercera columna. Usa un diccionario o Internet para verificar tus respuestas.

Target Words	Words Divided into Syllables	Number of Syllables
1. drinking	drink-ing	2
2. mentoring	men-tor-ing	3
3. spider	spi-der	2
4. Haiti	Hai-ti	2
5. kiwi	ki-wi	2
6. providing	pro-vid-ing	3
7. diner	din-er	2
8. beside	be-side	2
9. mineral	min-er-al	3
10. fictional	fic-tion-al	3

 Name: _____ Date: ___/___/_____ Score: _____

The Reading Challenge

Lesson 9.10

Reading Multisyllable Words

✓ Lesson Check Point

 Directions: Read each target word. Circle the word in the row that is divided correctly into syllables. Use a dictionary or the Internet to check your answers.

Direcciones: Lee cada palabra objetivo. Encierra en un círculo la palabra en la fila que esté correctamente separada en sílabas. Usa un diccionario o Internet para verificar tus respuestas.

Model

| interesting | a. in-ter-est-ing ⭕ | b. int-er-est-ing | c. inte-rest-ing |

1. bifocal	a. bif-o-cal	b. bi-fo-cal ⭕	c. bi-foc-al
2. hibernate	a. hi-ber-nate ⭕	b. hib-er-nate	c. hi-bern-ate
3. Malawi	a. Ma-la-wi ⭕	b. Ma-law-i	c. Mal-a-wi
4. tribunal	a. trib-un-al	b. trib-u-nal	c. tri-bu-nal ⭕
5. safari	a. sa-fa-ri ⭕	b. saf-a-ri	c. sa-far-i
6. unicorn	a. u-ni-corn ⭕	b. un-i-corn	c. u-nic-orn
7. imagine	a. im-a-gine	b. i-ma-gine	c. i-mag-ine ⭕
8. dialect	a. di-ale-ct	b. di-a-lect ⭕	c. dial-e-ct

Classwork

J.L Name: _____ Date: ___/___/_____ Score: _____

Lesson 9.11

Reading and Writing

Proper and Common Nouns and Adjectives

Directions: Read the words in the word box. Put an (X) on the line next to each word that is written incorrectly. Remember that all proper nouns and proper adjectives are capitalized. Use a dictionary or the Internet to check your answers.

Direcciones: Lee las palabras en el cuadro de texto. Coloca una (X) en la línea próxima a las palabras que estén escritas de forma incorrecta. Recuerda que todos los nombres propios y adjetivos propios empiezan con mayúscula. Usa un diccionario o Internet para verificar tus respuestas.

Word Box					
__	identify	X	illinois	X	Invincible
__	Iroquois	X	Insanity	__	illusion
__	Indo-European	__	itching	__	Ivory Coast
X	italy	X	irish	X	ida Mount

Directions: Read each unedited sentence and underline the word that is written incorrectly. Write each sentence correctly on the line.

Direcciones: Lee cada oración sin editar y subraya la palabra que está escrita de forma incorrecta. Escribe cada oración correctamente en la línea.

Model
New Delhi and Indore are beautiful cities in <u>india</u>.
New Delhi and Indore are beautiful cities in India.

1. My teacher said, "The <u>incas</u> inhabited the Americas."
My teacher said, "The Incas inhabited the Americas."

2. In April, Isabella will attend <u>iowa</u> Community College.
In April, Isabella will attend Iowa Community College.

3. Ida looked up information about <u>indonesia</u> on the Internet.
Ida looked up information about Indonesia on the Internet.

4. On <u>independence</u> Day, Ian ignited a massive display of fireworks.
On Independence Day, Ian ignited a massive display of fireworks.

Answer Key

 Name: _____ Date: ___/___/_____ Score: _____

Lesson 10.1

Reading Words with the Letter J/j

✓ **Lesson Check Point**

 Directions: Read each target word. Find the letter "j" and put a check (✓) in the column that identifies its position: beginning, within or end.
Direcciones: Lee cada palabra objetivo. Encuentra la letra "j" y coloca un signo de verificación (✓) en la columna que identifique su posición: inicio, interior o final.

Target Words	Beginning (First Letter)	Within	End (Last Letter)
1. conjunct		✓	
2. jacket	✓		
3. jersey	✓		
4. reject		✓	
5. jumbo	✓		

 Directions: Read each sentence and underline the words that begin with the letter "j." Write all the underlined words in alphabetical order on the lines below.
Direcciones: Lee cada oración y subraya las palabras que empiecen con la letra "j." Escribe todas las letras subrayadas en orden alfabético en las líneas que siguen.

6. Henry has a <u>jug</u> of apple <u>juice</u>.

7. The <u>jockey's</u> horse is named <u>Jupiter</u>.

8. We flew in a <u>jet</u> from New York to <u>Japan</u>.

9. Hadia took a long <u>journey</u> through the <u>jungle</u>.

10. In <u>January</u>, Mrs. Adams is going to <u>Jacksonville</u>, Florida.

Jacksonville	January	Japan
jet	jockey's	journey
juice	jug	jungle
	Jupiter	

Classwork

 Name: _____ Date:___/___/_____ Score:_____

The Reading Challenge

Lesson 10.2

Reading Multisyllable Words

✓ **Lesson Check Point**

 Directions: Read and divide each target word into syllables. Write each word and place a hyphen (-) between the syllables in the second column. Write the number of syllables in the third column. Use a dictionary or the Internet to check your answers.

Direcciones: Lee y separa en sílabas cada palabra objetivo. Escribe cada palabra y coloca un guión (-) entre las sílabas en la segunda columna. Escribe el número de sílabas en la tercera columna. Usa un diccionario o Internet para verificar tus respuestas.

Target Words	Words Divided into Syllables	Number of Syllables
1. jackpot	jack-pot	2
2. joey	jo-ey	2
3. jealous	jeal-ous	2
4. judgmental	judg-men-tal	3
5. journal	jour-nal	2
6. judo	ju-do	2
7. Japanese	Jap-a-nese	3
8. joyously	joy-ous-ly	3
9. justify	jus-ti-fy	3
10. juicy	juic-y	2

Answer Key

 Name: _____ Date: ___/___/_____ Score: _____

The Reading Challenge

Lesson 10.2

Reading Multisyllable Words

✓ **Lesson Check Point**

 Directions: Read each target word. Circle the word in the row that is divided correctly into syllables. Use a dictionary or the Internet to check your answers.

Direcciones: Lee cada palabra objetivo. Encierra en un círculo la palabra en la fila que esté correctamente separada en sílabas. Usa un diccionario o Internet para verificar tus respuestas.

Model

janitor	a. ja-ni-tor	b. jan-it-or	**c. jan-i-tor** ⭕

1. January	**a. Jan-u-ar-y** ⭕	b. Jan-u-ary	c. Jan-uar-y
2. jeopardize	**a. jeop-ard-ize** ⭕	b. jeop-ar-dize	c. jeo-pard-ize
3. jubilant	a. ju-bila-nt	**b. ju-bi-lant** ⭕	c. ju-bil-ant
4. javelin	a. javel-in	**b. jave-lin** ⭕	c. ja-vel-in
5. judgmental	**a. judg-men-tal** ⭕	b. jud-gmen-tal	c. judg-ment-al
6. jubilance	**a. ju-bi-lance** ⭕	b. ju-bil-ance	c. jub-i-lance
7. justify	a. ju-sti-fy	b. jus-tif-y	**c. jus-ti-fy** ⭕
8. jalopy	a. jal-o-py	**b. ja-lop-y** ⭕	c. jal-op-y

Learn To Read English With Directions In Spanish

Classwork

Name: _____ Date: ___/___/_____ Score: _____

Lesson 10.3

Reading and Writing

Proper and Common Nouns and Adjectives

Directions: Read the words in the word box. Put an (X) on the line next to each word that is written incorrectly. Remember that all proper nouns and proper adjectives are capitalized. Use a dictionary or the Internet to check your answers.

Direcciones: Lee las palabras en el cuadro de texto. Coloca una (X) en la línea próxima a las palabras que estén escritas de forma incorrecta. Recuerda que todos los nombres propios y adjetivos propios empiezan con mayúscula. Usa un diccionario o Internet para verificar tus respuestas.

Word Box					
__	Jasmine	X	jupiter	__	jigsaw
X	june	__	jelly	X	january
__	jersey	__	jockey	X	Juice
X	japan	X	Jewelry	__	Jackson

Directions: Read each unedited sentence and underline the word that is written incorrectly. Write each sentence correctly on the line.

Direcciones: Lee cada oración sin editar y subraya la palabra que está escrita de forma incorrecta. Escribe cada oración correctamente en la línea.

Model
Joey and his family live in New jersey.
Joey and his family live in New Jersey.

1. In january, Jack will wear a warm jacket.
In January, Jack will wear a warm jacket.

2. In june, Jordan had five jars of jalapenos.
In June, Jordan had five jars of jalapenos.

3. The kids are playing with a Jigsaw puzzle and a jet.
The kids are playing with a jigsaw puzzle and a jet.

4. jillian has a new job at Johnson and Johnson Incorporated.
Jillian has a new job at Johnson and Johnson Incorporated.

Answer Key

 Name: _____ Date: ___/___/_____ Score: _____

Lesson 11.1

Reading Words with the Letter K/k

✓ **Lesson Check Point**

 Directions: Read each target word. Find the letter "k" and put a check (✓) in the column that identifies its position: beginning, within or end.
Direcciones: Lee cada palabra objetivo. Encuentra la letra "k" y coloca un signo de verificación (✓) en la columna que identifique su posición: inicio, interior o final.

Target Words	Beginning (First Letter)	Within	End (Last Letter)
1. shock			✓
2. king	✓		
3. choke		✓	
4. homework			✓
5. keycard	✓		

 Directions: Read each sentence and underline the words that begin with the letter "k." Write all the underlined words in alphabetical order on the lines below.
Direcciones: Lee cada oración y subraya las palabras que empiecen con la letra "k." Escribe todas las letras subrayadas en orden alfabético en las líneas que siguen.

6. <u>Kangaroos</u> and <u>koalas</u> live in Australia.

7. Alex is learning to <u>kick</u> in his <u>karate</u> class.

8. <u>King</u> George III had a very powerful <u>kingdom</u>.

9. My friend, <u>Karen</u>, was born in <u>Kingston</u>, Jamaica.

10. Some <u>keys</u> on the computer <u>keyboard</u> are not working.

Kangaroos	karate	Karen
keyboard	keys	kick
King	kingdom	Kingston
	koalas	

Learn To Read English With Directions In Spanish

Classwork

Name: _____ Date: ___/___/_____ Score: _____

Lesson 11.2

Reading Words with the Letter "k" and "ck" Letter Combination

✓ **Lesson Check Point**

Directions: Read each target word. Put a check (✓) in the second column if the target word has one vowel. Put a check (✓) in the third column if the target word has two vowels.

Direcciones: Lee cada palabra objetivo. Coloca un signo de verificación (✓) en la segunda columna si la palabra objetivo tiene una vocal. Coloca un signo de verificación (✓) en la tercera columna si la palabra objetivo tiene dos vocales.

Target Words	Words with 1 Vowel	Words with 2 Vowels
1. pike		✓
2. smack	✓	
3. sneak		✓
4. lock	✓	
5. broke		✓

Directions: Read each target word in the first column and write the number of vowels within the word in the second column. Read each target word in the third column and write the number of vowels within the word in the fourth column.

Direcciones: Lee cada palabra objetivo en la primera columna y escribe el número de vocales que contiene en la segunda columna. Lee cada palabra objetivo en la tercera columna y escribe el número de vocales que contiene en la cuarta columna.

Target Words	Number of Vowels	Target Words	Number of Vowels
6. stoke	2	stock	1
7. smock	1	smoke	2
8. Blake	2	black	1
9. tack	1	take	2
10. pick	1	pike	2

Answer Key

 Name: _____ Date: ___/___/_____ Score: _____

Lesson 11.3

Reading Words with the "kle" Letter Combination

✓ **Lesson Check Point**

 Directions: Read each target word. Find the "kle" letter combination and put a check (✓) in the column that identifies its position: beginning, within or end.

Direcciones: Lee cada palabra objetivo. Encuentra la combinación de letras "kle" y coloca un signo de verificación (✓) en la columna que identifique su posición: inicio, interior o final.

Target Words	Beginning (First 3 Letters)	Within	End (Last 3 Letters)
1. knuckle			✓
2. Kleenex	✓		
3. anklets		✓	
4. sparkles		✓	
5. wrinkle			✓

 Directions: Read each target word. Put a check (✓) in the "yes" column if the "kle" letter combination has the /k/ + /ə/ + /l/ sounds. Put a check (✓) in the "no" column if the "kle" letter combination does not have the /k/ + /ə/ + /l/ sounds.

Direcciones: Lee cada palabra objetivo. Coloca un signo de verificación (✓) en la columna del "sí" si la combinación de letras "kle" tiene el sonidos /k/ + /ə/ + /l/. Coloca un signo de verificación (✓) en la columna del "no" si la combinación de letras "kle" no tiene el sonidos /k/ + /ə/ + /l/.

Target Words	Yes	No
6. knuckle	✓	
7. Kleenex		✓
8. anklets		✓
9. sparkles	✓	
10. wrinkle	✓	

Classwork

 Name: _____ Date:___/___/_____ Score:_____

Lesson 11.4

Reading Words with a Silent Letter "k"

✓ **Lesson Check Point**

 Directions: Read the target words in the word box. Write the words that have a silent letter "k" in the first column. Write the words that do not have a silent letter "k" in the second column.

Direcciones: Lee las palabras objetivo en el cuadro de texto. Escribe las palabras que tengan una letra muda "k" en la primera columna. Escribe las palabras que no tengan una letra muda "k" en la segunda columna.

Target Word Box				
knee	known	doorknob	seeking	knead
shaking	parking	knocking	keyboard	knew
keeping	karate	kennel	knap	sharks
knish	knives	knuckle	milky	kneed

Letter "k" is silent	Letter "k" has the /k/ sound
knee	milky
knew	knish
knap	sharks
knead	karate
kneed	kennel
known	parking
knives	seeking
knuckle	shaking
doorknob	keeping
knocking	keyboard

Learn To Read English With Directions In Spanish

Answer Key

Name: _____ Date: ___/___/_____ Score: _____

The Reading Challenge

Lesson 11.5

Reading Multisyllable Words

✓ **Lesson Check Point**

Directions: Read and divide each target word into syllables. Write each word and place a hyphen (-) between the syllables in the second column. Write the number of syllables in the third column. Use a dictionary or the Internet to check your answers.

Direcciones: Lee y separa en sílabas cada palabra objetivo. Escribe cada palabra y coloca un guión (-) entre las sílabas en la segunda columna. Escribe el número de sílabas en la tercera columna. Usa un diccionario o Internet para verificar tus respuestas.

Target Words	Words Divided into Syllables	Number of Syllables
1. kayak	kay-ak	2
2. Kenya	Ken-ya	2
3. Korean	Ko-re-an	3
4. kindly	kind-ly	2
5. ketchup	ketch-up	2
6. keyboard	key-board	2
7. Kuwaiti	Ku-wait-i	3
8. kidnap	kid-nap	2
9. knowledge	knowl-edge	2
10. kudos	ku-dos	2

Classwork

Name: _____ Date: ___/___/_____ Score: _____

The Reading Challenge

Lesson 11.5

Reading Multisyllable Words

✓ **Lesson Check Point**

Directions: Read each target word. Circle the word in the row that is divided correctly into syllables. Use a dictionary or the Internet to check your answers.

Direcciones: Lee cada palabra objetivo. Encierra en un círculo la palabra en la fila que esté correctamente separada en sílabas. Usa un diccionario o Internet para verificar tus respuestas.

Model

| kangaroo | a. kang-a-roo | (b. kan-ga-roo) | c. kan-gar-oo |

1. karate	(a. ka-ra-te)	b. ka-rate	c. kar-ate
2. kilobyte	a. ki-lo-byte	(b. kil-o-byte)	c. kil-ob-yte
3. Kentucky	a. Ken-tuc-ky	b. Kent-uck-y	(c. Ken-tuck-y)
4. kilowatt	a. ki-lo-watt	(b. kil-o-watt)	c. ki-low-att
5. keratin	a. ke-ra-tin	b. ker-at-in	(c. ker-a-tin)
6. Korea	a. Ko-r-ea	(b. Ko-re-a)	c. Kor-e-a
7. koala	(a. ko-a-la)	b. koa-la	c. ko-ala
8. kilogram	a. ki-log-ram	b. ki-lo-gram	(c. kil-o-gram)

Unit K
Lesson 11.5

Learn To Read English With Directions In Spanish

Answer Key

Name: _____ Date: ___/___/_____ Score: _____

Lesson 11.6

Reading and Writing

Proper and Common Nouns and Adjectives

Directions: Read the words in the word box. Put an (X) on the line next to each word that is written incorrectly. Remember that all proper nouns and proper adjectives are capitalized. Use a dictionary or the Internet to check your answers.

Direcciones: Lee las palabras en el cuadro de texto. Coloca una (X) en la línea próxima a las palabras que estén escritas de forma incorrecta. Recuerda que todos los nombres propios y adjetivos propios empiezan con mayúscula. Usa un diccionario o Internet para verificar tus respuestas.

Word Box					
__	Kenya	X	key Largo	__	Korea
X	Kept	__	Kensington	X	Know
X	Kid	__	knock	__	knight
X	kansas	X	kentucky	__	kind

Directions: Read each unedited sentence and underline the word that is written incorrectly. Write each sentence correctly on the line.

Direcciones: Lee cada oración sin editar y subraya la palabra que está escrita de forma incorrecta. Escribe cada oración correctamente en la línea.

Model
Helen <u>keller</u> was a kind person.
<u>Helen Keller was a kind person.</u>

1. <u>karen</u> and Kim speak Korean fluently.
<u>Karen and Kim speak Korean fluently.</u>

2. Kimberly is going to <u>kingston</u>, Jamaica.
<u>Kimberly is going to Kingston, Jamaica.</u>

3. My best friend, Kara, is from <u>kuwait</u>.
<u>My best friend, Kara, is from Kuwait.</u>

4. Kennedy and I are reading about <u>king</u> George III.
<u>Kennedy and I are reading about King George III.</u>

Classwork

L Name: _____ Date: ___/___/_____ Score: _____

Lesson 12.1

Reading Words with the Letter L/l

✓ **Lesson Check Point**

Directions: Read each target word. Find the letter "l" and put a check (✓) in the column that identifies its position: beginning, within or end.
Direcciones: Lee cada palabra objetivo. Encuentra la letra "l" y coloca un signo de verificación (✓) en la columna que identifique su posición: inicio, interior o final.

Target Words	Beginning (First Letter)	Within	End (Last Letter)
1. kneel			✓
2. imply		✓	
3. leave	✓		
4. juvenile		✓	
5. lasting	✓		

Directions: Read each sentence and underline the words that begin with the letter "l." Write all the underlined words in alphabetical order on the lines below.
Direcciones: Lee cada oración y subraya las palabras que empiecen con la letra "l." Escribe todas las letras subrayadas en orden alfabético en las líneas que siguen.

6. The <u>little</u> <u>light</u> bulb is very bright.

7. We are <u>learning</u> about <u>Lewis</u> and Clark.

8. Abraham <u>Lincoln</u> was a brilliant <u>lawyer</u>.

9. My friend, Tim, enjoys <u>licking</u> cherry <u>lollipops</u>.

10. Everyone in my <u>Latin</u> class speaks another <u>language</u>.

<u>language</u>   <u>Latin</u>   <u>lawyer</u>
<u>learning</u>   <u>Lewis</u>   <u>licking</u>
<u>light</u>   <u>Lincoln</u>   <u>little</u>
                 <u>lollipops</u>

Answer Key

 Name: _____ Date: ___/___/_____ Score: _____

Lesson 12.2

Reading Words with the Letter "l" Combinations: "cl," "fl," "pl" & "sl"

Dictionary Skills/ Vocabulary

✓ **Lesson Check Point**

 Directions: Read each target word and its definition. Write the target word on the line in front of its meaning. Use a dictionary or the Internet to check your answers.

Direcciones: Lee cada palabra objetivo y su definición. Escribe la palabra objetivo en la línea frente a su significado. Usa un diccionario o Internet para verificar tus respuestas.

Target Word Box				
class	flowers	placed	play	sleet

1. __play__ the act of doing something fun
2. __sleet__ small icy pieces that fall from the sky
3. __flowers__ the colorful part of a plant that contains seeds
4. __placed__ to put something in a particular position or location
5. __class__ group of students who is taught by the same teacher

 Directions: Read each sentence. Underline the word in the parentheses that correctly completes each sentence. Then, write the underlined word on the line.

Direcciones: Lee cada oración. Subraya la palabra entre paréntesis que completa correctamente cada oración. Luego, escribe la palabra subrayada en la línea.

6. I _____placed_____ two plants in large pots. (class, <u>placed</u>)

7. The kids like to _____play_____ at the playground. (placed, <u>play</u>)

8. The _____sleet_____ caused the skiers to stop skiing. (<u>sleet</u>, flowers)

9. The garden in your backyard has beautiful __flowers__ . (<u>flowers</u>, play)

10. Ms. Brown's _____class_____ is going on an exciting trip. (<u>class</u>, sleet)

Classwork

 Name: _____ Date: ___/___/_____ Score: _____

Lesson 12.3

Reading Words with a Silent Letter "l"

✓ Lesson Check Point

 Directions: Read the target words in the word box. Write the words that have a silent letter "l" in the first column. Write the words that do not have a silent letter "l" in the second column.

Direcciones: Lee las palabras objetivo en el cuadro de texto. Escribe las palabras que tengan una letra muda "l" en la primera columna. Escribe las palabras que no tengan una letra muda "l" en la segunda columna.

Target Word Box				
could	build	soul	cool	likes
yolk	halves	salmon	slam	behalf
calf	loves	talking	helpful	pencil
leaf	slime	chalk	should	almond

Letter "l" is silent

- calf
- yolk
- chalk
- behalf
- could
- halves
- almond
- should
- talking
- salmon

Letter "l" has the /l/ sound

- leaf
- likes
- slam
- loves
- soul
- cool
- build
- slime
- pencil
- helpful

Answer Key

Name: _____ Date: ___/___/_____ Score: _____

The Reading Challenge

Lesson 12.4

Reading Multisyllable Words

✓ **Lesson Check Point**

Directions: Read and divide each target word into syllables. Write each word and place a hyphen (-) between the syllables in the second column. Write the number of syllables in the third column. Use a dictionary or the Internet to check your answers.

Direcciones: Lee y separa en sílabas cada palabra objetivo. Escribe cada palabra y coloca un guión (-) entre las sílabas en la segunda columna. Escribe el número de sílabas en la tercera columna. Usa un diccionario o Internet para verificar tus respuestas.

Target Words	Words Divided into Syllables	Number of Syllables
1. limber	lim-ber	2
2. lumber	lum-ber	2
3. leveling	lev-el-ing	3
4. licensing	li-cens-ing	3
5. liberty	lib-er-ty	3
6. loyalty	loy-al-ty	3
7. landlord	land-lord	2
8. liable	li-a-ble	3
9. lioness	li-on-ess	3
10. leotard	le-o-tard	3

Learn To Read English With Directions In Spanish   Copyrighted Material

Classwork

 Name: _____ Date: ___/___/_____ Score: _____

The Reading Challenge

Lesson 12.4

Reading Multisyllable Words

✓ **Lesson Check Point**

 Directions: Read each target word. Circle the word in the row that is divided correctly into syllables. Use a dictionary or the Internet to check your answers.

Direcciones: Lee cada palabra objetivo. Encierra en un círculo la palabra en la fila que esté correctamente separada en sílabas. Usa un diccionario o Internet para verificar tus respuestas.

Model

| liberty | a. li-ber-ty | (b. lib-er-ty) | c. lib-ert-y |

| 1. luxury | (a. lux-u-ry) | b. lu-xu-ry | c. lux-ur-y |

| 2. lasagna | a. las-a-gna | (b. la-sa-gna) | c. la-sag-na |

| 3. lemonade | a. lem-o-nade | (b. lem-on-ade) | c. le-mo-nade |

| 4. limited | (a. lim-it-ed) | b. li-mit-ed | c. lim-i-ted |

| 5. levitate | a. le-vi-tate | (b. lev-i-tate) | c. lev-it-ate |

| 6. lavender | (a. lav-en-der) | b. lave-n-der | c. la-ven-der |

| 7. legislate | a. leg-i-slate | b. le-gis-late | (c. leg-is-late) |

| 8. levity | a. le-vit-y | b. le-vi-ty | (c. lev-i-ty) |

Answer Key

Name: _____ Date: ___/___/_____ Score: _____

Lesson 12.5

Reading and Writing

Proper and Common Nouns and Adjectives

Directions: Read the words in the word box. Put an (X) on the line next to each word that is written incorrectly. Remember that all proper nouns and proper adjectives are capitalized. Use a dictionary or the Internet to check your answers.

Direcciones: Lee las palabras en el cuadro de texto. Coloca una (X) en la línea próxima a las palabras que estén escritas de forma incorrecta. Recuerda que todos los nombres propios y adjetivos propios empiezan con mayúscula. Usa un diccionario o Internet para verificar tus respuestas.

Word Box					
__	ladder	__	leopard	X	Ladybug
X	lincoln	X	lebanon	__	language
__	Laos	X	Lobster	__	London
X	latin	__	Labrador	X	Lawyer

Directions: Read each unedited sentence and underline the word that is written incorrectly. Write each sentence correctly on the line.

Direcciones: Lee cada oración sin editar y subraya la palabra que está escrita de forma incorrecta. Escribe cada oración correctamente en la línea.

Model
I am studying <u>latin</u> at Lutheran Life Academy.
<u>I am studying Latin at Lutheran Life Academy.</u>

1. My family and I had a <u>Lovely</u> time in Liberia.
<u>My family and I had a lovely time in Liberia.</u>

2. Abraham <u>lincoln</u> was a loyal American president.
<u>Abraham Lincoln was a loyal American president.</u>

3. Lucy said, "The <u>labrador</u> Current is a cold ocean current."
<u>Lucy said, "The Labrador Current is a cold ocean current."</u>

4. Larry learned that the capital of Arkansas is <u>little</u> Rock.
<u>Larry learned that the capital of Arkansas is Little Rock.</u>

Classwork

✏ Name: _____ Date:___/___/_____ Score: _____

Lesson 13.1

Reading Words with the Letter M/m

✓ Lesson Check Point

Directions: Read each target word. Find the letter "m" and put a check (✓) in the column that identifies its position: beginning, within or end.
Direcciones: Lee cada palabra objetivo. Encuentra la letra "m" y coloca un signo de verificación (✓) en la columna que identifique su posición: inicio, interior o final.

Target Words	Beginning (First Letter)	Within	End (Last Letter)
1. money	✓		
2. common		✓	
3. multiple	✓		
4. eardrum			✓
5. dilemma		✓	

Directions: Read each sentence and underline the words that begin with the letter "m." Write all the underlined words in alphabetical order on the lines below.
Direcciones: Lee cada oración y subraya las palabras que empiecen con la letra "m." Escribe todas las letras subrayadas en orden alfabético en las líneas que siguen.

6. Danny has <u>more</u> <u>mittens</u> than gloves.

7. Our aunt, <u>Mary</u>, is baking <u>macaroons</u>.

8. Dan and <u>Madison</u> are from <u>Morocco</u>.

9. Did <u>Miller</u> eat the <u>mozzarella</u> cheese?

10. His <u>mom</u> baked <u>mini</u> pies for our snack.

macaroons	Madison	Mary
Miller	mini	mittens
mom	more	Morocco
	mozzarella	

Answer Key

 Name: _____ Date: ___/___/_____ Score: _____

Lesson 13.2

Reading Words with a Silent Letter "m"

✓ Lesson Check Point

Directions: Read each target word. Find the letter "m" and put a check (✓) in the column that identifies its position: beginning, within or end.
Direcciones: Lee cada palabra objetivo. Encuentra la letra "m" y coloca un signo de verificación (✓) en la columna que identifique su posición: inicio, interior o final.

Target Words	Beginning (First Letter)	Within	End (Last Letter)
1. program			✓
2. immediate		✓	
3. basement		✓	
4. submarine		✓	
5. moving	✓		

Directions: Read each target word. Put a check (✓) in the "yes" column if the target word has a silent letter "m." Put a check (✓) in the "no" column if the target word does not have a silent letter "m."
Direcciones: Lee cada palabra objetivo. Coloca un signo de verificación (✓) en la columna del "sí" si la palabra objetivo tiene una letra muda "m." Coloca un signo de verificación (✓) en la columna del "no" si la palabra objetivo no tiene una letra muda "m."

Target Words	Yes	No
6. mnemonic	✓	
7. immense	✓	
8. commit	✓	
9. compromise		✓
10. momentum		✓

Classwork

 Name: _____ Date:___/___/_____ Score:_____

The Reading Challenge

Lesson 13.3

Reading Multisyllable Words

✓ Lesson Check Point

 Directions: Read and divide each target word into syllables. Write each word and place a hyphen (-) between the syllables in the second column. Write the number of syllables in the third column. Use a dictionary or the Internet to check your answers.

Direcciones: Lee y separa en sílabas cada palabra objetivo. Escribe cada palabra y coloca un guión (-) entre las sílabas en la segunda columna. Escribe el número de sílabas en la tercera columna. Usa un diccionario o Internet para verificar tus respuestas.

Target Words	Words Divided into Syllables	Number of Syllables
1. menu	men-u	2
2. minuteman	min-ute-man	3
3. monsoon	mon-soon	2
4. meaningful	mean-ing-ful	3
5. migrant	mi-grant	2
6. monkey	mon-key	2
7. macaroni	mac-a-ro-ni	4
8. meadow	mead-ow	2
9. morsel	mor-sel	2
10. Mexico	Mex-i-co	3

Answer Key

 Name: _____ Date:___/___/_____ Score:_____

The Reading Challenge

Lesson 13.3

Reading Multisyllable Words

✓ **Lesson Check Point**

 Directions: Read each target word. Circle the word in the row that is divided correctly into syllables. Use a dictionary or the Internet to check your answers.

Direcciones: Lee cada palabra objetivo. Encierra en un círculo la palabra en la fila que esté correctamente separada en sílabas. Usa un diccionario o Internet para verificar tus respuestas.

Model

| magazine | **a. mag-a-zine** ⭕ | b. ma-ga-zine | c. mag-az-ine |

1. mineral	a. mi-ner-al	**b. min-er-al** ⭕	c. min-e-ral
2. magnify	**a. mag-ni-fy** ⭕	b. mag-nif-y	c. ma-gni-fy
3. malpractice	**a. mal-prac-tice** ⭕	b. mal-pract-ice	c. ma-lprac-tice
4. mechanics	a. mech-an-ics	b. me-cha-nics	**c. me-chan-ics** ⭕
5. monopoly	a. mon-op-o-ly	b. mo-no-po-ly	**c. mo-nop-o-ly** ⭕
6. metaphor	a. me-ta-phor	b. met-aph-or	**c. met-a-phor** ⭕
7. monument	a. mon-um-ent	**b. mon-u-ment** ⭕	c. mo-nu-ment
8. memorize	**a. mem-o-rize** ⭕	b. mem-or-ize	c. me-mor-ize

Learn To Read English With Directions In Spanish

Classwork

Name: _____ Date: ___/___/_____ Score: _____

Lesson 13.4

Reading and Writing

Proper and Common Nouns and Adjectives

Directions: Read the words in the word box. Put an (X) on the line next to each word that is written incorrectly. Remember that all proper nouns and proper adjectives are capitalized. Use a dictionary or the Internet to check your answers.

Direcciones: Lee las palabras en el cuadro de texto. Coloca una (X) en la línea próxima a las palabras que estén escritas de forma incorrecta. Recuerda que todos los nombres propios y adjetivos propios empiezan con mayúscula. Usa un diccionario o Internet para verificar tus respuestas.

Word Box					
X	Manager	X	Monkey	_	menu
_	Manchester	_	market	_	mentor
X	manhattan	_	Margaret	X	Mailbox
X	malawi	X	malta	_	Mother

Directions: Read each unedited sentence and underline the word that is written incorrectly. Write each sentence correctly on the line.

Direcciones: Lee cada oración sin editar y subraya la palabra que está escrita de forma incorrecta. Escribe cada oración correctamente en la línea.

Model
My son, Mark, is going to attend MIT in <u>massachusetts</u>.
My son, Mark, is going to attend MIT in Massachusetts.

1. My <u>Mom</u> is cooking macaroni and cheese for dinner.
My mom is cooking macaroni and cheese for dinner.

2. Mary and <u>max</u> read a book about the planet Mars.
Mary and Max read a book about the planet Mars.

3. Beth and Mom will meet in Midtown <u>manhattan</u>.
Beth and Mom will meet in Midtown Manhattan.

4. I received my master's degree from <u>mombasa</u> College.
I received my master's degree from Mombasa College.

Answer Key

Name: _____ Date: ___/___/_____ Score: _____

Lesson 14.1

Reading Words with the Letter N/n

✓ Lesson Check Point

Directions: Read each target word. Find the letter "n" and put a check (✓) in the column that identifies its position: beginning, within or end.
Direcciones: Lee cada palabra objetivo. Encuentra la letra "n" y coloca un signo de verificación (✓) en la columna que identifique su posición: inicio, interior o final.

Target Words	Beginning (First Letter)	Within	End (Last Letter)
1. university		✓	
2. glutton			✓
3. twin			✓
4. nurse	✓		
5. newspaper	✓		

Directions: Read each sentence and underline the words that begin with the letter "n." Write all the underlined words in alphabetical order on the lines below.
Direcciones: Lee cada oración y subraya las palabras que empiecen con la letra "n." Escribe todas las letras subrayadas en orden alfabético en las líneas que siguen.

6. Mommy never tasted chicken noodle soup.

7. Napoleon read ten books about the Nile River.

8. My neighbors enjoy celebrating New Year's Eve.

9. Nick wants to move from Kansas to North Dakota.

10. Everyone knows that many nice people live in Norway.

Napoleon	neighbors	never
New	nice	Nick
Nile	noodle	North
	Norway	

Learn To Read English With Directions In Spanish

Classwork

 Name: _____ Date: ___/___/_____ Score: _____

Lesson 14.2

Reading Words with the "ng" Letter Combination

✓ **Lesson Check Point**

 Directions: Read each target word. Circle the word in the column that has the same "ng" sound(s) as the target word.

Direcciones: Lee cada palabra objetivo. Encierra en un círculo la palabra en la columna que tenga el mismo sonido "ng" que la palabra objetivo.

| anger | a. exchange |
| | b. language (circled) |

| congratulate | a. congruence (circled) |
| | b. engineer |

| congeniality | a. jingle |
| | b. danger (circled) |

| singer | a. boxing (circled) |
| | b. triangle |

 Directions: Read each target word. Put a check (✓) under the correct column heading.

Direcciones: Lee cada palabra objetivo. Coloca un signo de verificación (✓) bajo el encabezado de la columna correcta.

Target Words	"ng" has the /n/ + /g/ sounds as in the word <u>ingrain</u>	"ng" has the /n/ + /j/ sounds as in the word <u>ginger</u>	"ng" has the /ng/ sound as in the word <u>bang</u>	"ng" has the /ng/ + /g/ sounds as in the word <u>congress</u>
1. anger				✓
2. congratulate	✓			
3. congeniality		✓		
4. singer			✓	

Answer Key

 Name: _____ Date:___/___/_____ Score:_____

Lesson 14.3

Reading Words with a Silent Letter "n"

✓ **Lesson Check Point**

 Directions: Read the target words in the word box. Write the words that have a silent letter "n" in the first column. Write the words that do not have a silent letter "n" in the second column.

Direcciones: Lee las palabras objetivo en el cuadro de texto. Escribe las palabras que tengan una letra muda "n" en la primera columna. Escribe las palabras que no tengan una letra muda "n" en la segunda columna.

Target Word Box				
animals	hymn	encounter	botanical	annex
comments	behind	hunter	nouns	penny
autumn	annual	cinnamon	monsieur	condemn
chimneys	tennis	handy	nominate	columns

Letter "n" is silent	Letter "n" has the /n/ sound
hymn	handy
annex	nouns
tennis	hunter
penny	animals
annual	behind
autumn	botanical
monsieur	comments
condemn	encounter
columns	chimneys
cinnamon	nominate

Unit N
Lesson 14.3

Classwork

 Name: _____ Date:___/___/_____ Score:_____

The Reading Challenge

Lesson 14.4

Reading Multisyllable Words

✓ Lesson Check Point

 Directions: Read and divide each target word into syllables. Write each word and place a hyphen (-) between the syllables in the second column. Write the number of syllables in the third column. Use a dictionary or the Internet to check your answers.

Direcciones: Lee y separa en sílabas cada palabra objetivo. Escribe cada palabra y coloca un guión (-) entre las sílabas en la segunda columna. Escribe el número de sílabas en la tercera columna. Usa un diccionario o Internet para verificar tus respuestas.

Target Words	Words Divided into Syllables	Number of Syllables
1. nighttime	night-time	2
2. nationwide	na-tion-wide	3
3. nuance	nu-ance	2
4. needlessly	need-less-ly	3
5. normalize	nor-mal-ize	3
6. ninety	nine-ty	2
7. nimbleness	nim-ble-ness	3
8. noble	no-ble	2
9. nectarine	nec-tar-ine	3
10. notion	no-tion	2

Answer Key

 Name: _____ Date: ___/___/_____ Score: _____

The Reading Challenge

Lesson 14.4

Reading Multisyllable Words

✓ Lesson Check Point

 Directions: Read each target word. Circle the word in the row that is divided correctly into syllables. Use a dictionary or the Internet to check your answers.

Direcciones: Lee cada palabra objetivo. Encierra en un círculo la palabra en la fila que esté correctamente separada en sílabas. Usa un diccionario o Internet para verificar tus respuestas.

Model

| napkin | a. na-pkin | b. napk-in | **c. nap-kin** |

1. neighbor	a. neighb-or	**b. neigh-bor**	c. nei-gh-bor
2. notify	**a. no-ti-fy**	b. no-tif-y	c. not-i-fy
3. natural	**a. nat-u-ral**	b. na-tu-ral	c. na-tur-al
4. nevermore	a. ne-ver-more	b. nev-erm-ore	**c. nev-er-more**
5. nobody	**a. no-bod-y**	b. no-body	c. no-bo-dy
6. newcomer	a. ne-wcom-er	b. new-co-mer	**c. new-com-er**
7. nutrition	**a. nu-tri-tion**	b. nut-ri-tion	c. nu-trit-ion
8. nausea	a. na-us-ea	b. n-au-sea	**c. nau-se-a**

Unit N
Lesson 14.4

Classwork

Name: _____ Date: ___/___/_____ Score: _____

Lesson 14.5

Reading and Writing

Proper and Common Nouns and Adjectives

Directions: Read the words in the word box. Put an (X) on the line next to each word that is written incorrectly. Remember that all proper nouns and proper adjectives are capitalized. Use a dictionary or the Internet to check your answers.

Direcciones: Lee las palabras en el cuadro de texto. Coloca una (X) en la línea próxima a las palabras que estén escritas de forma incorrecta. Recuerda que todos los nombres propios y adjetivos propios empiezan con mayúscula. Usa un diccionario o Internet para verificar tus respuestas.

Word Box					
X	Nugget	X	north Africa	X	nigeria
__	Nepal	X	nile	__	napkin
__	Napoleon	__	news	X	Noodle
__	New Delhi	X	Number	__	Nicaragua

Directions: Read each unedited sentence and underline the word that is written incorrectly. Write each sentence correctly on the line.

Direcciones: Lee cada oración sin editar y subraya la palabra que está escrita de forma incorrecta. Escribe cada oración correctamente en la línea.

Model
Nick and Nancy live in the <u>netherlands</u>.
<u>Nick and Nancy live in the Netherlands.</u>

1. I received a <u>Needle</u> from Nurse Nutley.
<u>I received a needle from Nurse Nutley.</u>

2. The <u>Newscasters</u> collaborate about national news stories.
<u>The newscasters collaborate about national news stories.</u>

3. Mrs. Newton taught a lesson about the <u>Nervous</u> system.
<u>Mrs. Newton taught a lesson about the nervous system.</u>

4. The <u>nile</u> River derives its name from the Greek word, Nelios.
<u>The Nile River derives its name from the Greek word, Nelios.</u>

Answer Key

 Name: _____ Date: ___/___/_____ Score: _____

Lesson 15.1

Reading Words with the Letter O/o

✓ **Lesson Check Point**

 Directions: Read each target word. Find the letter "o" and put a check (✓) in the column that identifies its position: beginning, within or end.
Direcciones: Lee cada palabra objetivo. Encuentra la letra "o" y coloca un signo de verificación (✓) en la columna que identifique su posición: inicio, interior o final.

Target Words	Beginning (First Letter)	Within	End (Last Letter)
1. combine		✓	
2. older	✓		
3. outreach	✓		
4. cargo			✓
5. embargo			✓

 Directions: Read each target word. Read the words in the row and circle the word that has a different vowel "o" sound.
Direcciones: Lee cada palabra objetivo. Lee las palabras en la fila y encierra la palabra que tenga un sonido vocal "o" diferente.

Target Words				
6. almost	go	code	(song)	dole
7. drop	(host)	prom	stop	clog
8. solo	(lock)	joke	tone	coat
9. gold	soap	(toss)	aloe	so
10. shopping	rock	clock	frost	(poll)

Unit O Lesson 15.1

Classwork

 Name: _____ Date: ___/___/_____ Score: _____

Lesson 15.2

Reading Words with the Short Vowel "o" Sound

✓ Lesson Check Point

 Directions: Read the words in the four boxes. Circle two words with the short vowel /ŏ/ or /ô/ sound. The anchor word for the short vowel /ŏ/ and /ô/ sounds is frog.

Direcciones: Lee las palabras en las cuatro cajas. Encierra en un círculo dos palabras con el sonido vocal corto /ŏ/ o /ô/. La palabra ejemplo para el sonido vocal corto /ŏ/ y /ô/ es la palabra, frog.

(stop)	poll	colt	(flog)	post	both
old	(plot)	host	(drop)	(slot)	(chop)

(fond)	(prom)	(blot)	mole	(rock)	(clop)
told	go	(knot)	don't	hold	roll

 Directions: Read the words in the four boxes. Circle two words that rhyme. Rhyming words have the same ending sound, such as hot and not.

Direcciones: Lee las palabras en las cuatro cajas. Encierra en un círculo dos que rimen. Las palabras que riman tienen el mismo sonido al final, como hot y not.

(shot)	(spot)	(shop)	roll	hydro	phone
no	chosen	solo	(crop)	(bond)	(pond)

ago	(lock)	(boss)	(toss)	(long)	joke
gold	(dock)	ocean	hotel	(song)	sold

Answer Key

Name: _____ Date: ___/___/_____ Score: _____

Lesson 15.2

Reading & Writing Words with the Short Vowel "o" Sound

✓ **Lesson Check Point**

Directions: Read each sentence and underline three words with the short vowel /ŏ/ or /ô/ sound. Then, write the underlined words on the lines below. The anchor word for the short vowel /ŏ/ and /ô/ sounds is frog.

Direcciones: Lee cada oración y subraya tres palabras con el sonido vocal corto /ŏ/ o /ô/. Luego, escribe las palabras subrayadas en las líneas siguientes. La palabra ejemplo para el sonido vocal corto /ŏ/ y /ô/ es la palabra, frog.

Model
Everyone saw the frog hop close to the rock.

   frog   hop   rock

1. The ropes on the mop are very soft.

   on   mop   soft

2. The policeman stopped the robber in the office.

   stopped   robber   office

3. Tom walked around the block in his socks.

   Tom   block   socks

4. Joan's job assignment is to mop the spotty tiles.

   job   mop   spotty

5. Moss develops from spores and grows in damp logs.

   Moss   from   logs

Learn To Read English With Directions In Spanish

Classwork

 Name: _____ Date:___/___/_____ Score:_____

Lesson 15.3

Reading Words with the Long Vowel "o" Sound

✓ Lesson Check Point

 Directions: Read the words in the four boxes. Circle two words with the long vowel /ō/ sound. The anchor word for the long vowel /ō/ sound is open.

Direcciones: Lee las palabras en las cuatro cajas. Encierra en un círculo dos palabras con el sonido vocal largo /ō/. La palabra ejemplo para el sonido vocal largo /ō/ es la palabra, open.

cross	(yo-yo)	boss	(joke)	rock	took
(roll)	lock	lost	(so)	(pony)	sold

(both)	pond	drop	shop	prompt	(soap)
(boat)	sock	(poke)	(toad)	floss	(poll)

 Directions: Read the words in the four boxes. Circle two words that rhyme. Rhyming words have the same ending sound, such as hope and soap.

Direcciones: Lee las palabras en las cuatro cajas. Encierra en un círculo dos palabras que rimen. Las palabras que riman tienen el mismo sonido al final, como hope y soap.

go	(folk)	(boat)	(coat)	toss	home
(yolk)	clock	rose	song	(post)	(most)

frost	(pole)	so	(cold)	poet	(roast)
told	(role)	strong	(sold)	(toast)	spot

Answer Key

Name: _____ Date: ___/___/_____ Score: _____

Lesson 15.3

Reading & Writing Words with the Long Vowel "o" Sound

✓ **Lesson Check Point**

Directions: Read each sentence and underline three words with the long vowel /ō/ sound. Then, write the underlined words on the lines below. The anchor word for the long vowel /ō/ sound is <u>open</u>.

Direcciones: Lee cada oración y subraya tres palabras con el sonido vocal largo /ō/. Luego, escribe las palabras subrayadas en las líneas siguientes. La palabra ejemplo para el sonido vocal largo /ō/ es la palabra, <u>open</u>.

Model

We will <u>go</u> to the <u>rodeo</u> and <u>limbo</u> competitions for fun.

go	rodeo	limbo

1. <u>Owen</u> said <u>hello</u> to the <u>ponies</u> in the zoo.

Owen	hello	ponies

2. The <u>hotel's</u> <u>frozen</u> <u>donuts</u> do not taste good.

hotel's	frozen	donuts

3. The <u>coeducational</u> golf team is <u>going</u> to <u>enroll</u> in the competition.

coeducational	going	enroll

4. Tom, the <u>yodeler</u>, will change his <u>tempo</u> in a <u>moment</u>.

yodeler	tempo	moment

5. My son said, "<u>Both</u> <u>hippos</u> and <u>dodo</u> birds are interesting animals."

Both	hippos	dodo

Learn To Read English With Directions In Spanish

Classwork

✏ Name: _____ Date: ___/___/_____ Score: _____

Review Lessons 15.2 & 15.3

Reading Short Vowel and Long Vowel Words

Directions: Read the target words in the word box. In the first column, write the words that have the short vowel /ŏ/ or /ô/ sound, as in the word <u>frog</u>. In the second column, write the words that have the long vowel /ō/ sound, as in the word <u>open</u>.

Direcciones: Lee las palabras objetivo en el cuadro de texto. En la primera columna, escribe las palabras que tengan el sonido vocal corto /ŏ/ o /ô/, como en la palabra inglés <u>frog</u>. En la segunda columna, escribe las palabras que tengan el sonido vocal largo /ō/, como en la palabra inglés <u>open</u>.

Target Word Box				
scaffold	cross	billfold	prompt	shopping
disposal	postal	bonding	going	rocking
stock	revolt	lost	enroll	grocery
plot	clock	mostly	strong	hippos

Letter "o" has the /ŏ/ or /ô/ sound as in the word <u>frog</u>

- plot
- lost
- clock
- cross
- stock
- strong
- prompt
- rocking
- bonding
- shopping

Letter "o" has the /ō/ sound as in the word <u>open</u>

- enroll
- revolt
- grocery
- mostly
- postal
- hippos
- going
- billfold
- scaffold
- disposal

Name: _____ Date: ___/___/_____ Score: _____

Lesson 15.4

Reading Words with Letter "o" Vowel Pairs

✓ Lesson Check Point

 Directions: Read each target word. Circle the word in the column that has the same vowel "oa," "oe," "oo" or "ou" sound(s) as the target word.
Direcciones: Lee cada palabra objetivo. Encierra en un círculo la palabra en la columna que tenga el mismo sonido vocal "oa," "oe," "oo" o "ou" que la palabra objetivo.

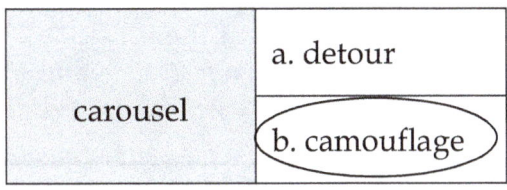
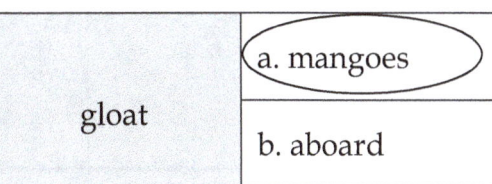
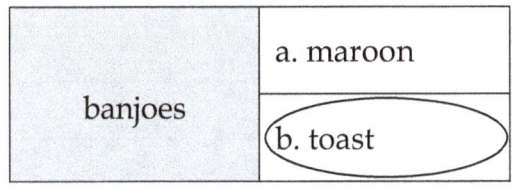
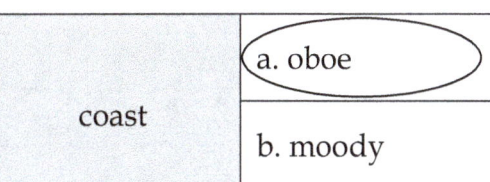

 Directions: Read each target word. Put a check (✓) under the correct column heading.
Direcciones: Lee cada palabra objetivo. Coloca un signo de verificación (✓) bajo el encabezado de la columna correcta.

Target Words	Words have the long "o" sound as in the word <u>coat</u>	Words do not have the long "o" sound
1. carousel		✓
2. gloat	✓	
3. banjoes	✓	
4. coast	✓	

Classwork

 Name: _____ Date:___/___/_____ Score:_____

Lesson 15.5

Reading Words with the Final Letter "o"

✓ **Lesson Check Point**

 Directions: Read each target word. Find the letter "o" and put a check (✓) in the column that identifies its position within the syllable.
Direcciones: Lee cada palabra objetivo. Encuentra la letra "o" y coloca un signo de verificación (✓) en la columna que identifique su posición dentro de la sílaba.

Target Words	"o" is at the end of a one syllable word	"o" is at the end of the first syllable	"o" is at the end of a multi-syllable word
1. m<u>o</u>tor		✓	
2. piano			✓
3. chosen		✓	
4. go	✓		
5. ago			✓

 Directions: Read each target word. Put a check (✓) under the correct column heading.
Direcciones: Lee cada palabra objetivo. Coloca un signo de verificación (✓) bajo el encabezado de la columna correcta.

Target Words	"o" has the /ŏ/ sound as in the word <u>frog</u>	"o" has the /ō/ sound as in the word <u>go</u>	"o" has the /ə/ sound as in the word <u>carrot</u>	"o" is silent as in the word <u>people</u>
6. roaches		✓		
7. turbo		✓		
8. contain			✓	
9. mopping	✓			
10. vaporize			✓	

 Name: _____ Date: ___/___/_____ Score: _____

Answer Key

Lesson 15.6

Reading Letter "o" Words with the Schwa Vowel Sound

✓ **Lesson Check Point**

 Directions: Read each target word. Circle the word in the column that has the same "o" sound as the target word.

Direcciones: Lee cada palabra objetivo. Lee las palabras en la columna y encierra la palabra que tenga el mismo sonido "o" que la palabra objetivo.

other	a. opening
	(b. sons)

collector	a. socks
	(b. inspector)

factor	**(a. occur)**
	b. toads

parrot	**(a. lemons)**
	b. boxer

 Directions: Read each sentence and underline the letter "o" word that has the schwa vowel /ə/ sound or short vowel /ŭ/ sound. The anchor word for the letter "o" schwa vowel /ə/ sound is <u>carrot</u> and the letter "o" short vowel /ŭ/ sound is <u>dove</u>.

Direcciones: Lee cada oración y subraya la letra "o" en palabras que tengan el sonido schwa /ə/ o /ŭ/. La palabra ejemplo para el sonido schwa de la letra "o" /ə/ es la palabra, <u>carrot</u> y para la letra "o" corta /ŭ/ es <u>dove</u>.

1. The orange <u>sponge</u> is in the old pot.

2. The boys <u>won</u> the bowling tournament.

3. Mommy enjoys eating <u>onion</u> noodle soup.

4. This year, our school will start at eight <u>o'clock</u>.

5. On <u>Monday</u>, I closed the window before the storm.

6. In October, my <u>doctor</u> gave me an intensive examination.

Classwork

 Name: _____ Date: ___/___/_____ Score: _____

Lesson 15.7

Reading Words with Vowel "o" Sounds: /ŏ/, /ō/ & /o͞o/

✓ Lesson Check Point

 Directions: Read each target word. Put a check (✓) under the correct column heading.

Direcciones: Lee cada palabra objetivo. Coloca un signo de verificación (✓) bajo el encabezado de la columna correcta.

Target Words	"o" has the /ŏ/ sound as in the word frog	"o" has the /ō/ sound as in the word go	"o" has the /o͞o/ sound as in the word to
1. mopping	✓		
2. who			✓
3. moving			✓
4. October	✓		
5. soul		✓	

 Directions: Read each sentence and underline the word that has a letter "o" that has the vowel /o͞o/ sound, as in the word two.

Direcciones: Lee cada oración y subraya la palabra con la letra "o" que tenga el sonido /o͞o/, como en la palabra inglés two.

6. Do we have a box of colorful rocks?

7. On Monday, Ron and Tom will move out.

8. We may lose our money in the stock market.

9. Who read the book about the fox in the woods?

10. The outspoken lawyer proved that his client is not guilty.

Answer Key

 Name: _____ Date: ___/___/_____ Score: _____

Lesson 15.8

Reading Words with the "or" Letter Combination

✓ **Lesson Check Point**

 Directions: Read each target word. Circle the word in the column that has the same "o" + "r" sounds as the target word.
Direcciones: Lee cada palabra objetivo. Encierra en un círculo la palabra en la columna que tenga los mismos sonidos "o" + "r" que la palabra objetivo.

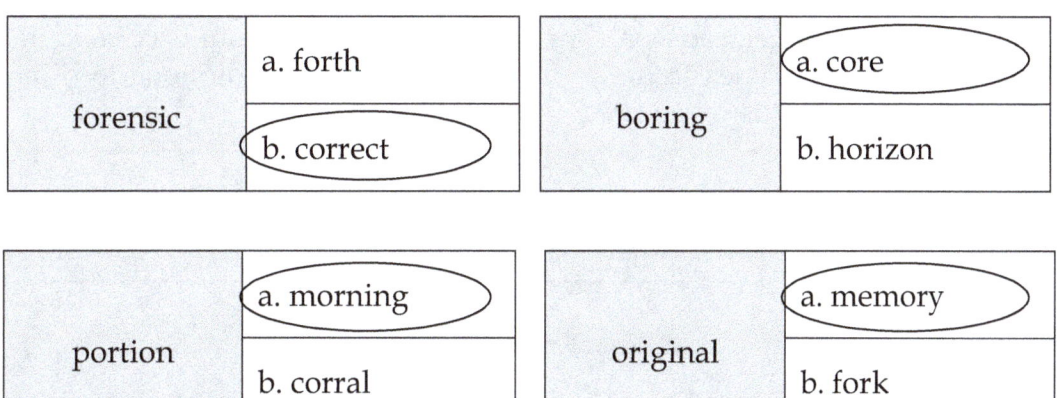

 Directions: Read each target word. Put a check (✓) under the correct column heading.
Direcciones: Lee cada palabra objetivo. Coloca un signo de verificación (✓) bajo el encabezado de la columna correcta.

Target Words	"or" has the /ô/ + /r/ sounds as in the word <u>door</u>	"or" has the /ə/ + /r/ sounds as in the word <u>doctor</u>
1. forensic		✓
2. boring	✓	
3. portion	✓	
4. original		✓

Learn To Read English With Directions In Spanish   153   Copyrighted Material

Classwork

Name: _____ Date: ___/___/_____ Score: _____

Lesson 15.8

Reading Words with the "or" Letter Combination

Dictionary Skills/ Vocabulary

✓ Lesson Check Point

Directions: Read each target word and its definition. Write the target word on the line in front of its meaning. Use a dictionary or the Internet to check your answers.

Direcciones: Lee cada palabra objetivo y su definición. Escribe la palabra objetivo en la línea frente a su significado. Usa un diccionario o Internet para verificar tus respuestas.

Target Word Box				
worn	orbits	important	story	forgot

1. __forgot__   inability to remember
2. __important__   something or someone of great value
3. __worn__   fabric that has become thinner or damaged
4. __orbits__   the act of moving around another object
5. __story__   a spoken or written description of characters and events

Directions: Read each sentence and write the target word that correctly completes the sentence.

Direcciones: Lee cada oración y escribe la palabra objetivo que complete la oración.

6. My old blue jeans are ____worn____ out.

7. The science teacher said, "The Earth __orbits__ the Sun."

8. It is ____important____ to attend school every day.

9. Molly told the teacher she ____forgot____ to do her homework.

10. The ____story____ "The Fox and the Wise Owl" has a great plot.

Answer Key

 Name: _____ Date:___/___/_____ Score:_____

Lesson 15.9

Reading Words with a Silent Letter "o"

✓ **Lesson Check Point**

 Directions: Read the target words in the word box. Write the words that have a silent letter "o" in the first column. Write the words that do not have a silent letter "o" in the second column.

Direcciones: Lee las palabras objetivo en el cuadro de texto. Escribe las palabras que tengan una letra muda "o" en la primera columna. Escribe las palabras que no tengan una letra muda "o" en la segunda columna.

Target Word Box				
combat	leopards	horse	Phoenician	subpoena
body	jeopardy	subpoenas	know	hold
Leonard	assort	open	leopard	collect
expose	phoenix	people	octopus	jeopardize

Letter "o" is silent

- leopards
- jeopardy
- leopard
- people
- phoenix
- subpoena
- subpoenas
- Leonard
- jeopardize
- Phoenician

Letter "o" has a letter "o" sound

- open
- horse
- know
- body
- hold
- assort
- combat
- collect
- expose
- octopus

Classwork

Name: _____ Date:___/___/_____ Score:_____

Unit Review - O/o

Reading Words with Vowel "o" Sounds: /ŏ/, /ō/, /ə/ & Silent

✓ **Lesson Check Point**

Directions: Read each target word. Circle the word in the column that has the same "o" sound as the target word.

Direcciones: Lee cada palabra objetivo. Lee las palabras en la columna y encierra la palabra que tenga el mismo sonido "o" que la palabra objetivo.

| forget | (a. corral) |
| | b. avoid |

| toaster | a. spotted |
| | (b. goals) |

| jeopardy | a. ponder |
| | (b. people) |

| robbing | (a. hopping) |
| | b. hoping |

Directions: Read each target word. Put a check (✓) under the correct column heading.

Direcciones: Lee cada palabra objetivo. Coloca un signo de verificación (✓) bajo el encabezado de la columna correcta.

Target Words	"o" has the /ŏ/ sound as in the word <u>frog</u>	"o" has the /ō/ sound as in the word <u>go</u>	"o" has the /ə/ sound as in the word <u>carrot</u>	"o" is silent as in the word <u>people</u>
1. forget			✓	
2. toaster		✓		
3. jeopardy				✓
4. robbing	✓			

Answer Key

 Name: _____ Date:___/___/_____ Score: _____

The Reading Challenge

Lesson 15.10

Reading Multisyllable Words

✓ **Lesson Check Point**

 Directions: Read and divide each target word into syllables. Write each word and place a hyphen (-) between the syllables in the second column. Write the number of syllables in the third column. Use a dictionary or the Internet to check your answers.

Direcciones: Lee y separa en sílabas cada palabra objetivo. Escribe cada palabra y coloca un guión (-) entre las sílabas en la segunda columna. Escribe el número de sílabas en la tercera columna. Usa un diccionario o Internet para verificar tus respuestas.

Target Words	Words Divided into Syllables	Number of Syllables
1. solar	so-lar	2
2. motel	mo-tel	2
3. token	to-ken	2
4. composer	com-pos-er	3
5. Romania	Ro-ma-ni-a	4
6. lotion	lo-tion	2
7. orderly	or-der-ly	3
8. rodent	ro-dent	2
9. provoking	pro-vok-ing	3
10. Bohemian	Bo-he-mi-an	4

Classwork

 Name: _____ Date: ___/___/_____ Score: _____

The Reading Challenge

Lesson 15.10

Reading Multisyllable Words

✓ **Lesson Check Point**

 Directions: Read each target word. Circle the word in the row that is divided correctly into syllables. Use a dictionary or the Internet to check your answers.

Direcciones: Lee cada palabra objetivo. Encierra en un círculo la palabra en la fila que esté correctamente separada en sílabas. Usa un diccionario o Internet para verificar tus respuestas.

Model

| proposal | a. prop-o-sal | b. pro-po-sal | c. pro-pos-al ⭕ |

| 1. portable | a. por-table | b. por-ta-ble ⭕ | c. port-a-ble |

| 2. asteroid | a. as-te-roid | b. ast-e-roid | c. as-ter-oid ⭕ |

| 3. corporate | a. cor-po-rate ⭕ | b. corpo-ra-te | c. corp-o-rate |

| 4. potato | a. pot-at-o | b. po-ta-to ⭕ | c. pot-a-to |

| 5. repertoire | a. rep-er-toire ⭕ | b. re-pert-oire | c. re-per-toire |

| 6. investor | a. in-ves-tor ⭕ | b. in-vest-or | c. i-nvest-or |

| 7. cockatoo | a. cock-at-oo | b. co-cka-too | c. cock-a-too ⭕ |

| 8. October | a. Oct-o-ber | b. Oc-to-ber ⭕ | c. Oct-ob-er |

Answer Key

Name: _____ Date: ___/___/_____ Score: _____

Lesson 15.11

Reading and Writing

Proper and Common Nouns and Adjectives

Directions: Read the words in the word box. Put an (X) on the line next to each word that is written incorrectly. Remember that all proper nouns and proper adjectives are capitalized. Use a dictionary or the Internet to check your answers.

Direcciones: Lee las palabras en el cuadro de texto. Coloca una (X) en la línea próxima a las palabras que estén escritas de forma incorrecta. Recuerda que todos los nombres propios y adjetivos propios empiezan con mayúscula. Usa un diccionario o Internet para verificar tus respuestas.

Word Box					
__	Oxbridge	__	octopus	X	orlando
X	ontario	__	Onega Bay	__	organizer
__	Old English	X	october	X	Atlantic ocean
X	Occasion	__	objective	X	Original

Directions: Read each unedited sentence and underline the word that is written incorrectly. Write each sentence correctly on the line.

Direcciones: Lee cada oración sin editar y subraya la palabra que está escrita de forma incorrecta. Escribe cada oración correctamente en la línea.

Model
At <u>One</u> o'clock, the Owens family went to Onega Bay.
<u>At one o'clock, the Owens family went to Onega Bay.</u>

1. Mr. <u>o'Connor</u> is planning an outstanding trip to the Orient.
<u>Mr. O'Connor is planning an outstanding trip to the Orient.</u>

2. Marie, Octavia and I are <u>Overjoyed</u> about our trip to Oktoberfest.
<u>Marie, Octavia and I are overjoyed about our trip to Oktoberfest.</u>

3. Mr. O'Keeffe gave the class a fact sheet about the <u>oregon</u> Trail.
<u>Mr. O'Keeffe gave the class a fact sheet about the Oregon Trail.</u>

4. In October, the official <u>olympic</u> Games tryouts will begin.
<u>In October, the official Olympic Games tryouts will begin.</u>

Classwork

✍ Name: _____ Date: ___/___/_____ Score: _____

Lesson 16.1

Reading Words with the Letter P/p

✓ Lesson Check Point

Directions: Read each target word. Find the letter "p" and put a check (✓) in the column that identifies its position: beginning, within or end.
Direcciones: Lee cada palabra objetivo. Encuentra la letra "p" y coloca un signo de verificación (✓) en la columna que identifique su posición: inicio, interior o final.

Target Words	Beginning (First Letter)	Within	End (Last Letter)
1. price	✓		
2. pest	✓		
3. plans	✓		
4. asleep			✓
5. concept		✓	

Directions: Read each sentence and underline the words that begin with the letter "p." Write all the underlined words in alphabetical order on the lines below.
Direcciones: Lee cada oración y subraya las palabras que empiecen con la letra "p." Escribe todas las letras subrayadas en orden alfabético en las líneas que siguen.

6. The pitcher threw powerful fastballs.

7. Lydia is sending a package to Panama.

8. Gabby's pageant gown is white and purple.

9. The police officer is patrolling our college campus.

10. People in the courtroom said the plaintiff has a strong case.

package   pageant   Panama
patrolling   People   pitcher
plaintiff   police   powerful
                 purple

Answer Key

Name: _____ Date: ___/___/_____ Score: _____

Lesson 16.2

Reading Words with the "ph" Letter Combination

✓ Lesson Check Point

Directions: Read each target word. Circle the word in the column that has the same "ph" sound(s) as the target word.

Direcciones: Lee cada palabra objetivo. Encierra en un círculo la palabra en la columna que tenga el mismo sonido "ph" que la palabra objetivo.

| orphan | **a. pamphlet** (circled) |
| | b. haphazard |

| upheaval | **a. haphazard** (circled) |
| | b. photograph |

| alphabet | a. uphold |
| | **b. biography** (circled) |

| amphibian | **a. esophagus** (circled) |
| | b. shepherd |

Directions: Read each target word. Put a check (✓) under the correct column heading.

Direcciones: Lee cada palabra objetivo. Coloca un signo de verificación (✓) bajo el encabezado de la columna correcta.

Target Words	"ph" has the /f/ sound as in the word phone	"ph" has the /p/ + /h/ sounds as in the word uphill
1. orphan	✓	
2. upheaval		✓
3. alphabet	✓	
4. amphibian	✓	

Classwork

Name: _____ Date: ___/___/_____ Score: _____

Lesson 16.3

Reading Words with the "pr" Letter Combination

Dictionary Skills/ Vocabulary

✓ **Lesson Check Point**

Directions: Read each target word and its definition. Write the letter of the definition on the line of each target word. Use a dictionary or the Internet to check your answers.

Direcciones: Lee cada palabra objetivo y su definición. Escribe la letra de la definición en la línea de cada palabra objetivo. Usa un diccionario o Internet para verificar tus respuestas.

Target Words   **Definitions**

1. _b_ praised   a. an educator/instructor at a university or college
2. _c_ predators   b. to have expressed words of admiration or approval
3. _d_ president   c. animals that kill and eat other animals for survival
4. _a_ professor   d. an elected or appointed leader of a country
5. _e_ program   e. an organized business that provides activities

Directions: Read each sentence and write the target word that correctly completes the sentence.

Direcciones: Lee cada oración y escribe la palabra objetivo que complete la oración.

6. The great white whales and lions are alpha ___predators___.

7. Dr. Pringle is a ___professor___ at Pratt University.

8. The ___president___ was elected for a four-year term.

9. The teacher ___praised___ her hardworking students.

10. My sister and I attend an after-school ___program___.

Answer Key

 Name: _____ Date: ___/___/_____ Score: _____

Lesson 16.4

Reading Words with the "pl" Letter Combination

Dictionary Skills/ Vocabulary

✓ **Lesson Check Point**

 Directions: Read each target word and its definition. Write the target word on the line in front of its meaning. Use a dictionary or the Internet to check your answers.

Direcciones: Lee cada palabra objetivo y su definición. Escribe la palabra objetivo en la línea frente a su significado. Usa un diccionario o Internet para verificar tus respuestas.

Target Word Box				
plaintiff	pleasure	plowing	plum	plush

1. <u>plowing</u>   the act of breaking up the land for farming
2. <u>plush</u>   a luxury item that is nice and expensive
3. <u>plaintiff</u>   a person or group of people who file a lawsuit
4. <u>pleasure</u>   an experience that is enjoyable or satisfying
5. <u>plum</u>   purple, smooth-skinned fruit that is very sweet

 Directions: Read each sentence. Underline the word in the parentheses that correctly completes each sentence. Then, write the underlined word on the line.

Direcciones: Lee cada oración. Subraya la palabra entre paréntesis que completa correctamente cada oración. Luego, escribe la palabra subrayada en la línea.

6. The <u>plaintiff</u> filed a case at the courthouse. (pleasure, <u>plaintiff</u>)

7. The farmer is <u>plowing</u> the center of his field. (<u>plowing</u>, plush)

8. I spent a lot of money for my <u>plush</u> condo. (plum, <u>plush</u>)

9. I bought peaches and <u>plums</u> from the fruit store. (<u>plums</u>, pleasure)

10. I agree that it is a <u>pleasure</u> to work with children. (<u>pleasure</u>, plaintiff)

Classwork

Name: _____ Date: ___/___/_____ Score: _____

Lesson 16.4

Reading Words with the "ple" Letter Combination

 Lesson Check Point

Directions: Read each target word. Find the "ple" letter combination and put a check (✓) in the column that identifies its position: beginning, within or end.

Direcciones: Lee cada palabra objetivo. Encuentra la combinación de letras "ple" y coloca un signo de verificación (✓) en la columna que identifique su posición: inicio, interior o final.

Target Words	Beginning (First 3 Letters)	Within	End (Last 3 Letters)
1. participle			✓
2. multiple			✓
3. displeased		✓	
4. simple			✓
5. plentiful	✓		

Directions: Read each target word. Put a check (✓) in the "yes" column if the "ple" letter combination has the /p/ + /ə/ + /l/ sounds. Put a check (✓) in the "no" column if the "ple" letter combination does not have the /p/ + /ə/ + /l/ sounds.

Direcciones: Lee cada palabra objetivo. Coloca un signo de verificación (✓) en la columna del "sí" si la combinación de letras "ple" tiene el sonidos /p/ + /ə/ + /l/. Coloca un signo de verificación (✓) en la columna del "no" si la combinación de letras "ple" no tiene el sonidos /p/ + /ə/ + /l/.

Target Words	Yes	No
6. participle	✓	
7. multiple	✓	
8. displeased		✓
9. simple	✓	
10. plentiful		✓

Answer Key

 Name: _____ Date: ___/___/_____ Score: _____

Lesson 16.5

Reading Words with a Silent Letter "p"

✓ Lesson Check Point

 Directions: Read the target words in the word box. Write the words that have a silent letter "p" in the first column. Write the words that do not have a silent letter "p" in the second column.

Direcciones: Lee las palabras objetivo en el cuadro de texto. Escribe las palabras que tengan una letra muda "p" en la primera columna. Escribe las palabras que no tengan una letra muda "p" en la segunda columna.

Target Word Box				
apple	receipt	sleep	compose	slippery
suppose	point	puppy	hopping	raspberry
tips	sample	corps	predict	play
plot	psychic	cupboard	stamps	surprise

Letter "p" is silent

- corps
- apple
- receipt
- slippery
- puppy
- psychic
- raspberry
- cupboard
- suppose
- hopping

Letter "p" has the /p/ sound

- plot
- tips
- play
- sleep
- point
- predict
- sample
- stamps
- surprise
- compose

Classwork

 Name: _____ Date: ___/___/_____ Score: _____

The Reading Challenge

Lesson 16.6

Reading Multisyllable Words

✓ Lesson Check Point

 Directions: Read and divide each target word into syllables. Write each word and place a hyphen (-) between the syllables in the second column. Write the number of syllables in the third column. Use a dictionary or the Internet to check your answers.

Direcciones: Lee y separa en sílabas cada palabra objetivo. Escribe cada palabra y coloca un guión (-) entre las sílabas en la segunda columna. Escribe el número de sílabas en la tercera columna. Usa un diccionario o Internet para verificar tus respuestas.

Target Words	Words Divided into Syllables	Number of Syllables
1. people	peo-ple	2
2. plural	plu-ral	2
3. powder	pow-der	2
4. privatized	pri-va-tized	3
5. platform	plat-form	2
6. politeness	po-lite-ness	3
7. plastic	plas-tic	2
8. persistence	per-sis-tence	3
9. parsley	pars-ley	2
10. peanut	pea-nut	2

Answer Key

Name: _____ Date: ___/___/_____ Score: _____

The Reading Challenge

Lesson 16.6

Reading Multisyllable Words

✓ **Lesson Check Point**

Directions: Read each target word. Circle the word in the row that is divided correctly into syllables. Use a dictionary or the Internet to check your answers.

Direcciones: Lee cada palabra objetivo. Encierra en un círculo la palabra en la fila que esté correctamente separada en sílabas. Usa un diccionario o Internet para verificar tus respuestas.

Model

paragraph	**a. par-a-graph** (circled)	b. pa-ra-graph	c. par-ag-raph
1. period	a. per-i-od	**b. pe-ri-od** (circled)	c. pe-r-iod
2. pyramid	**a. pyr-a-mid** (circled)	b. py-ra-mid	c. pyr-am-id
3. personal	**a. per-son-al** (circled)	b. pers-on-al	c. per-so-nal
4. parakeet	a. pa-ra-keet	**b. par-a-keet** (circled)	c. pa-rak-eet
5. punctual	a. pun-ctu-al	b. punc-t-ual	**c. punc-tu-al** (circled)
6. Panama	a. Pan-am-a	**b. Pan-a-ma** (circled)	c. Pa-na-ma
7. perigee	a. pe-rig-ee	**b. per-i-gee** (circled)	c. per-ig-ee
8. peculiar	a. pec-u-liar	b. pe-cul-iar	**c. pe-cu-liar** (circled)

Learn To Read English With Directions In Spanish   Copyrighted Material

Classwork

Name: _____ Date: ___/___/_____ Score: _____

Lesson 16.7

Reading and Writing

Proper and Common Nouns and Adjectives

Directions: Read the words in the word box. Put an (X) on the line next to each word that is written incorrectly. Remember that all proper nouns and proper adjectives are capitalized. Use a dictionary or the Internet to check your answers.

Direcciones: Lee las palabras en el cuadro de texto. Coloca una (X) en la línea próxima a las palabras que estén escritas de forma incorrecta. Recuerda que todos los nombres propios y adjetivos propios empiezan con mayúscula. Usa un diccionario o Internet para verificar tus respuestas.

Word Box					
__	Poland	X	philippine	__	place
__	passport	__	Peruvian	X	panama
X	Penguin	__	people	X	Passenger
__	pharmacist	X	pennsylvania	X	Poodle

Directions: Read each unedited sentence and underline the word that is written incorrectly. Write each sentence correctly on the line.

Direcciones: Lee cada oración sin editar y subraya la palabra que está escrita de forma incorrecta. Escribe cada oración correctamente en la línea.

Model
The poem, "puddles," was written by Patrick Parker.
The poem, "Puddles," was written by Patrick Parker.

1. The panama Canal is a powerful structure.
The Panama Canal is a powerful structure.

2. The City of philadelphia is located in Pennsylvania.
The City of Philadelphia is located in Pennsylvania.

3. The peruvian coast bordering the Pacific Ocean is a desert strip.
The Peruvian coast bordering the Pacific Ocean is a desert strip.

4. perry the Platypus is the star of the hit show "Phineas and Ferb."
Perry the Platypus is the star of the hit show "Phineas and Ferb."

Answer Key

Name: _____ Date: ___/___/_____ Score: _____

Lesson 17.1

Reading Words with the Letter Q/q

✓ **Lesson Check Point**

Directions: Read each target word. Find the letter "q" and put a check (✓) in the column that identifies its position: beginning, within or end.
Direcciones: Lee cada palabra objetivo. Encuentra la letra "q" y coloca un signo de verificación (✓) en la columna que identifique su posición: inicio, interior o final.

Target Words	Beginning (First Letter)	Within	End (Last Letter)
1. question	✓		
2. squabbled		✓	
3. quotation	✓		
4. Iraq			✓
5. consequent		✓	

Directions: Read each sentence and underline the words that begin with the letter "q." Write all the underlined words in alphabetical order on the lines below.
Direcciones: Lee cada oración y subraya las palabras que empiecen con la letra "q." Escribe todas las letras subrayadas en orden alfabético en las líneas que siguen.

6. <u>Quincy</u> and his family are from <u>Quebec</u>, Canada.

7. The new <u>quilts</u> are made with high <u>quality</u> fabrics.

8. My sister, <u>Queenisha</u>, sleeps on a <u>queen-sized</u> bed.

9. All the children in the <u>Quinn</u> family have four <u>quarters</u>.

10. All the candidates are highly <u>qualified</u> for the job at <u>Quick</u> Inc.

qualified   quality   quarters
Quebec   Queenisha   queen-sized
Quick   quilts   Quincy
                   Quinn

Classwork

 Name: _____ Date: ___/___/_____ Score: _____

Lesson 17.2

Reading Words with the Letter "q" and "qu" Letter Combination

✓ **Lesson Check Point**

 Directions: Read each target word. Circle the word in the column that has the same "q" or "qu" sound(s) as the target word.

Direcciones: Lee cada palabra objetivo. Encierra en un círculo la palabra en la columna que tenga el mismo sonido "q" o "qu" que la palabra objetivo.

| equip | a. antique |
| | b. quickly (circled) |

| conquer | a. liquid |
| | b. Qatar (circled) |

| equal | a. queen (circled) |
| | b. quetzal |

| conquest | a. opaque |
| | b. quench (circled) |

 Directions: Read each target word. Put a check (✓) under the correct column heading.

Direcciones: Lee cada palabra objetivo. Coloca un signo de verificación (✓) bajo el encabezado de la columna correcta.

Target Words	"qu" has the /k/ sound as in the word <u>plaque</u>	"qu" has the /k/ + /w/ sounds as in the word <u>queen</u>
1. equip		✓
2. conquer	✓	
3. equal		✓
4. conquest		✓

Answer Key

 Name: _____ Date:___/___/_____ Score:_____

Lesson 17.2

Reading Words with the "qu" Letter Combination

✓ **Lesson Check Point**

 Directions: Read each target word. Circle the word in the column that has the same "qu" sound(s) as the target word.

Direcciones: Lee cada palabra objetivo. Encierra en un círculo la palabra en la columna que tenga el mismo sonido "qu" que la palabra objetivo.

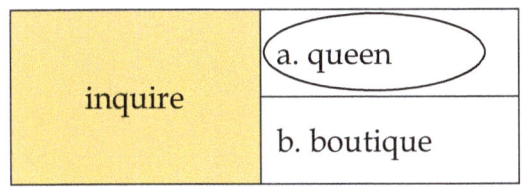
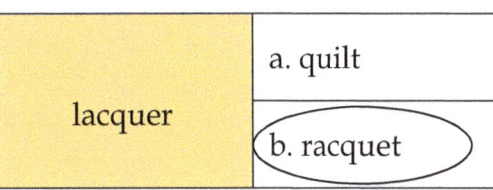
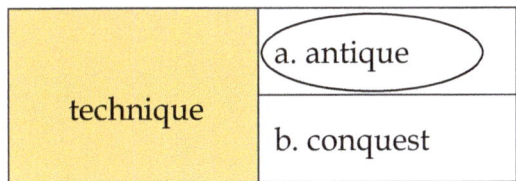
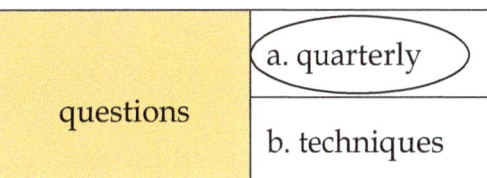

 Directions: Read each target word. Put a check (✓) under the correct column heading.

Direcciones: Lee cada palabra objetivo. Coloca un signo de verificación (✓) bajo el encabezado de la columna correcta.

Target Words	"qu" has the /k/ + /w/ sounds as in the word queen	"qu" has the /k/ sound as in the word plaque	"qu" is silent as in the word racquet
1. inquire	✓		
2. lacquer			✓
3. technique		✓	
4. questions	✓		

Classwork

Name: _____ Date:___/___/_____ Score: _____

The Reading Challenge

Lesson 17.3

Reading Multisyllable Words

✓ **Lesson Check Point**

Directions: Read and divide each target word into syllables. Write each word and place a hyphen (-) between the syllables in the second column. Write the number of syllables in the third column. Use a dictionary or the Internet to check your answers.

Direcciones: Lee y separa en sílabas cada palabra objetivo. Escribe cada palabra y coloca un guión (-) entre las sílabas en la segunda columna. Escribe el número de sílabas en la tercera columna. Usa un diccionario o Internet para verificar tus respuestas.

Target Words	Words Divided into Syllables	Number of Syllables
1. quarantine	quar-an-tine	3
2. quintet	quin-tet	2
3. quiver	quiv-er	2
4. quota	quo-ta	2
5. query	que-ry	2
6. quartet	quar-tet	2
7. quantities	quan-ti-ties	3
8. qualified	qual-i-fied	3
9. quadruple	quad-ru-ple	3
10. quietness	qui-et-ness	3

Answer Key

 Name: _____ Date: ___/___/_____ Score: _____

The Reading Challenge

Lesson 17.3

Reading Multisyllable Words

✓ **Lesson Check Point**

 Directions: Read each target word. Circle the word in the row that is divided correctly into syllables. Use a dictionary or the Internet to check your answers.

Direcciones: Lee cada palabra objetivo. Encierra en un círculo la palabra en la fila que esté correctamente separada en sílabas. Usa un diccionario o Internet para verificar tus respuestas.

Model

| quarter | a. quart-er | **(b. quar-ter)** | c. qu-arter |

1. quantum	**(a. quan-tum)**	b. quant-um	c. qua-ntum
2. qualify	**(a. qual-i-fy)**	b. qua-li-fy	c. qua-lif-y
3. quiver	a. qui-ver	**(b. quiv-er)**	c. qu-iver
4. question	**(a. ques-tion)**	b. quest-ion	c. que-stion
5. quotient	a. quot-ient	b. qu-otient	**(c. quo-tient)**
6. quota	a. qu-ota	**(b. quo-ta)**	c. quot-a
7. Quebec	a. Qu-ebec	**(b. Que-bec)**	c. Queb-ec
8. quietude	**(a. qui-e-tude)**	b. quiet-ude	c. quie-tu-de

Learn To Read English With Directions In Spanish

Classwork

Name: _____ Date:___/___/_____ Score:_____

Lesson 17.4

Reading and Writing

Proper and Common Nouns and Adjectives

Directions: Read the words in the word box. Put an (X) on the line next to each word that is written incorrectly. Remember that all proper nouns and proper adjectives are capitalized. Use a dictionary or the Internet to check your answers.

Direcciones: Lee las palabras en el cuadro de texto. Coloca una (X) en la línea próxima a las palabras que estén escritas de forma incorrecta. Recuerda que todos los nombres propios y adjetivos propios empiezan con mayúscula. Usa un diccionario o Internet para verificar tus respuestas.

Word Box					
__	quarrel	X	quebec	__	Quakers
X	Quotient	__	Qatar	__	questionable
X	Quotes	__	quickly	X	queen Anne
X	Quiver	X	Quiche	__	Quincy

Directions: Read each unedited sentence and underline the word that is written incorrectly. Write each sentence correctly on the line.

Direcciones: Lee cada oración sin editar y subraya la palabra que está escrita de forma incorrecta. Escribe cada oración correctamente en la línea.

Model
The queen of England is very quiet.
The Queen of England is very quiet.

1. According to my Quartz watch, it is a Quarter after two.
   According to my Quartz watch, it is a quarter after two.

2. My good friends, Mr. and Mrs. Quinn, are quakers.
   My good friends, Mr. and Mrs. Quinn, are Quakers.

3. The queen is going to visit quezon City in the Philippines.
   The queen is going to visit Quezon City in the Philippines.

4. After reading the article, I asked a Question about Queen Elizabeth.
   After reading the article, I asked a question about Queen Elizabeth.

Answer Key

L Name: _____ Date: ___/___/_____ Score: _____

Lesson 18.1

Reading Words with the Letter R/r

✓ **Lesson Check Point**

Directions: Read each target word. Find the letter "r" and put a check (✓) in the column that identifies its position: beginning, within or end.
Direcciones: Lee cada palabra objetivo. Encuentra la letra "r" y coloca un signo de verificación (✓) en la columna que identifique su posición: inicio, interior o final.

Target Words	Beginning (First Letter)	Within	End (Last Letter)
1. cashier			✓
2. recent	✓		
3. folder			✓
4. grape		✓	
5. runaway	✓		

Directions: Read each sentence and underline the words that begin with the letter "r." Write all the underlined words in alphabetical order on the lines below.
Direcciones: Lee cada oración y subraya las palabras que empiecen con la letra "r." Escribe todas las letras subrayadas en orden alfabético en las líneas que siguen.

6. At <u>recess</u>, Brianna and I <u>ran</u> quickly on the track.

7. The green <u>rowboat</u> is floating along the Nile <u>River</u>.

8. Brian <u>rode</u> his bike along the base of the <u>Rocky</u> Mountains.

9. The <u>residents</u> have the new Long Island <u>Railroad</u> schedule.

10. We can preserve our planet by <u>recycling</u> and <u>reusing</u> items.

Railroad	ran	recess
recycling	residents	reusing
River	Rocky	rode
	rowboat	

Learn To Read English With Directions In Spanish

Classwork

Name: _____ Date:___/___/_____ Score:_____

Lesson 18.2

Reading Words with the Letter "r" Combinations: "br," "cr," "dr," "fr," "gr," "pr" and "tr"

✓ **Lesson Check Point**

Directions: Read the target words in the word box. Identify the words with the following letter combinations: "br," "cr," "dr," "fr," "gr," "pr" and "tr." Write the target word on the line that correctly completes each sentence.

Direcciones: Lee las palabras objetivo en el cuadro de texto. Identifica las palabras con las siguientes combinaciones de letras: "br," "cr," "dr," "fr," "gr," "pr" y "tr." Escribe la palabra objetivo en la línea que complete correctamente la oración.

Target Word Box			
friends	traveling	bread	groom
principal		cruise	drifting
brochure		program	trucks

1. The ____cruise____ brochure is on the brass table.

2. Francis and Brad are best ____friends____.

3. The new ____principal____ is our school's leader.

4. Yesterday, I saw logs ____drifting____ along the riverbank.

5. The two loaves of ____bread____ are fresh out of the oven.

6. The train is ____traveling____ from New York to Chicago.

7. The college admission ____brochure____ is very informative.

8. My social service ____program____ distributes food to needy families.

9. Testa's electric ____trucks____ travel up to 100 miles without recharging.

10. The bride and ____groom____ received lots of expensive wedding presents.

Answer Key

Name: _____ Date: ___/___/_____ Score: _____

The Reading Challenge

Lesson 18.3

Reading Multisyllable Words

✓ Lesson Check Point

Directions: Read and divide each target word into syllables. Write each word and place a hyphen (-) between the syllables in the second column. Write the number of syllables in the third column. Use a dictionary or the Internet to check your answers.

Direcciones: Lee y separa en sílabas cada palabra objetivo. Escribe cada palabra y coloca un guión (-) entre las sílabas en la segunda columna. Escribe el número de sílabas en la tercera columna. Usa un diccionario o Internet para verificar tus respuestas.

Target Words	Words Divided into Syllables	Number of Syllables
1. reviewing	re-view-ing	3
2. rigorously	rig-or-ous-ly	4
3. rapidly	rap-id-ly	3
4. ready	read-y	2
5. rocky	rock-y	2
6. rather	rath-er	2
7. reading	read-ing	2
8. rapture	rap-ture	2
9. reflection	re-flec-tion	3
10. reporting	re-port-ing	3

Classwork

 Name: _____ Date: ___/___/_____ Score: _____

The Reading Challenge
Lesson 18.3
Reading Multisyllable Words

✓ Lesson Check Point

 Directions: Read each target word. Circle the word in the row that is divided correctly into syllables. Use a dictionary or the Internet to check your answers.

Direcciones: Lee cada palabra objetivo. Encierra en un círculo la palabra en la fila que esté correctamente separada en sílabas. Usa un diccionario o Internet para verificar tus respuestas.

Model

| runaway | a. ru-na-way | **(b. run-a-way)** | c. run-aw-ay |

| 1. robotics | **(a. ro-bot-ics)** | b. rob-ot-ics | c. ro-bo-tics |

| 2. radius | **(a. ra-di-us)** | b. rad-i-us | c. ra-diu-s |

| 3. radical | **(a. rad-i-cal)** | b. ra-dic-al | c. ra-di-cal |

| 4. reception | **(a. re-cept-ion)** | b. rec-ep-tion | **(c. re-cep-tion)** |

| 5. royalist | a. ro-yal-ist | b. roy-a-list | **(c. roy-al-ist)** |

| 6. reconcile | a. re-con-cile | **(b. rec-on-cile)** | c. rec-onc-ile |

| 7. recliner | a. rec-lin-er | b. re-cli-ner | **(c. re-clin-er)** |

| 8. refresher | **(a. re-fresh-er)** | b. ref-res-her | c. ref-resh-er |

Answer Key

Name: _____ Date: ___/___/_____ Score: _____

Lesson 18.4

Reading and Writing

Proper and Common Nouns and Adjectives

Directions: Read the words in the word box. Put an (X) on the line next to each word that is written incorrectly. Remember that all proper nouns and proper adjectives are capitalized. Use a dictionary or the Internet to check your answers.

Direcciones: Lee las palabras en el cuadro de texto. Coloca una (X) en la línea próxima a las palabras que estén escritas de forma incorrecta. Recuerda que todos los nombres propios y adjetivos propios empiezan con mayúscula. Usa un diccionario o Internet para verificar tus respuestas.

Word Box					
__	runner	X	Amazon river	X	Red CRoss
__	Richard	__	Ryan	__	rainforest
X	romanian	__	Richmond, VA	X	Railroad
X	The rockies	__	roaches	X	rome

Directions: Read each unedited sentence and underline the word that is written incorrectly. Write each sentence correctly on the line.

Direcciones: Lee cada oración sin editar y subraya la palabra que está escrita de forma incorrecta. Escribe cada oración correctamente en la línea.

Model
We saw two <u>Retired</u> racehorses at Richardson Ranch.
<u>We saw two retired racehorses at Richardson Ranch.</u>

1. Raphael said, "<u>russia</u> is the world's largest country."
<u>Raphael said, "Russia is the world's largest country."</u>

2. My friends, Rachel and Ricky, went to the Amazon <u>rainforest</u>.
<u>My friends, Rachel and Ricky, went to the Amazon Rainforest.</u>

3. Mr. Richards received the <u>rockefeller</u> Merit Award for Excellence.
<u>Mr. Richards received the Rockefeller Merit Award for Excellence.</u>

4. Do you know that Rose Robin <u>restaurant</u> serves the best ribs?
<u>Do you know that Rose Robin Restaurant serves the best ribs?</u>

Classwork

Name: _____ Date: ___/___/_____ Score: _____

Lesson 19.1

Reading Words with the Letter S/s

✓ **Lesson Check Point**

Directions: Read each target word. Find the letter "s" and put a check (✓) in the column that identifies its position: beginning, within or end.
Direcciones: Lee cada palabra objetivo. Encuentra la letra "s" y coloca un signo de verificación (✓) en la columna que identifique su posición: inicio, interior o final.

Target Words	Beginning (First Letter)	Within	End (Last Letter)
1. safety	✓		
2. matches			✓
3. runners			✓
4. shower	✓		
5. construct		✓	

Directions: Read each sentence and underline the words that begin with the letter "s." Write all the underlined words in alphabetical order on the lines below.
Direcciones: Lee cada oración y subraya las palabras que empiecen con la letra "s." Escribe todas las letras subrayadas en orden alfabético en las líneas que siguen.

6. Dexter ate a tasty <u>salami</u> <u>sandwich</u> for lunch.

7. My brother received two <u>scholarships</u> for <u>school</u>.

8. Melanie <u>said</u>, "My grandmother is a great <u>singer</u>."

9. Melissa is using <u>scissors</u> to cut ten <u>sheets</u> of paper.

10. Both Josiah and <u>Simone</u> are <u>seventy-six</u> years old.

said _____   salami _____   sandwich _____
scholarship _____   school _____   scissors _____
singer _____   seventy-six _____   sheets _____
                        Simone _____

Learn To Read English With Directions In Spanish

Answer Key

Name: _____ Date: ___/___/_____ Score: _____

Lesson 19.1

Reading Words with the Letter S/s

✓ **Lesson Check Point**

Directions: Read each target word. Circle the word in the column that has the same "s" sound as the target word.

Direcciones: Lee cada palabra objetivo. Encierra en un círculo la palabra en la columna que tenga el mismo sonido "s" que la palabra objetivo.

| aspect | (a. summer) |
| | b. diversion |

| instant | a. insurance |
| | (b. cross) |

| cheese | (a. music) |
| | b. swim |

| issue | (a. assurance) |
| | b. jets |

Directions: Read each target word. Put a check (✓) under the correct column heading.

Direcciones: Lee cada palabra objetivo. Coloca un signo de verificación (✓) bajo el encabezado de la columna correcta.

Target Words	"s" has the /s/ sound as in the word <u>sun</u>	"s" has the /sh/ sound as in the word <u>sugar</u>	"s" has the /z/ sound as in the word <u>his</u>	"s" has the /zh/ sound as in the word <u>vision</u>
1. aspect	✓			
2. instant	✓			
3. cheese			✓	
4. issue		✓		

Classwork

Name: _____ Date: ___/___/_____ Score: _____

Lesson 19.2

Reading Words with the "sion," "sial" & "scious" Suffixes

✓ **Lesson Check Point**

Directions: Read each target word. Circle the word in the column that has the same "sion," "sial" or "scious" sound as the target word.

Direcciones: Lee cada palabra objetivo. Identifica las palabras que tengan los mismos sonidos "sion," "sial" o "scious" que la palabra objetivo.

| commission | a. controversial |
| | b. (passion) |

| conversion | a. (fusion) |
| | b. percussion |

| compulsion | a. (inclusion) |
| | b. ambrosial |

| unconscious | a. vision |
| | b. (conscious) |

Directions: Read each target word. Put a check (✓) under the correct column heading.

Direcciones: Lee cada palabra objetivo. Coloca un signo de verificación (✓) bajo el encabezado de la columna correcta.

Target Words	"sion" has the /sh/ +/ə/+/n/ sounds as in the word <u>passion</u>	"sion" has the /zh/ +/ə/+/n/ sounds as in the word <u>vision</u>	"scious" has the /sh/ +/ə/+/s/ sounds as in the word <u>conscious</u>
1. commission	✓		
2. conversion		✓	
3. compulsion	✓		
4. unconscious			✓

Answer Key

 Name: _____ Date: ___/___/_____ Score: _____

Lesson 19.3

Reading Words with the "sch" Letter Combination

✓ Lesson Check Point

 Directions: Read each target word. Circle the word in the column that has the same "sch" sound(s) as the target word.
Direcciones: Lee cada palabra objetivo. Encierra en un círculo la palabra en la columna que tenga el mismo sonido "sch" que la palabra objetivo.

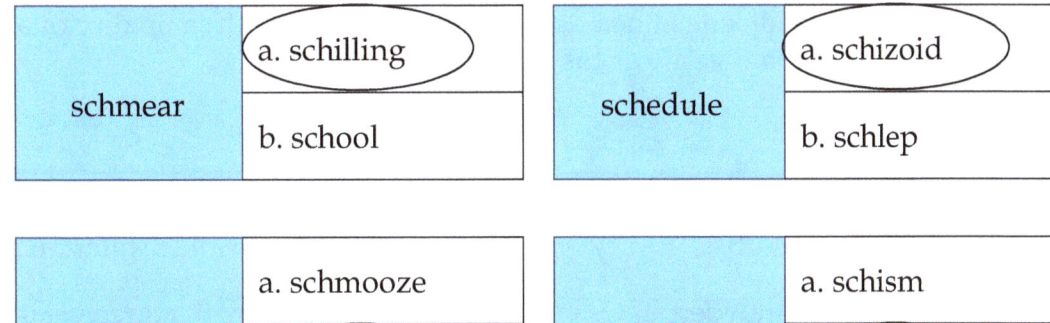

 Directions: Read each target word. Put a check (✓) under the correct column heading.
Direcciones: Lee cada palabra objetivo. Coloca un signo de verificación (✓) bajo el encabezado de la columna correcta.

Target Words	"sch" has the /s/ + /k/ sounds as in the word <u>school</u>	"sch" has the /sh/ sound as in the word <u>schilling</u>
1. schmear		✓
2. schedule	✓	
3. schema	✓	
4. scholarly	✓	

Learn To Read English With Directions In Spanish

Classwork

Name: _____ Date: ___/___/_____ Score: _____

Lesson 19.4

Reading Words with the "scr," "shr," "spr" & "str" Letter Combinations

Dictionary Skills/ Vocabulary

✓ **Lesson Check Point**

Directions: Read each target word and its definition. Write the letter of the definition on the line of each target word. Use a dictionary or the Internet to check your answers.

Direcciones: Lee cada palabra objetivo y su definición. Escribe la letra de la definición en la línea de cada palabra objetivo. Usa un diccionario o Internet para verificar tus respuestas.

Target Words	Definitions
1. _c_ scrub	a. a device used to sprinkle water on a lawn
2. _b_ strawberries	b. sweet, red berries with a green leaf on top
3. _e_ shredder	c. to clean something by brushing
4. _d_ street	d. a paved road in a town or city
5. _a_ sprinkler	e. a machine that cuts paper into small pieces

Directions: Read each sentence. Underline the word in the parentheses that correctly completes each sentence. Then, write the underlined word on the line.

Direcciones: Lee cada oración. Subraya la palabra entre paréntesis que completa correctamente cada oración. Luego, escribe la palabra subrayada en la línea.

6. I will water my grass with a __sprinkler__ system. (street, <u>sprinkler</u>)

7. She will __scrub__ the dirty floor with a firm brush. (street, <u>scrub</u>)

8. Stan shreds documents with a __shredder__. (<u>shredder</u>, sprinkler)

9. The driver drove down the __street__ at a high speed. (<u>street</u>, scrub)

10. I enjoy __strawberries__ with my breakfast cereal. (shredder, <u>strawberries</u>)

Answer Key

 Name: _____ Date: ___/___/_____ Score: _____

Lesson 19.5

Reading Words with the "sl" & "sle" Letter Combinations

Dictionary Skills/ Vocabulary

✓ **Lesson Check Point**

    Directions: Read each target word and its definition. Write the target word on the line in front of its meaning. Use a dictionary or the Internet to check your answers.

Direcciones: Lee cada palabra objetivo y su definición. Escribe la palabra objetivo en la línea frente a su significado. Usa un diccionario o Internet para verificar tus respuestas.

Target Word Box				
sleeves	slippery	slope	sloth	sly

1. <u>slippery</u>   causing to slip and/or slide
2. <u>sly</u>   a characteristic of a tricky person
3. <u>sloth</u>   a furry mammal that moves very slowly
4. <u>slopes</u>   a falling or rising land surface
5. <u>sleeves</u>   the parts of a garment that cover a person's arms

    Directions: Read each sentence. Underline the word in the parentheses that correctly completes each sentence. Then, write the underlined word on the line.

Direcciones: Lee cada oración. Subraya la palabra entre paréntesis que completa correctamente cada oración. Luego, escribe la palabra subrayada en la línea.

6. In the woods, the tricky fox has a <u>sly</u> smile. (sloth, <u>sly</u>)

7. I could not hold the <u>slippery</u> starfish. (<u>slippery</u>, slopes)

8. The <u>sloth</u> is hanging on the tropical tree. (<u>sloth</u>, slippery)

9. Sam is wearing a shirt with short <u>sleeves</u>. (sly, <u>sleeves</u>)

10. The ski <u>slopes</u> are covered with snow and ice. (<u>slopes</u>, sleeves)

Classwork

 Name: _____ Date: ___/___/_____ Score: _____

Lesson 19.5

Reading Words with the "sle" Letter Combination

✓ **Lesson Check Point**

 Directions: Read each target word. Find the "sle" letter combination and put a check (✓) in the column that identifies its position: beginning, within or end.

Direcciones: Lee cada palabra objetivo. Encuentra la combinación de letras "sle" y coloca un signo de verificación (✓) en la columna que identifique su posición: inicio, interior o final.

Target Words	Beginning (First 3 Letters)	Within	End (Last 3 Letters)
1. sleet	✓		
2. sleeves	✓		
3. sleigh	✓		
4. tussle			✓
5. measles		✓	

 Directions: Read each target word. Put a check (✓) in the "yes" column if the "sle" letter combination has the /s/ + /ə/ + /l/ or /z/ + /ə/ + /l/ sounds. Put a check (✓) in the "no" column if the "sle" letter combination does not have the /s/ + /ə/ + /l/ or /z/ + /ə/ + /l/ sounds.

Direcciones: Lee cada palabra objetivo. Coloca un signo de verificación (✓) en la columna del "sí" si la combinación de letras "sle" tiene el sonidos /s/ + /ə/ + /l/ o /z/ + /ə/ + /l/. Coloca un signo de verificación (✓) en la columna del "no" si la combinación de letras "sle" no tiene el sonidos /s/ + /ə/ + /l/ o /z/ + /ə/ + /l/.

Target Words	Yes	No
6. sleet		✓
7. sleeves		✓
8. sleigh		✓
9. tussle	✓	
10. measles	✓	

Answer Key

 Name: _____ Date: ___/___/_____ Score: _____

Lesson 19.6

Reading Words with the "sm" Letter Combination

✓ Lesson Check Point

 Directions: Read each target word. Circle the word in the column that has the same "sm" sounds as the target word.
Direcciones: Lee cada palabra objetivo. Encierra en un círculo la palabra en la columna que tenga el mismo sonido "sm" que la palabra objetivo.

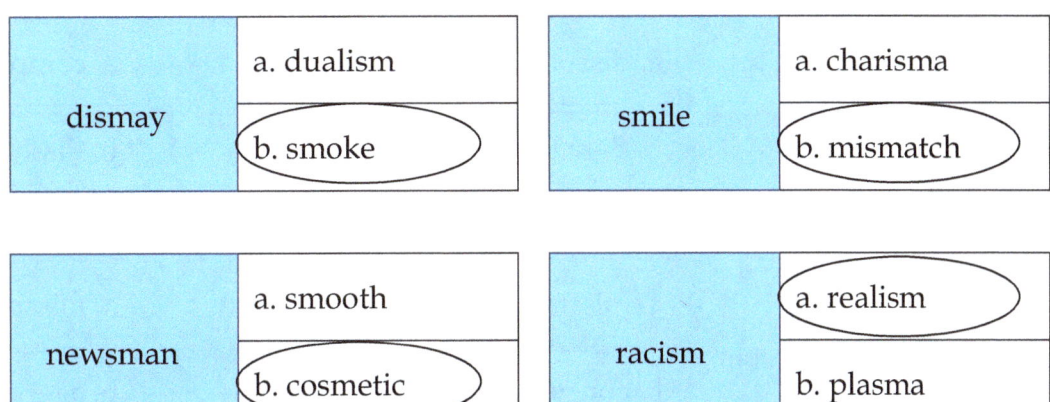

 Directions: Read each target word. Put a check (✓) under the correct column heading.
Direcciones: Lee cada palabra objetivo. Coloca un signo de verificación (✓) bajo el encabezado de la columna correcta.

Target Words	"sm" has the /s/ + /m/ sounds as in the word smell	"sm" has the /z/ + /m/ sounds as in the word cosmic	"sm" has the /z/ + /ə/ + /m/ sounds as in the word autism
1. dismay	✓		
2. smile	✓		
3. newsman		✓	
4. racism			✓

Classwork

 Name: _____ Date: ___/___/_____ Score: _____

Lesson 19.7

Reading Words with the "ss" Letter Combination

✓ Lesson Check Point

 Directions: Read each target word. Circle the word in the column that has the same "ss" sound(s) as the target word.

Direcciones: Lee cada palabra objetivo. Encierra en un círculo la palabra en la columna que tenga el mismo sonido "ss" que la palabra objetivo.

misshaped	a. dissolving
	b. dissatisfy (circled)

Missouri	a. compassion
	b. dissolve (circled)

expression	a. misstated
	b. concussion (circled)

mission	a. misspell
	b. aggression (circled)

 Directions: Read each target word. Put a check (✓) under the correct column heading.

Direcciones: Lee cada palabra objetivo. Coloca un signo de verificación (✓) bajo el encabezado de la columna correcta.

Target Words	"ss" has the /sh/ sound as in the word tissue	"ss" has the /s/ + /s/ sounds as in the word misspell	"ss" has the /z/ sound as in the word dissolve
1. misshaped		✓	
2. Missouri			✓
3. expression	✓		
4. mission	✓		

Answer Key

 Name: _____ Date: ___/___/_____ Score: _____

Lesson 19.8

Reading Words with a Silent Letter "s"

✓ **Lesson Check Point**

 Directions: Read the target words in the word box. Write the words that have a silent letter "s" in the first column. Write the words that do not have a silent letter "s" in the second column.

Direcciones: Lee las palabras objetivo en el cuadro de texto. Escribe las palabras que tengan una letra muda "s" en la primera columna. Escribe las palabras que no tengan una letra muda "s" en la segunda columna.

Target Word Box				
class	horses	handsome	island	debris
aisle	passage	estate	assess	becomes
request	hotels	Arkansas	consider	aside
optimist	address	discover	embassy	isle

Letter "s" is silent

- isle
- aisle
- assess
- class
- debris
- island
- address
- embassy
- passage
- Arkansas

Letter "s" has the /s/, /z/ or /sh/ sound

- aside
- estate
- hotels
- becomes
- request
- horses
- consider
- optimist
- discover
- handsome

Classwork

 Name: _____ Date: ___/___/_____ Score: _____

The Reading Challenge

Lesson 19.9

Reading Multisyllable Words

✓ **Lesson Check Point**

 Directions: Read and divide each target word into syllables. Write each word and place a hyphen (-) between the syllables in the second column. Write the number of syllables in the third column. Use a dictionary or the Internet to check your answers.

Direcciones: Lee y separa en sílabas cada palabra objetivo. Escribe cada palabra y coloca un guión (-) entre las sílabas en la segunda columna. Escribe el número de sílabas en la tercera columna. Usa un diccionario o Internet para verificar tus respuestas.

Target Words	Words Divided into Syllables	Number of Syllables
1. safety	safe-ty	2
2. senior	sen-ior	2
3. sampling	sam-pling	2
4. shampoo	sham-poo	2
5. seaport	sea-port	2
6. soldiers	sol-diers	2
7. satisfaction	sat-is-fac-tion	4
8. sequential	se-quen-tial	3
9. shadowing	shad-ow-ing	3
10. sisterhood	sis-ter-hood	3

Answer Key

 Name: _____ Date: ___/___/_____ Score: _____

The Reading Challenge

Lesson 19.9

Reading Multisyllable Words

✓ Lesson Check Point

 Directions: Read each target word. Circle the word in the row that is divided correctly into syllables. Use a dictionary or the Internet to check your answers.

Direcciones: Lee cada palabra objetivo. Encierra en un círculo la palabra en la fila que esté correctamente separada en sílabas. Usa un diccionario o Internet para verificar tus respuestas.

Model

| Saturday | a. Sa-tur-day | **b. Sat-ur-day** ⭕ | c. Sa-turd-ay |

1. seminar	**a. sem-i-nar** ⭕	b. se-mi-nar	c. se-min-ar
2. satisfy	a. sa-tis-fy	b. sa-tisf-y	**c. sat-is-fy** ⭕
3. seasonal	a. seas-on-al	b. sea-so-nal	**c. sea-son-al** ⭕
4. several	a. se-ver-al	**b. sev-er-al** ⭕	c. sev-e-ral
5. singular	a. sing-u-lar	**b. sin-gu-lar** ⭕	c. sin-gul-ar
6. semester	a. se-mest-er	b. sem-est-er	**c. se-mes-ter** ⭕
7. skeleton	**a. skel-e-ton** ⭕	b. ske-le-ton	c. ske-let-on
8. salary	a. sa-lar-y	b. sal-ar-y	**c. sal-a-ry** ⭕

Classwork

Name: _____ Date: ___/___/_____ Score: _____

Lesson 19.10

Reading and Writing

Proper and Common Nouns and Adjectives

Directions: Read the words in the word box. Put an (X) on the line next to each word that is written incorrectly. Remember that all proper nouns and proper adjectives are capitalized. Use a dictionary or the Internet to check your answers.

Direcciones: Lee las palabras en el cuadro de texto. Coloca una (X) en la línea próxima a las palabras que estén escritas de forma incorrecta. Recuerda que todos los nombres propios y adjetivos propios empiezan con mayúscula. Usa un diccionario o Internet para verificar tus respuestas.

Word Box					
X	Sandbox	X	siberia	__	Samoa
X	Salon	__	shrimp	X	Dr. samuel
__	San Juan	__	sample	X	Sailor
__	seagull	X	senator Sam	__	seahorse

Directions: Read each unedited sentence and underline the word that is written incorrectly. Write each sentence correctly on the line.

Direcciones: Lee cada oración sin editar y subraya la palabra que está escrita de forma incorrecta. Escribe cada oración correctamente en la línea.

Model
<u>sandy</u> is going to Salt Lake City on Sunday.
Sandy is going to Salt Lake City on Sunday.

1. On <u>saturday</u>, we are going sailing around South Bay.
   On Saturday, we are going sailing around South Bay.

2. My <u>Siblings</u> received scholarships to Sidney School.
   My siblings received scholarships to Sidney School.

3. On Sunday, I am going to have lunch with <u>sergeant</u> Smith.
   On Sunday, I am going to have lunch with Sergeant Smith.

4. My grandparents, Samuel and Samantha, are <u>Senior</u> citizens.
   My grandparents, Samuel and Samantha, are senior citizens.

Answer Key

 Name: _____ Date:___/___/_____ Score:_____

Lesson 20.1

Reading Words with the Letter T/t

✓ Lesson Check Point

Directions: Read each target word. Find the letter "t" and put a check (✓) in the column that identifies its position: beginning, within or end.
Direcciones: Lee cada palabra objetivo. Encuentra la letra "t" y coloca un signo de verificación (✓) en la columna que identifique su posición: inicio, interior o final.

Target Words	Beginning (First Letter)	Within	End (Last Letter)
1. reporter		✓	
2. teenager	✓		
3. merchant			✓
4. Tuesday	✓		
5. section		✓	

Directions: Read each sentence and underline the words that begin with the letter "t." Write all the underlined words in alphabetical order on the lines below.
Direcciones: Lee cada oración y subraya las palabras que empiecen con la letra "t." Escribe todas las letras subrayadas en orden alfabético en las líneas que siguen.

6. My <u>teacher</u>, Ms. Peters, does not like <u>tarantulas</u>.

7. My sister <u>tossed</u> her interactive <u>toys</u> everywhere.

8. At <u>Thanksgiving</u> dinner, Danny ate rice and <u>turkey</u>.

9. <u>Terrence</u> likes putting <u>tartar</u> sauce on his fish sandwiches.

10. An intense <u>thunderstorm</u> caused damage <u>throughout</u> our county.

tarantulas	tartar	teacher
Terrence	Thanksgiving	throughout
thunderstorm	tossed	toys
	turkey	

Classwork

 Name: _____ Date:___/___/_____ Score:_____

Lesson 20.2

Reading Words with the "thm" Letter Combination

✓ Lesson Check Point

 Directions: Read each target word. Circle the word in the column that has the same "thm" sound(s) as the target word.

Direcciones: Lee cada palabra objetivo. Encierra en un círculo la palabra en la columna que tenga el mismo sonido "thm" que la palabra objetivo.

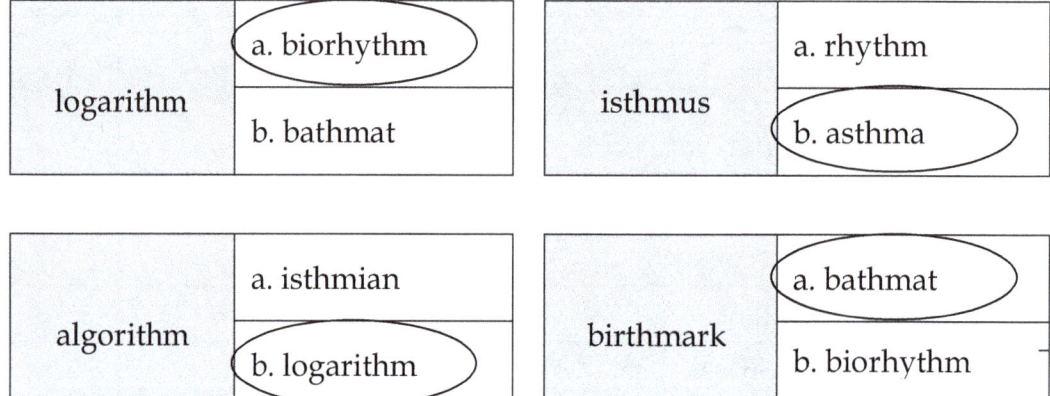

 Directions: Read each target word. Put a check (✓) under the correct column heading.

Direcciones: Lee cada palabra objetivo. Coloca un signo de verificación (✓) bajo el encabezado de la columna correcta.

Target Words	"thm" has the /th/ + /ə/ + /m/ sounds as in the word <u>rhythm</u>	"thm" has the /th/ + /m/ sounds as in the word <u>bathmat</u>	"thm" silent "th" + /m/ sound as in the word <u>asthma</u>
1. logarithm	✓		
2. isthmus			✓
3. algorithm	✓		
4. birthmark		✓	

Answer Key

 Name: _____ Date:___/___/_____ Score:_____

Lesson 20.3

Reading Words with the "tion," "tial" & "tious" Suffixes

✓ **Lesson Check Point**

 Directions: Read each target word. Circle the word in the column that has the same "tion," "tial" or "tious" sound as the target word.

Direcciones: Lee cada palabra objetivo. Identifica las palabras que tengan los mismos sonidos "tion," "tial" o "tious" que la palabra objetivo.

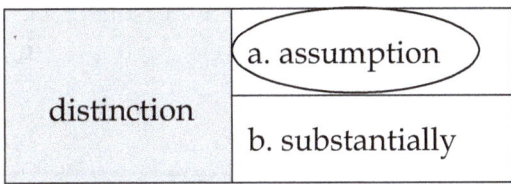

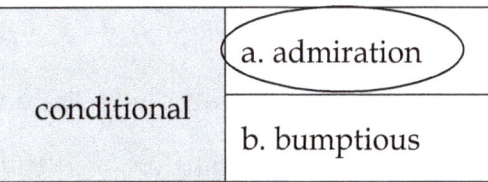

	a. cautiously	
infectious		
	b. animation	

(circled: a. cautiously)

	a. admiration	
conditional		
	b. bumptious	

(circled: a. admiration)

 Directions: Read each target word. Put a check (✓) under the correct column heading.

Direcciones: Lee cada palabra objetivo. Coloca un signo de verificación (✓) bajo el encabezado de la columna correcta.

Target Words	"tion" has the /sh/ +/ə/+/n/ sounds as in the word <u>education</u>	"tial" has the /sh/ +/ə/+/l/ sounds as in the word <u>partial</u>	"tious" has the /sh/ +/ə/+/s/ sounds as in the word <u>ambitious</u>
1. distinction	✓		
2. substantial		✓	
3. infectious			✓
4. conditional	✓		

Classwork

Name: _____ Date: ___/___/_____ Score: _____

Lesson 20.4

Reading Words with the "tr" Letter Combination

Dictionary Skills/ Vocabulary

✓ **Lesson Check Point**

Directions: Read each target word and its definition. Write the letter of the definition on the line of each target word. Use a dictionary or the Internet to check your answers.

Direcciones: Lee cada palabra objetivo y su definición. Escribe la letra de la definición en la línea de cada palabra objetivo. Usa un diccionario o Internet para verificar tus respuestas.

Target Words	Definitions
1. _d_ tragic	a. a problematic situation, a conflict
2. _e_ trampled	b. to write words from one language to another
3. _c_ transfer	c. to move from one place to another
4. _b_ translate	d. a disastrous occurrence or event
5. _a_ trouble	e. the act of beating a surface down with one's feet

Directions: Read each sentence. Underline the word in the parentheses that correctly completes each sentence. Then, write the underlined word on the line.

Direcciones: Lee cada oración. Subraya la palabra entre paréntesis que completa correctamente cada oración. Luego, escribe la palabra subrayada en la línea.

6. I ___translated___ the report from English to Arabic. (translated, tragic)

7. He got in ___trouble___ for breaking the class rules. (trouble, transfer)

8. Tress cried when she read the story's ___tragic___ ending. (tragic, trample)

9. Terrance will ___transfer___ to his connecting flight. (transfer, translate)

10. The horse ___trampled___ the crops in the field. (trouble, trampled)

Answer Key

 Name: _____ Date: ___/___/_____ Score: _____

Lesson 20.5

Reading Words with the "tle" Letter Combination

✓ **Lesson Check Point**

Directions: Read each target word. Find the "tle" letter combination and put a check (✓) in the column that identifies its position: beginning, within or end.

Direcciones: Lee cada palabra objetivo. Encuentra la combinación de letras "tle" y coloca un signo de verificación (✓) en la columna que identifique su posición: inicio, interior o final.

Target Words	Beginning (First 3 Letters)	Within	End (Last 3 Letters)
1. hurtle			✓
2. cutlet		✓	
3. outlet		✓	
4. settle			✓
5. countless		✓	

Directions: Read each target word. Put a check (✓) in the "yes" column if the "tle" letter combination has the /t/ + /ə/ + /l/ sounds. Put a check (✓) in the "no" column if the "tle" letter combination does not have the /t/ + /ə/ + /l/ sounds.

Direcciones: Lee cada palabra objetivo. Coloca un signo de verificación (✓) en la columna del "sí" si la combinación de letras "tle" tiene el sonidos /t/ + /ə/ + /l/. Coloca un signo de verificación (✓) en la columna del "no" si la combinación de letras "tle" no tiene el sonidos /t/ + /ə/ + /l/.

Target Words	Yes	No
6. hurtle	✓	
7. cutlet		✓
8. outlet		✓
9. settle	✓	
10. countless		✓

Learn To Read English With Directions In Spanish

Classwork

 Name: _____ Date: ___/___/_____ Score: _____

Lesson 20.6

Reading Words with the Letter "t" Sounds

✓ Lesson Check Point

 Directions: Read each target word. Circle the word in the column that has the same "t" sound as the target word.

Direcciones: Lee cada palabra objetivo. Encierra en un círculo la palabra en la columna que tenga el mismo sonido "t" que la palabra objetivo.

mention	(a. ambition)
	b. righteous

culture	(a. picture)
	b. contact

electric	(a. connect)
	b. action

actual	(a. denture)
	b. expect

 Directions: Read each target word. Put a check (✓) under the correct column heading.

Direcciones: Lee cada palabra objetivo. Coloca un signo de verificación (✓) bajo el encabezado de la columna correcta.

Target Words	"t" has the /t/ sound as in the word <u>multiply</u>	"t" has the /ch/ sound as in the word <u>picture</u>	"t" has the /sh/ sound as in the word <u>position</u>
1. mention			✓
2. culture		✓	
3. electric	✓		
4. actual		✓	

Answer Key

 Name: _____ Date: ___/___/_____ Score: _____

Lesson 20.7

Reading Words with a Silent Letter "t"

✓ Lesson Check Point

 Directions: Read the target words in the word box. Write the words that have a silent letter "t" in the first column. Write the words that do not have a silent letter "t" in the second column.

Direcciones: Lee las palabras objetivo en el cuadro de texto. Escribe las palabras que tengan una letra muda "t" en la primera columna. Escribe las palabras que no tengan una letra muda "t" en la segunda columna.

Target Word Box				
continue	itch	crochet	entrance	totally
pottery	curtain	kitchen	heart	factory
clothes	defeat	denote	listening	dieting
castle	postman	sitting	mortgage	snitch

Letter "t" is silent

- itch
- kitchen
- castle
- clothes
- snitch
- sitting
- pottery
- crochet
- listening
- mortgage

Letter "t" has the /t/ sound

- heart
- denote
- defeat
- curtain
- totally
- factory
- entrance
- dieting
- continue
- postman

Learn To Read English With Directions In Spanish

Classwork

 Name: _____ Date:___/___/_____ Score: _____

The Reading Challenge

Lesson 20.8

Reading Multisyllable Words

✓ **Lesson Check Point**

 Directions: Read and divide each target word into syllables. Write each word and place a hyphen (-) between the syllables in the second column. Write the number of syllables in the third column. Use a dictionary or the Internet to check your answers.

Direcciones: Lee y separa en sílabas cada palabra objetivo. Escribe cada palabra y coloca un guión (-) entre las sílabas en la segunda columna. Escribe el número de sílabas en la tercera columna. Usa un diccionario o Internet para verificar tus respuestas.

Target Words	Words Divided into Syllables	Number of Syllables
1. traveling	trav-el-ing	3
2. tiny	ti-ny	2
3. treasure	treas-ure	2
4. textbooks	text-books	2
5. tonight	to-night	2
6. timbering	tim-ber-ing	3
7. tweezers	tweez-ers	2
8. turquoise	tur-quoise	2
9. transplanting	trans-plant-ing	3
10. title	ti-tle	2

Answer Key

 Name: _____ Date:___/___/_____ Score:_____

The Reading Challenge

Lesson 20.8

Reading Multisyllable Words

✓ **Lesson Check Point**

 Directions: Read each target word. Circle the word in the row that is divided correctly into syllables. Use a dictionary or the Internet to check your answers.

Direcciones: Lee cada palabra objetivo. Encierra en un círculo la palabra en la fila que esté correctamente separada en sílabas. Usa un diccionario o Internet para verificar tus respuestas.

Model

| telephone | a. te-lep-hone | **b. tel-e-phone** ⭕ | c. te-le-phone |

| 1. teenager | **a. teen-ag-er** ⭕ | b. teen-a-ger | c. teena-g-er |

| 2. taxicab | a. ta-xic-ab | b. tax-ic-ab | **c. tax-i-cab** ⭕ |

| 3. technical | a. te-chnic-al | b. tech-nic-al | **c. tech-ni-cal** ⭕ |

| 4. triangle | a. tri-ang-le | **b. tri-an-gle** ⭕ | c. tria-n-gle |

| 5. testify | **a. tes-ti-fy** ⭕ | b. te-stif-y | c. tes-tif-y |

| 6. temperate | a. temp-er-ate | b. tem-pe-rate | **c. tem-per-ate** ⭕ |

| 7. typical | a. ty-pi-cal | b. ty-pic-al | **c. typ-i-cal** ⭕ |

| 8. translated | **a. trans-lat-ed** ⭕ | b. transl-a-ted | c. tran-slat-ed |

Classwork

Name: _____ Date: ___/___/_____ Score: _____

Lesson 20.9

Reading and Writing

Proper and Common Nouns and Adjectives

Directions: Read the words in the word box. Put an (X) on the line next to each word that is written incorrectly. Remember that all proper nouns and proper adjectives are capitalized. Use a dictionary or the Internet to check your answers.

Direcciones: Lee las palabras en el cuadro de texto. Coloca una (X) en la línea próxima a las palabras que estén escritas de forma incorrecta. Recuerda que todos los nombres propios y adjetivos propios empiezan con mayúscula. Usa un diccionario o Internet para verificar tus respuestas.

Word Box					
X	taiwan	X	thursday	_	thousand
_	Togo	X	Today	_	Tonga
_	thunder	_	Tokyo	X	tunisia
X	Twins	_	target	X	Tomato

Directions: Read each unedited sentence and underline the word that is written incorrectly. Write each sentence correctly on the line.

Direcciones: Lee cada oración sin editar y subraya la palabra que está escrita de forma incorrecta. Escribe cada oración correctamente en la línea.

Model
On <u>thursday</u>, a tornado destroyed my hometown.
<u>On Thursday, a tornado destroyed my hometown.</u>

1. I ate tasty <u>thai</u> food at Lemongrass Thailand Restaurant.
   <u>I ate tasty Thai food at Lemongrass Thailand Restaurant.</u>

2. My dentist, Dr. Tracks, <u>Takes</u> good care of my teeth.
   <u>My dentist, Dr. Tracks, takes good care of my teeth.</u>

3. In <u>tanzania</u>, the townspeople have tremendous hearts.
   <u>In Tanzania, the townspeople have tremendous hearts.</u>

4. I will travel to the beautiful twin islands of Trinidad and <u>tobago</u>.
   <u>I will travel to the beautiful twin islands of Trinidad and Tobago.</u>

Answer Key

 Name: _____ Date: ___/___/_____ Score: _____

Lesson 21.1

Reading Words with the Letter U/u

✓ Lesson Check Point

 Directions: Read each target word. Find the letter "u" and put a check (✓) in the column that identifies its position: beginning, within or end.
Direcciones: Lee cada palabra objetivo. Encuentra la letra "u" y coloca un signo de verificación (✓) en la columna que identifique su posición: inicio, interior o final.

Target Words	Beginning (First Letter)	Within	End (Last Letter)
1. under	✓		
2. menu			✓
3. success		✓	
4. you			✓
5. university	✓		

 Directions: Read each target word. Read the words in the row and circle the word that has a different vowel "u" sound.
Direcciones: Lee cada palabra objetivo. Lee las palabras en la fila y encierra la palabra que tenga un sonido vocal "u" diferente.

Target Words					
6. swum	mud	(June)	tug	sub	
7. chum	(thru)	bum	cut	hum	
8. snub	nut	bud	(tube)	bun	
9. thug	pun	cub	nun	(juke)	
10. funny	(burst)	makeup	snuff	tux	

Learn To Read English With Directions In Spanish

Classwork

 Name: _____ Date: ___/___/_____ Score: _____

Lesson 21.2

Reading Words with the Short Vowel "u" Sound

✓ Lesson Check Point

 Directions: Read the words in the four boxes. Circle two words with the short vowel /ŭ/ sound. The anchor word for the short vowel /ŭ/ sound is up.

Direcciones: Lee las palabras en las cuatro cajas. Encierra en un círculo dos palabras con el sonido vocal corto /ŭ/. La palabra ejemplo para el sonido vocal corto /ŭ/ es la palabra, up.

fume	(buck)	(bump)	(rust)	(suck)	(null)
June	(dull)	crude	brute	rule	truce

chute	(lush)	(drunk)	mute	dune	flute
used	(punch)	fuse	(plush)	(duck)	(buff)

 Directions: Read the words in the four boxes. Circle two words that rhyme. Rhyming words have the same ending sound, such as just and must.

Direcciones: Lee las palabras en las cuatro cajas. Encierra en un círculo dos que rimen. Las palabras que riman tienen el mismo sonido al final, como just y must.

tuba	(dump)	(luck)	gush	grub	(rush)
(lump)	drug	tuck	flu	(hush)	use

stub	(rust)	cute	slug	super	(much)
tune	(dust)	(brush)	(crush)	smug	(such)

Answer Key

Name: _____ Date: ___/___/_____ Score: _____

Lesson 21.2

Reading & Writing Words with the Short Vowel "u" Sound

✓ **Lesson Check Point**

Directions: Read each sentence and underline three words with the short vowel /ŭ/ sound. Then, write the underlined words on the lines below. The anchor word for the short vowel /ŭ/ sound is <u>up</u>.

Direcciones: Lee las palabras en las cuatro cajas. Encierra en un círculo dos palabras con el sonido vocal corto /ŭ/. La palabra ejemplo para el sonido vocal corto /ŭ/ es la palabra, <u>up</u>.

Model

Ulysses, the <u>drummer</u>, <u>jumps</u> when he plays the <u>drums</u>.

    drummer   jumps   drums

1. As Luke <u>trudged</u> in, he got <u>mud</u> on the <u>rug</u>.

    trudged   mud   rug

2. The oatmeal in the <u>cup</u> is usually not <u>lumpy</u> and <u>mushy</u>.

    cup   lumpy   mushy

3. The groomer <u>brushed</u> the <u>puppy's</u> fur with a soft <u>brush</u>.

    brushed   puppy's   brush

4. In June, I was <u>lucky</u> to see the <u>ducks</u> and <u>cubs</u> at the zoo.

    lucky   ducks   cubs

5. The <u>club's</u> members sat on the <u>rug</u> and ate blueberry <u>muffins</u>.

    club's   rug   muffins

Unit U
Lesson 21.2

Classwork

Name: _____ Date: ___/___/_____ Score: _____

Lesson 21.3

Reading Words with the Long Vowel "u" Sound

✓ **Lesson Check Point**

Directions: Read the words in the four boxes. Circle two words with the long vowel /yōō/ or /ōō/ sound. The anchor word for the long vowel /yōō/ and /ōō/ sounds is <u>tube</u>.

Direcciones: Lee las palabras en las cuatro cajas. Encierra en un círculo dos palabras con el sonido vocal largo /yōō/ o /ōō/. La palabra ejemplo para el sonido vocal largo /yōō/ y /ōō/ es la palabra, <u>tube</u>.

guard	(June)	(brute)	junk	yucky	(dilute)
biscuit	(use)	bunch	(volume)	guest	(reduce)

stump	gulp	must	(prune)	sunken	(salute)
(nude)	(accuse)	(confuse)	quiet	lungs	(include)

Directions: Read the words in the four boxes. Circle two words that rhyme. Rhyming words have the same ending sound, such as <u>rule</u> and <u>mule</u>.

Direcciones: Lee las palabras en las cuatro cajas. Encierra en un círculo dos palabras que rimen. Las palabras que riman tienen el mismo sonido al final, como <u>rule</u> y <u>mule</u>.

dump	(cruel)	dusk	lumpy	(June)	duckling
Just	(fuel)	(glue)	(blue)	lucky	(tune)

(mute)	Dutch	sung	(rude)	munch	rushing
(flute)	pumps	(crude)	bumper	(excuse)	(refuse)

Answer Key

L! Name: _____ Date: ___/___/_____ Score: _____

Lesson 21.3

Reading & Writing Words with the Long Vowel "u" Sound

✓ **Lesson Check Point**

Directions: Read each sentence and underline three words with the long vowel /yoō/ or /oō/ sound. Then, write the underlined words on the lines below. The anchor word for the long vowel /yoō/ and /oō/ sounds is tube.

Direcciones: Lee cada oración y subraya tres palabras con el sonido vocal largo /yoō/ o /oō/. Luego, escribe las palabras subrayadas en las líneas siguientes. La palabra ejemplo para el sonido vocal largo /yoō/ y /oō/ es la palabra, tube.

Model

Bruce is going to play the tuba and drums in Uganda.

Bruce   tuba   Uganda

1. At lunch, Lucy enjoys eating juicy fruits.

   Lucy   juicy   fruits

2. The students' blue uniforms are dull and unattractive.

   students'   blue   uniforms

3. My aunt used flowers to produce a fragrant perfume.

   used   produce   perfume

4. In June, the club's rules gradually changed for the better.

   June   rules   gradually

5. Mr. Gus Underhill refused to accept the students' excuses.

   refused   students'   excuses

Classwork

Name: _____ Date: ___/___/_____ Score: _____

Review Lessons 21.2 & 21.3

Reading Short Vowel and Long Vowel Words

Directions: Read the target words in the word box. In the first column, write the words that have the short vowel /ŭ/ sound, as in the word <u>up</u>. In the second column, write the words that have the long vowel /yo͞o/ or /o͞o/ sound, as in the word <u>tube</u>.

Direcciones: Lee las palabras objetivo en el cuadro de texto. En la primera columna, escribe las palabras que tengan el sonido vocal corto /ŭ/, como en la palabra inglés <u>up</u>. En la segunda columna, escribe las palabras que tengan el sonido vocal largo /yo͞o/ o /o͞o/, como en la palabra inglés <u>tube</u>.

Target Word Box				
lucky	bunch	consume	hunter	rung
using	dull	bumpers	accuse	truce
computer	tofu	lungs	commute	jumping
rushing	debut	music	dusty	uniform

Letter "u" has the /ŭ/ sound as in the word <u>up</u>

- dull
- rung
- lungs
- lucky
- dusty
- bunch
- hunter
- jumping
- rushing
- bumpers

Letter "u" has the /yo͞o/ or /o͞o/ sound as in the word <u>tube</u>

- tofu
- truce
- music
- debut
- using
- accuse
- uniform
- consume
- commute
- computer

Answer Key

 Name: _____ Date: ___/___/_____ Score: _____

Lesson 21.4

Reading Words with Letter "u" Vowel Pairs

✓ **Lesson Check Point**

 Directions: Read each target word. Circle the word in the column that has the same vowel "ua," "ue" or "ui" sound(s) as the target word.

Direcciones: Lee cada palabra objetivo. Encierra en un círculo la palabra en la columna que tenga el mismo sonido vocal "ua," "ue," o "ui" que la palabra objetivo.

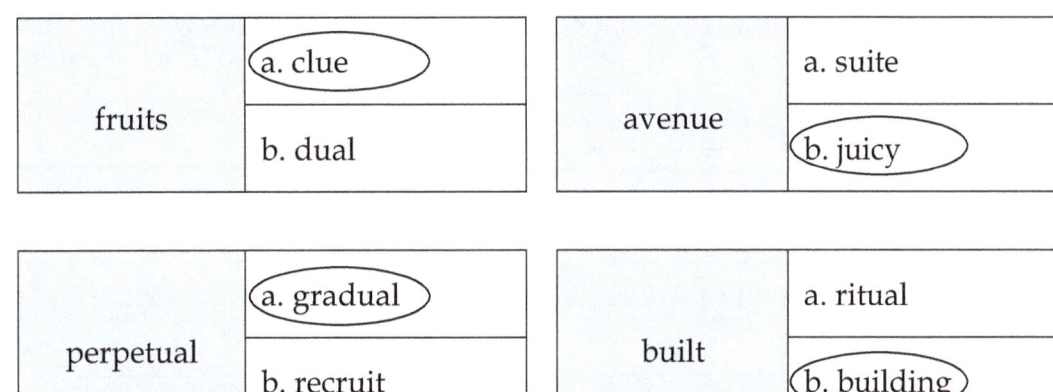

 Directions: Read each target word. Put a check (✓) under the correct column heading.

Direcciones: Lee cada palabra objetivo. Coloca un signo de verificación (✓) bajo el encabezado de la columna correcta.

Target Words	Words have the long "u" sound as in the word <u>blue</u>	Words do not have the long "u" sound
1. builds		✓
2. affluent	✓	
3. factual	✓	
4. suites		✓

Classwork

 Name: _____ Date: ___/___/_____ Score: _____

Lesson 21.5

Reading Words with the Final Letter "u"

✓ **Lesson Check Point**

 Directions: Read each target word. Find the letter "u" and put a check (✓) in the column that identifies its position within the syllable.
Direcciones: Lee cada palabra objetivo. Encuentra la letra "u" y coloca un signo de verificación (✓) en la columna que identifique su posición dentro de la sílaba.

Target Words	"u" is at the end of a one syllable word	"u" is at the end of the first syllable	"u" is at the end of a multi-syllable word
1. July		✓	
2. you	✓		
3. impromptu			✓
4. Utah		✓	
5. uniform		✓	

 Directions: Read each target word. Put a check (✓) under the correct column heading.
Direcciones: Lee cada palabra objetivo. Coloca un signo de verificación (✓) bajo el encabezado de la columna correcta.

Target Words	"u" has the /ŭ/ sound as in the word tub	"u" has the /yoo/ sound as in the word tube	"u" has the /ə/ sound as in the word circus	"u" is silent as in the word build
6. vague				✓
7. radius			✓	
8. clue		✓		
9. drums	✓			
10. survive			✓	

Answer Key

 Name: _____ Date: ___/___/_____ Score: _____

Lesson 21.6

Reading Letter "u" Words with the Schwa Vowel Sound

✓ Lesson Check Point

 Directions: Read each target word. Circle the word in the column that has the same "u" sound as the target word.

Direcciones: Lee cada palabra objetivo. Encierra en un círculo la palabra en la columna que tenga el mismo sonido "u" que la palabra objetivo.

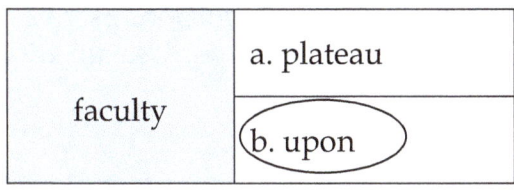
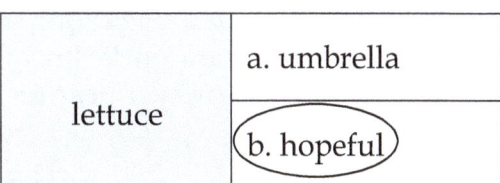
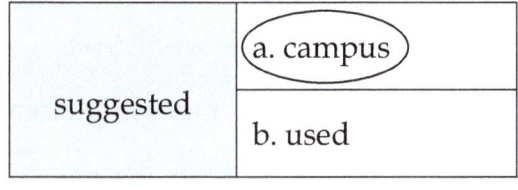
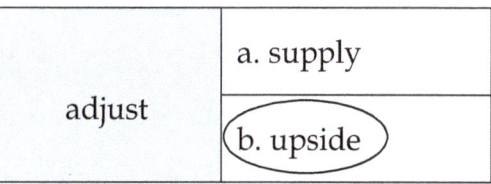

 Directions: Read each sentence and underline the letter "u" word that has the schwa vowel /ə/ sound. The anchor word for the letter "u" schwa vowel sound is campus.

Direcciones: Lee cada oración y subraya la letra "u" en palabras que tengan el sonido schwa /ə/. La palabra ejemplo para el sonido schwa de la letra "u" es la palabra, campus.

1. The umpire is not very popular.

2. Some of my students are very playful.

3. Hugo has nice pictures and gifts from Guyana.

4. In January, Eugene will visit Portugal and Uganda.

5. The Museum of Urban Studies is close to Pace University.

6. During class, I tend to focus on the bilingual presentations.

Classwork

Name: _____ Date: ___/___/_____ Score: _____

Lesson 21.7

Reading Words with the "ur" Letter Combination

Dictionary Skills/ Vocabulary

✓ Lesson Check Point

Directions: Read each target word and its definition. Write the letter of the definition on the line of each target word. Use a dictionary or the Internet to check your answers.

Direcciones: Lee cada palabra objetivo y su definición. Escribe la letra de la definición en la línea de cada palabra objetivo. Usa un diccionario o Internet para verificar tus respuestas.

Target Words	Definitions
1. _b_ purse	a. the possessive form of the word, you
2. _c_ journey	b. a small bag used to carry money and items
3. _a_ Your	c. a trip; to go from one place to another
4. _e_ Failure	d. to have felt extreme sadness or sorrow
5. _d_ mourned	e. act of not succeeding

Directions: Read each sentence and write the target word on the line that correctly completes the sentence.
Direcciones: Lee cada oración y escribe la palabra objetivo que complete la oración.

6. My teacher shouted, "__Failure__ in school is unacceptable."

7. Jimmy _____mourned_____ the loss of his pet goldfish.

8. Grandma carries keys and money in her _____purse_____.

9. __Your_____ brother is going to join the basketball team.

10. The characters are on a dangerous __journey__ in the woods.

Answer Key

Name: _____ Date: ___/___/_____ Score: _____

Lesson 21.8

Reading Words with a Silent Letter "u"

✓ Lesson Check Point

Directions: Read the target words in the word box. Write the words that have a silent letter "u" in the first column. Write the words that do not have a silent letter "u" in the second column.

Direcciones: Lee las palabras objetivo en el cuadro de texto. Escribe las palabras que tengan una letra muda "u" en la primera columna. Escribe las palabras que no tengan una letra muda "u" en la segunda columna.

Target Word Box				
fatigue	continuum	circuit	laughing	Guinea
guiding	avenue	Tuesday	rulers	attitude
unison	under	annual	guessing	visual
impromptu	building	tongues	biscuit	shoulder

Letter "u" is silent	Letter "u" has a letter "u" sound
fatigue	unison
circuit	avenue
laughing	Tuesday
Guinea	rulers
guiding	attitude
guessing	under
building	annual
biscuit	visual
shoulder	impromptu
tongues	continuum

Classwork

Name: _____ Date: ___/___/_____ Score: _____

Unit Review - U/u

Reading Words with Vowel "u" Sounds: /ŭ/, /o͞o/, /ə/ & Silent

✓ **Lesson Check Point**

Directions: Read each target word. Circle the word in the column that has the same "u" sound as the target word.

Direcciones: Lee cada palabra objetivo. Encierra en un círculo la palabra en la columna que tenga el mismo sonido "u" que la palabra objetivo.

suggest	a. unicorn
	(b. subtract)

duckling	(a. hutch)
	b. music

student	(a. super)
	b. dumping

tongue	a. menu
	(b. guests)

Directions: Read each target word. Put a check (✓) under the correct column heading.

Direcciones: Lee cada palabra objetivo. Coloca un signo de verificación (✓) bajo el encabezado de la columna correcta.

Target Words	"u" has the /ŭ/ sound as in the word **tub**	"u" has the /o͞o/ sound as in the word **tube**	"u" has the /ə/ sound as in the word **circus**	"u" is silent as in the word **build**
1. suggest			✓	
2. duckling	✓			
3. student		✓		
4. tongue				✓

Answer Key

Name: _____ Date: ___/___/_____ Score: _____

The Reading Challenge

Lesson 21.9

Reading Multisyllable Words

✓ Lesson Check Point

Directions: Read and divide each target word into syllables. Write each word and place a hyphen (-) between the syllables in the second column. Write the number of syllables in the third column. Use a dictionary or the Internet to check your answers.

Direcciones: Lee y separa en sílabas cada palabra objetivo. Escribe cada palabra y coloca un guión (-) entre las sílabas en la segunda columna. Escribe el número de sílabas en la tercera columna. Usa un diccionario o Internet para verificar tus respuestas.

Target Words	Words Divided into Syllables	Number of Syllables
1. luncheon	lunch-eon	2
2. bunches	bunch-es	2
3. duckling	duck-ling	2
4. crushing	crush-ing	2
5. sugary	sug-ar-y	3
6. pulpit	pul-pit	2
7. bumper	bump-er	2
8. intruding	in-trud-ing	3
9. denouncing	de-nounc-ing	3
10. capsulate	cap-su-late	3

Classwork

 Name: _____ Date:___/___/_____ Score:_____

The Reading Challenge

Lesson 21.9

Reading Multisyllable Words

✓ Lesson Check Point

 Directions: Read each target word. Circle the word in the row that is divided correctly into syllables. Use a dictionary or the Internet to check your answers.

Direcciones: Lee cada palabra objetivo. Encierra en un círculo la palabra en la fila que esté correctamente separada en sílabas. Usa un diccionario o Internet para verificar tus respuestas.

Model

| visualize | a. vis-ua-lize | **b. vi-su-al-ize** ⭕ | c. vis-u-a-lize |

| 1. habitual | **a. ha-bit-u-al** ⭕ | b. ha-bit-ual | c. hab-it-ual |

| 2. avenue | **a. av-e-nue** ⭕ | b. ave-nu-e | c. a-ve-nue |

| 3. diluting | a. dil-u-ting | **b. di-lut-ing** ⭕ | c. di-lu-ting |

| 4. amusing | a. a-mu-sing | **b. a-mus-ing** ⭕ | c. am-u-sing |

| 5. confusion | **a. con-fu-sion** ⭕ | b. con-fus-ion | c. conf-u-sion |

| 6. saluting | **a. sa-lut-ing** ⭕ | b. sal-u-ting | c. sa-lu-ting |

| 7. fortunate | a. fort-u-nate | b. for-tun-ate | **c. for-tu-nate** ⭕ |

| 8. truancy | a. tru-anc-y | b. tru-a-ncy | **c. tru-an-cy** ⭕ |

Answer Key

Name: _____ Date: ___/___/_____ Score: _____

Lesson 21.10

Reading and Writing

Proper and Common Nouns and Adjectives

Directions: Read the words in the word box. Put an (X) on the line next to each word that is written incorrectly. Remember that all proper nouns and proper adjectives are capitalized. Use a dictionary or the Internet to check your answers.

Direcciones: Lee las palabras en el cuadro de texto. Coloca una (X) en la línea próxima a las palabras que estén escritas de forma incorrecta. Recuerda que todos los nombres propios y adjetivos propios empiezan con mayúscula. Usa un diccionario o Internet para verificar tus respuestas.

Word Box					
X	University	X	ukraine	__	URL
__	USSR	X	ubangi	__	upbeat
X	Universal	__	umbrella	__	Uncle
X	Ultra	__	Uruguay	X	Uncovered

Directions: Read each unedited sentence and underline the word that is written incorrectly. Write each sentence correctly on the line.

Direcciones: Lee cada oración sin editar y subraya la palabra que está escrita de forma incorrecta. Escribe cada oración correctamente en la línea.

Model
Mrs. Ubangi usually has union meetings at a local <u>University</u>.
<u>Mrs. Ubangi usually has union meetings at a local university.</u>

1. We are studying the planet Uranus in Mrs. <u>ubet's</u> class.
<u>We are studying the planet Uranus in Mrs. Ubet's class.</u>

2. Professor Utrecht said, "The <u>united</u> Nations is very influential."
<u>Professor Utrecht said, "The United Nations is very influential."</u>

3. In 1971, <u>uzbekistan</u> became independent from the U.S.S.R.
<u>In 1971, Uzbekistan became independent from the U.S.S.R.</u>

4. I found information about two universities in <u>upper</u> Canada.
<u>I found information about two universities in Upper Canada.</u>

Classwork

Name: _____ **Date:** ___/___/_____ **Score:** _____

Lesson 22.1

Reading Words with the Letter V/v

✓ **Lesson Check Point**

Directions: Read each target word. Find the letter "v" and put a check (✓) in the column that identifies its position: beginning, within or end.
Direcciones: Lee cada palabra objetivo. Encuentra la letra "v" y coloca un signo de verificación (✓) en la columna que identifique su posición: inicio, interior o final.

Target Words	Beginning (First Letter)	Within	End (Last Letter)
1. visitor	✓		
2. travel		✓	
3. veterans	✓		
4. silver		✓	
5. Yugoslav			✓

Directions: Read each sentence and underline the words that begin with the letter "v." Write all the underlined words in alphabetical order on the lines below.
Direcciones: Lee cada oración y subraya las palabras que empiecen con la letra "v." Escribe todas las letras subrayadas en orden alfabético en las líneas que siguen.

6. My guitar case has a <u>valuable</u> <u>velvet</u> lining.

7. Samantha's <u>vintage</u> dress is <u>violet</u> and white.

8. Our <u>vice</u> president has a <u>vibrant</u> personality.

9. The character in the <u>video</u> game <u>vanished</u> into thin air.

10. Joshua plays <u>volleyball</u> for his school's team, The <u>Vikings</u>.

<u>valuable</u>   <u>vanished</u>   <u>velvet</u>
<u>vibrant</u>   <u>vice</u>   <u>video</u>
<u>Vikings</u>   <u>vintage</u>   <u>violet</u>
                <u>volleyball</u>

Answer Key

 Name: _____ Date: ___/___/_____ Score: _____

The Reading Challenge

Lesson 22.2

Reading Multisyllable Words

✓ **Lesson Check Point**

 Directions: Read and divide each target word into syllables. Write each word and place a hyphen (-) between the syllables in the second column. Write the number of syllables in the third column. Use a dictionary or the Internet to check your answers.

Direcciones: Lee y separa en sílabas cada palabra objetivo. Escribe cada palabra y coloca un guión (-) entre las sílabas en la segunda columna. Escribe el número de sílabas en la tercera columna. Usa un diccionario o Internet para verificar tus respuestas.

Target Words	Words Divided into Syllables	Number of Syllables
1. visionary	vi-sion-ar-y	4
2. vocalized	vo-cal-ized	3
3. vantage	van-tage	2
4. visiting	vis-it-ing	3
5. volume	vol-ume	2
6. verdict	ver-dict	2
7. vanishing	van-ish-ing	3
8. victorious	vic-to-ri-ous	4
9. vineyard	vine-yard	2
10. various	var-i-ous	3

Learn To Read English With Directions In Spanish

Classwork

Name: _____   Date: ___/___/_____   Score: _____

The Reading Challenge

Lesson 22.2

Reading Multisyllable Words

✓ Lesson Check Point

Directions: Read each target word. Circle the word in the row that is divided correctly into syllables. Use a dictionary or the Internet to check your answers.

Direcciones: Lee cada palabra objetivo. Encierra en un círculo la palabra en la fila que esté correctamente separada en sílabas. Usa un diccionario o Internet para verificar tus respuestas.

Model

volcano	a. vo-lcan-o	b. vol-can-o	c. vol-ca-no ⭕

1. victory	a. vic-tor-y	b. vic-to-ry ⭕	c. vi-ctor-y

2. varsity	a. var-sit-y	b. va-rsi-ty	c. var-si-ty ⭕

3. visual	a. vis-u-al	b. vi-su-al ⭕	c. visu-a-l

4. vacation	a. va-cat-ion	b. vac-a-tion	c. va-ca-tion ⭕

5. volunteer	a. vol-un-teer ⭕	b. vo-lun-teer	c. vol-u-nteer

6. vitamin	a. vit-a-min	b. vi-tam-in	c. vi-ta-min ⭕

7. vehement	a. ve-hem-ent	b. veh-e-ment	c. ve-he-ment ⭕

8. vehicle	a. ve-hi-cle ⭕	b. veh-i-cle	c. ve-hicl-e

Answer Key

Name: _____ Date: ___/___/_____ Score: _____

Lesson 22.3

Reading and Writing

Proper and Common Nouns and Adjectives

Directions: Read the words in the word box. Put an (X) on the line next to each word that is written incorrectly. Remember that all proper nouns and proper adjectives are capitalized. Use a dictionary or the Internet to check your answers.

Direcciones: Lee las palabras en el cuadro de texto. Coloca una (X) en la línea próxima a las palabras que estén escritas de forma incorrecta. Recuerda que todos los nombres propios y adjetivos propios empiezan con mayúscula. Usa un diccionario o Internet para verificar tus respuestas.

Word Box					
__	vision	X	vienna	X	vikings
X	Las vegas	__	Vietnam	__	velvet
X	Village	__	vehicle	__	Virginia
X	Volume	__	VIP	X	Vice president

Directions: Read each unedited sentence and underline the word that is written incorrectly. Write each sentence correctly on the line.

Direcciones: Lee cada oración sin editar y subraya la palabra que está escrita de forma incorrecta. Escribe cada oración correctamente en la línea.

Model
In the fall, the leaves in <u>vermont</u> have vibrant colors.
<u>In the fall, the leaves in Vermont have vibrant colors.</u>

1. <u>valerie</u> is attending Valor Vocational School.
<u>Valerie is attending Valor Vocational School.</u>

2. Vince voted to go to the British <u>virgin</u> Islands.
<u>Vince voted to go to the British Virgin Islands.</u>

3. Washington's troops were victorious at <u>valley</u> Forge.
<u>Washington's troops were victorious at Valley Forge.</u>

4. This summer, I am going on <u>Vacation</u> to Victoria Falls.
<u>This summer, I am going on vacation to Victoria Falls.</u>

Classwork

L Name: _____ Date: ___/___/_____ Score: _____

Lesson 23.1

Reading Words with the Letter W/w

✓ Lesson Check Point

Directions: Read each target word. Find the letter "w" and put a check (✓) in the column that identifies its position: beginning, within or end.
Direcciones: Lee cada palabra objetivo. Encuentra la letra "w" y coloca un signo de verificación (✓) en la columna que identifique su posición: inicio, interior o final.

Target Words	Beginning (First Letter)	Within	End (Last Letter)
1. bowling		✓	
2. arrow			✓
3. western	✓		
4. bookworm		✓	
5. shadow			✓

Directions: Read each sentence and underline the words that begin with the letter "w." Write all the underlined words in alphabetical order on the lines below.
Direcciones: Lee cada oración y subraya las palabras que empiecen con la letra "w." Escribe todas las letras subrayadas en orden alfabético en las líneas que siguen.

6. The <u>wildcats</u> have very long <u>whiskers</u>.

7. The tourists are <u>walking</u> along the <u>waterfront</u>.

8. The <u>wilderness</u> is home to <u>wolves</u> and eagles.

9. There are beautiful <u>waterfalls</u> in the <u>West</u> Indies.

10. My <u>wife</u> placed the clothes in the new <u>washing</u> machine.

walking	washing	waterfalls
waterfront	West	whiskers
wife	wildcats	wilderness
	wolves	

Learn To Read English With Directions In Spanish

Name: _____ Date: ___/___/_____ Score: _____

Answer Key

Lesson 23.2

Reading Words with a Vowel before the Letter "w"

✓ Lesson Check Point

 Directions: Read each target word. Circle the word in the column that has the same "aw," "ew" or "ow" sound as the target word.
Direcciones: Lee cada palabra objetivo. Encierra en un círculo la palabra en la columna que tenga el mismo sonido vocal "aw," "ew," o "ow" que la palabra objetivo.

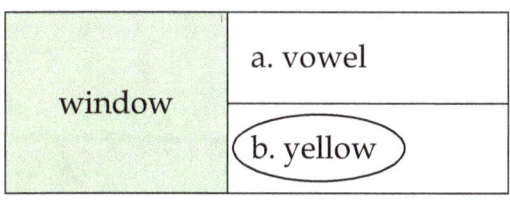
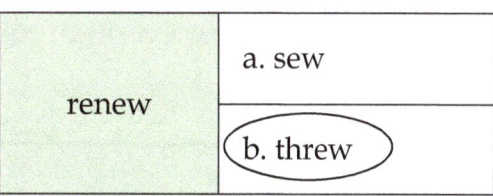
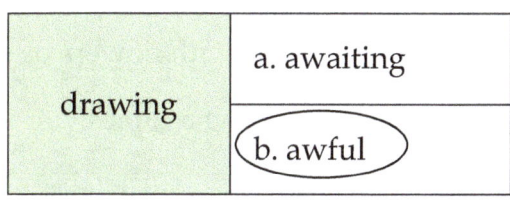
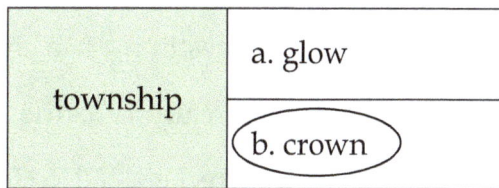

window — a. vowel / (b. yellow)
renew — a. sew / (b. threw)
drawing — a. awaiting / (b. awful)
township — a. glow / (b. crown)

 Directions: Read each target word. Put a check (✓) under the correct column heading.
Direcciones: Lee cada palabra objetivo. Coloca un signo de verificación (✓) bajo el encabezado de la columna correcta.

Target Words	Underlined letters have /o͞o/ sound as in the word <u>few</u>	Underlined letters have /ȯ/ sound as in the word <u>law</u>	Underlined letters have /ō/ sound as in the word <u>sew</u>	Underlined letters have /ou/ sound as in the word <u>cow</u>
1. wind<u>ow</u>			✓	
2. ren<u>ew</u>	✓			
3. dr<u>aw</u>ing		✓		
4. t<u>ow</u>nship				✓

Classwork

Name: _____ Date: ___/___/_____ Score: _____

Lesson 23.3

Reading Words with a Silent "w" and "wr" Letter Combination

Dictionary Skills/ Vocabulary

✓ Lesson Check Point

Directions: Read each target word and its definition. Write the letter of the definition on the line of each target word. Use a dictionary or the Internet to check your answers

Direcciones: Lee cada palabra objetivo y su definición. Escribe la letra de la definición en la línea de cada palabra objetivo. Usa un diccionario o Internet para verificar tus respuestas.

Target Words	Definitions
1. _d_ wrap	a. to have destroyed something with intense force
2. _e_ wrestling	b. a circular decoration made with flowers or evergreens
3. _b_ wreath	c. the act of arguing or debating a topic
4. _a_ wrecked	d. to fold in a fitted covering
5. _c_ wrangling	e. a physical sport

Directions: Read each sentence. Underline the word in the parentheses that correctly completes each sentence. Then, write the underlined word on the line.
Direcciones: Lee cada oración. Subraya la palabra entre paréntesis que completa correctamente cada oración. Luego, escribe la palabra subrayada en la línea.

6. Wendy placed a beautiful ___wreath___ on the door. (wrestling, <u>wreath</u>)

7. His house was ___wrecked___ by the tornado. (wrangling, <u>wrecked</u>)

8. The wrestler has a ___wrestling___ match tonight. (<u>wrestling</u>, wrap)

9. The mothers will __wrap__ their babies in warm blankets. (<u>wrap</u>, wreath)

10. He was __wrangling__ with his teacher over an unfair grade. (<u>wrangling</u>, wrap)

Answer Key

 Name: _____ Date: ___/___/_____ Score: _____

Lesson 23.3

Reading Words with a Silent Letter "w"

✓ Lesson Check Point

 Directions: Read the target words in the word box. Write the words that have a silent letter "w" in the first column. Write the words that do not have a silent letter "w" in the second column.

Direcciones: Lee las palabras objetivo en el cuadro de texto. Escribe las palabras que tengan una letra muda "w" en la primera columna. Escribe las palabras que no tengan una letra muda "w" en la segunda columna.

Target Word Box				
sword	tomorrow	below	dwell	disown
winner	bandwidth	eastward	two	freewill
afterward	answer	farewell	firewall	writing
wrap	doorway	wreck	wrongly	went

Letter "w" is silent

- two
- wrap
- below
- disown
- wreck
- sword
- answer
- writing
- wrongly
- tomorrow

Letter "w" has the /w/ sound

- went
- dwell
- winner
- eastward
- freewill
- afterward
- farewell
- firewall
- doorway
- bandwidth

Learn To Read English With Directions In Spanish

Classwork

 Name: _____ Date: ___/___/_____ Score: _____

The Reading Challenge

Lesson 23.4

Reading Multisyllable Words

✓ Lesson Check Point

Directions: Read and divide each target word into syllables. Write each word and place a hyphen (-) between the syllables in the second column. Write the number of syllables in the third column. Use a dictionary or the Internet to check your answers.

Direcciones: Lee y separa en sílabas cada palabra objetivo. Escribe cada palabra y coloca un guión (-) entre las sílabas en la segunda columna. Escribe el número de sílabas en la tercera columna. Usa un diccionario o Internet para verificar tus respuestas.

Target Words	Words Divided into Syllables	Number of Syllables
1. waistband	waist-band	2
2. woman	wom-an	2
3. whistle	whis-tle	2
4. western	west-ern	2
5. wondering	won-der-ing	3
6. washing	wash-ing	2
7. writer	writ-er	2
8. worthless	worth-less	2
9. willful	will-ful	2
10. waterfall	wa-ter-fall	3

Answer Key

 Name: _____ Date: ___/___/_____ Score: _____

The Reading Challenge

Lesson 23.4

Reading Multisyllable Words

✓ Lesson Check Point

 Directions: Read each target word. Circle the word in the row that is divided correctly into syllables. Use a dictionary or the Internet to check your answers.

Direcciones: Lee cada palabra objetivo. Encierra en un círculo la palabra en la fila que esté correctamente separada en sílabas. Usa un diccionario o Internet para verificar tus respuestas.

Model

| wonderful | a. wo-nder-ful | **(b. won-der-ful)** | c. won-derf-ul |

| 1. waterbed | **(a. wa-ter-bed)** | b. wa-terb-ed | c. wat-er-bed |

| 2. wandering | a. wand-er-ing | b. wand-e-ring | **(c. wan-der-ing)** |

| 3. Wyoming | **(a. Wy-o-ming)** | b. Wy-om-ing | c. Wyo-mi-ng |

| 4. whenever | a. whe-nev-er | **(b. when-ev-er)** | c. wh-ene-ver |

| 5. withdrawal | a. withdr-aw-al | **(b. with-draw-al)** | c. with-dra-wal |

| 6. watermark | a. wat-er-mark | b. wa-term-ark | **(c. wa-ter-mark)** |

| 7. workable | a. wor-ka-ble | b. wor-kab-le | **(c. work-a-ble)** |

| 8. weekender | a. wee-kend-er | **(b. week-end-er)** | c. week-en-der |

Unit W
Lesson 23.4

Learn To Read English With Directions In Spanish

Classwork

Name: _____ Date: ___/___/_____ Score: _____

Lesson 23.5

Reading and Writing

Proper and Common Nouns and Adjectives

Directions: Read the words in the word box. Put an (X) on the line next to each word that is written incorrectly. Remember that all proper nouns and proper adjectives are capitalized. Use a dictionary or the Internet to check your answers.

Direcciones: Lee las palabras en el cuadro de texto. Coloca una (X) en la línea próxima a las palabras que estén escritas de forma incorrecta. Recuerda que todos los nombres propios y adjetivos propios empiezan con mayúscula. Usa un diccionario o Internet para verificar tus respuestas.

Word Box					
X	wakefield, NY	__	wrappers	__	whiplash
X	Wealth	X	wisconsin	__	West Virginia
__	Washington	X	Wheelchair	X	white House
__	waterfall	__	Wake Island	X	Workforce

Directions: Read each unedited sentence and underline the word that is written incorrectly. Write each sentence correctly on the line.
Direcciones: Lee cada oración sin editar y subraya la palabra que está escrita de forma incorrecta. Escribe cada oración correctamente en la línea.

Model

We walked along the winding path that led to the <u>Waterfalls</u>.
<u>We walked along the winding path that led to the waterfalls.</u>

1. The <u>Warden</u> works for the Wisconsin Prison System.
<u>The warden works for the Wisconsin Prison System.</u>

2. The waterfalls in the <u>west</u> Indies are breathtaking.
<u>The waterfalls in the West Indies are breathtaking.</u>

3. The new <u>Waitress</u> is from Washington, D.C.
<u>The new waitress is from Washington, D.C.</u>

4. The woodpeckers made their homes in <u>wilmington</u>.
<u>The woodpeckers made their homes in Wilmington.</u>

   Answer Key

Name: _____   Date:___/___/_____   Score:_____

Lesson 24.1

Reading Words with the Letter X/x

✓ Lesson Check Point

 Directions: Read each target word. Find the letter "x" and put a check (✓) in the column that identifies its position: beginning, within or end.
Direcciones: Lee cada palabra objetivo. Encuentra la letra "x" y coloca un signo de verificación (✓) en la columna que identifique su posición: inicio, interior o final.

Target Words	Beginning (First Letter)	Within	End (Last Letter)
1. sixty		✓	
2. oxen		✓	
3. prefix			✓
4. x-ray	✓		
5. wax			✓

 Directions: Read each sentence and underline the words that begin with the letter "x." Write all the underlined words in alphabetical order on the lines below.
Direcciones: Lee cada oración y subraya las palabras que empiecen con la letra "x." Escribe todas las letras subrayadas en orden alfabético en las líneas que siguen.

6. <u>Xaria</u> has to go to the hospital for chest <u>x-rays</u>.

7. <u>Xavier</u> enjoys playing the <u>xylophone</u> at concerts.

8. <u>Xianna</u> used the <u>Xerox</u> machine to make photocopies.

9. <u>Xander</u> said, "<u>Xiamen</u> is an island of Southeast China."

10. I have worked for <u>Xola's</u> company for <u>x</u> number of years.

x_____   Xander_____   Xaria_____
Xavier_____   Xerox_____   Xiamen_____
Xianna_____   Xola's_____   x-rays_____
                    xylophone_____

Classwork

 Name: _____ Date: _____/ ___/ _____ Score: _____

Lesson 24.1

Reading Words with the Letter X/x

✓ **Lesson Check Point**

 Directions: Read each target word. Circle the word in the column that has the same "x" sound(s) as the target word.

Direcciones: Lee cada palabra objetivo. Encierra en un círculo la palabra en la columna que tenga el mismo sonido "x" que la palabra objetivo.

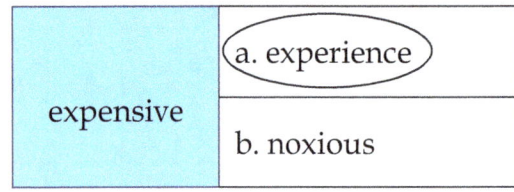

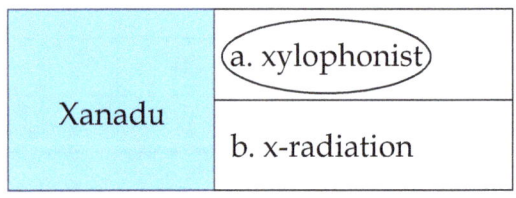 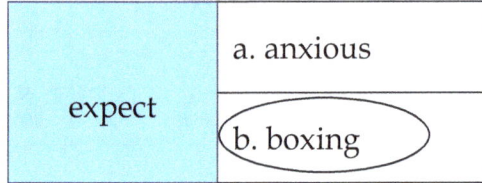

 Directions: Read each target word. Put a check (✓) under the correct column heading.

Direcciones: Lee cada palabra objetivo. Coloca un signo de verificación (✓) bajo el encabezado de la columna correcta.

Target Words	"x" has the /k/ + /s/ sounds as in the word <u>box</u>	"x" has the /z/ sound as in the word <u>xylophone</u>	"x" has the /g/ + /z/ sounds as in the word <u>exhibit</u>	"x" has the /k/ + /sh/ sounds as in the word <u>anxious</u>
1. expect	✓			
2. complexion				✓
3. Xanadu		✓		
4. expensive	✓			

Answer Key

 Name: _____ Date: ___/___/_____ Score: _____

The Reading Challenge

Lesson 24.2

Reading Multisyllable Words

✓ Lesson Check Point

 Directions: Read and divide each target word into syllables. Write each word and place a hyphen (-) between the syllables in the second column. Write the number of syllables in the third column. Use a dictionary or the Internet to check your answers.

Direcciones: Lee y separa en sílabas cada palabra objetivo. Escribe cada palabra y coloca un guión (-) entre las sílabas en la segunda columna. Escribe el número de sílabas en la tercera columna. Usa un diccionario o Internet para verificar tus respuestas.

Target Words	Words Divided into Syllables	Number of Syllables
1. boxer	box-er	2
2. prefix	pre-fix	2
3. saxophone	sax-o-phone	3
4. complexion	com-plex-ion	3
5. index	in-dex	2
6. textual	tex-tu-al	3
7. sixteen	six-teen	2
8. perplexing	per-plex-ing	3
9. taxicab	tax-i-cab	3
10. oxygen	ox-y-gen	3

Classwork

 Name: _____ Date: ___/___/_____ Score: _____

The Reading Challenge

Lesson 24.2

Reading Multisyllable Words

✓ **Lesson Check Point**

 Directions: Read each target word. Circle the word in the row that is divided correctly into syllables. Use a dictionary or the Internet to check your answers.

Direcciones: Lee cada palabra objetivo. Encierra en un círculo la palabra en la fila que esté correctamente separada en sílabas. Usa un diccionario o Internet para verificar tus respuestas.

Model

| oxidized | **a. ox-i-dized** ✓ | b. oxi-d-ized | c. o-xi-dized |

| 1. paradox | a. pa-rad-ox | b. par-ad-ox | **c. par-a-dox** ✓ |

| 2. explorer | **a. ex-plor-er** ✓ | b. exp-lo-rer | c. expl-or-er |

| 3. taxable | a. ta-xa-ble | **b. tax-a-ble** ✓ | c. ta-xab-le |

| 4. existence | a. exi-ste-nce | **b. ex-is-tence** ✓ | c. ex-i-stence |

| 5. hexagon | a. he-xa-gon | b. he-xag-on | **c. hex-a-gon** ✓ |

| 6. exciting | **a. ex-cit-ing** ✓ | b. exc-i-ting | c. exc-it-ing |

| 7. lexical | a. le-xic-al | b. le-xi-cal | **c. lex-i-cal** ✓ |

| 8. expanding | a. ex-pan-ding | **b. ex-pand-ing** ✓ | c. exp-and-ing |

Answer Key

Name: _____ Date: ___/___/_____ Score: _____

Lesson 24.3

Reading and Writing

Proper and Common Nouns and Adjectives

Directions: Read the words in the word box. Put an (X) on the line next to each word that is written incorrectly. Remember that all proper nouns and proper adjectives are capitalized. Use a dictionary or the Internet to check your answers.

Direcciones: Lee las palabras en el cuadro de texto. Coloca una (X) en la línea próxima a las palabras que estén escritas de forma incorrecta. Recuerda que todos los nombres propios y adjetivos propios empiezan con mayúscula. Usa un diccionario o Internet para verificar tus respuestas.

Word Box					
X	xerox Inc.	__	xylems	X	King xerxes I
__	xanthium	__	xenon	X	Xylophone
__	xylene	__	Xiang	X	Xanthic acid
X	X-ray	X	xavier	__	xebec

Directions: Read each unedited sentence and underline the word that is written incorrectly. Write each sentence correctly on the line.
Direcciones: Lee cada oración sin editar y subraya la palabra que está escrita de forma incorrecta. Escribe cada oración correctamente en la línea.

Model
Xia said, "The population of xankandi is 33,000 people."
<u>Xia said, "The population of Xankandi is 33,000 people."</u>

1. Xia is reading about xanthus, the ancient City of Lycia.
<u>Xia is reading about Xanthus, the ancient City of Lycia.</u>

2. Mr. and Mrs. Xem visited the Chinese province of xuzhou.
<u>Mr. and Mrs. Xem visited the Chinese province of Xuzhou.</u>

3. My friend, xavier, is scheduled to have an x-ray at six o'clock.
<u>My friend, Xavier, is scheduled to have an x-ray at six o'clock.</u>

4. My dentist, Dr. Xu, applied a local anesthetic, Xylocaine, to my gums.
<u>My dentist, Dr. Xu, applied a local anesthetic, xylocaine, to my gums.</u>

Classwork

 Name: _____ Date: ___/___/_____ Score: _____

Lesson 25.1

Reading Words with the Letter Y/y

✓ Lesson Check Point

 Directions: Read each target word. Find the letter "y" and put a check (✓) in the column that identifies its position: beginning, within or end.
Direcciones: Lee cada palabra objetivo. Encuentra la letra "y" y coloca un signo de verificación (✓) en la columna que identifique su posición: inicio, interior o final.

Target Words	Beginning (First Letter)	Within	End (Last Letter)
1. galaxy			✓
2. yellow	✓		
3. hyperactive		✓	
4. strawberry			✓
5. younger	✓		

 Directions: Read each sentence and underline the words that begin with the letter "y." Write all the underlined words in alphabetical order on the lines below.
Direcciones: Lee cada oración y subraya las palabras que empiecen con la letra "y." Escribe todas las letras subrayadas en orden alfabético en las líneas que siguen.

6. <u>Yesterday</u>, I had a relaxing <u>yoga</u> class.

7. <u>Yolanda</u> and Nancy enjoyed my <u>yodeling</u> contest.

8. In <u>Yorktown</u>, I saw a pair of oxen <u>yoked</u> together.

9. The <u>yellow</u> car stopped at the triangular <u>yield</u> sign.

10. Mr. <u>Young</u> lives close to <u>Yellowstone</u> National Park.

<u>yellow</u>   <u>Yellowstone</u>   <u>Yesterday</u>
<u>yield</u>   <u>yodeling</u>   <u>yoga</u>
<u>yoked</u>   <u>Yolanda</u>   <u>Yorktown</u>
             <u>Young</u>

Answer Key

 Name: _____ Date: ___/___/_____ Score: _____

Lesson 25.1

Reading Words with the Letter Y/y

✓ **Lesson Check Point**

 Directions: Read each target word. Circle the word in the row that has a different "y" sound than the target word.
Direcciones: Lee cada palabra objetivo. Encierra en un círculo la palabra en la columna que tenga un sonido "y" diferente al de la palabra objetivo.

Target Words				
1. yours	young	(candy)	year	yield
2. lyric	(myself)	gymnast	cylinders	symbols
3. Polynesia	sibyl	vinyl	(younger)	polymer
4. community	energy	baby	penny	(pyramid)
5. young	(money)	yours	yes	youth

 Directions: Read the words in the four boxes. Circle two words that have the same "y" sound.
Direcciones: Lee las palabras en las cuatro cajas. Encierra en un círculo dos palabras que tengan el mismo sonido "y."

young	(belly)
reply	(city)

cylinder	(yesterday)
cycles	(yahoo)

(very)	apply
your	(jelly)

(happy)	(shiny)
ratify	years

penny	July
(syringe)	(vinyl)

(plywood)	baby
cylinder	(identify)

Unit Y
Lesson 25.1

Classwork

 Name: _____ Date:___/___/_____ Score:_____

Lesson 25.2

Reading Words with a Vowel before the Letter "y"

✓ Lesson Check Point

 Directions: Read each target word. Circle the word in the column that has the same "y" sound as the target word.

Direcciones: Lee cada palabra objetivo. Encierra en un círculo la palabra en la columna que tenga un sonido "y" diferente al de la palabra objetivo.

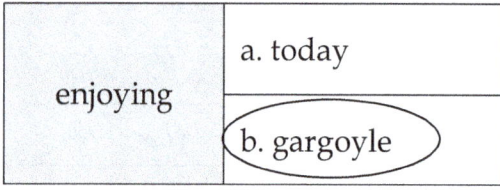
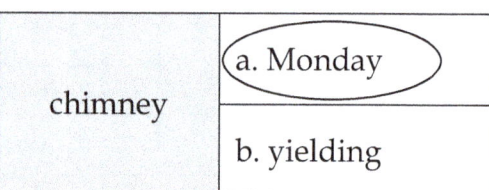
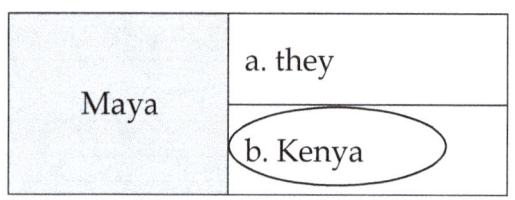
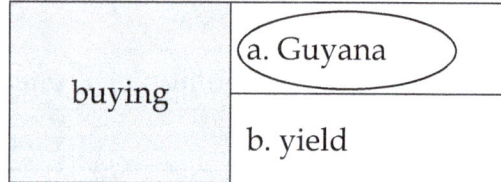

 Directions: Read each target word. Put a check (✓) under the correct column heading.

Direcciones: Lee cada palabra objetivo. Coloca un signo de verificación (✓) bajo el encabezado de la columna correcta.

Target Words	"y" has the /y/ sound as in the word yes	"oy" has the /oi/ sound as in the word boy	"y" has the /ī/ sound as in the word by	"y" is silent as in the word day
1. enjoying		✓		
2. chimney				✓
3. Maya	✓			
4. buying			✓	

Name: _____ Date: ___/___/_____ Score: _____

Answer Key

Lesson 25.3

Reading Words with the "cy" Letter Combination

✓ Lesson Check Point

 Directions: Read each target word. Find the "cy" letter combination and put a check (✓) in the column to identify its position in the word: beginning, within or end.

Direcciones: Lee cada palabra objetivo. Encuentra la combinación de letras "cy" y coloca un signo de verificación (✓) en la columna que identifique su posición: inicio, interior o final.

Target Words	Beginning (First 2 Letters)	Within	End (Last 2 Letters)
1. Nancy			✓
2. bicyclist		✓	
3. cymbal	✓		
4. regency			✓
5. cytoplasm	✓		

 Directions: Read each target word. Put a check (✓) under the correct column heading.

Direcciones: Lee cada palabra objetivo. Coloca un signo de verificación (✓) bajo el encabezado de la columna correcta.

Target Words	"cy" has the /s/ + /ĭ/ sounds as in the word cylinder	"cy" has the /s/ + /ī/ sounds as in the word cycle	"cy" has the /s/ + /ē/ sounds as in the word agency
6. Nancy			✓
7. bicyclist	✓		
8. cymbal	✓		
9. regency			✓
10. cytoplasm		✓	

Classwork

 Name: _____ Date: ___/___/_____ Score: _____

Lesson 25.4

Reading Words with the Final Letter "y"

✓ Lesson Check Point

 Directions: Read each target word. Find the letter "y" and put a check (✓) in the column that identifies its position within the word.
Direcciones: Lea cada palabra objetivo. Busque la letra "y" y marque (✓) en la columna que identifica su posición dentro de la palabra.

Target Words	"y" is at the end of a one syllable word	"y" is at the end of the first syllable	"y" is at the end of a multi-syllable word
1. myself		✓	
2. community			✓
3. cry	✓		
4. discovery			✓
5. tycoon		✓	

 Directions: Read each target word. Put a check (✓) under the correct column heading.
Direcciones: Lee cada palabra objetivo. Coloca un signo de verificación (✓) bajo el encabezado de la columna correcta.

Target Words	"y" has the /ē/ sound as in the word agency	"y" has the /ī/ sound as in the word flying
6. myself		✓
7. community	✓	
8. cry		✓
9. discovery	✓	
10. tycoon		✓

Name: _____ Date: ___/___/_____ Score: _____

Answer Key

Lesson 25.5

Reading Words with the "yr" Letter Combination

✓ **Lesson Check Point**

 Directions: Read each target word. Circle the word in the column that has the same "yr" sounds as the target word.
Direcciones: Lee cada palabra objetivo. Encierra en un círculo la palabra en la columna que tenga el mismo sonido "yr" que la palabra objetivo.

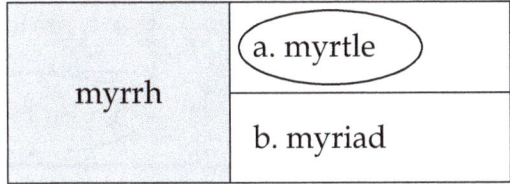

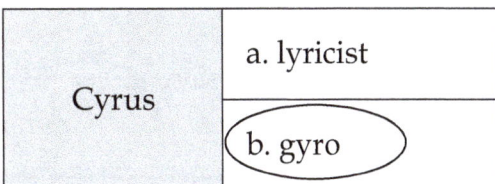

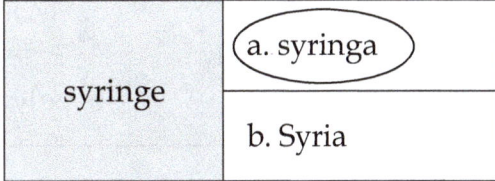

 Directions: Read each target word. Put a check (✓) under the correct column heading.
Direcciones: Lee cada palabra objetivo. Coloca un signo de verificación (✓) bajo el encabezado de la columna correcta.

Target Words	"yr" has the /û/ + /r/ sounds as in the word myrtle	"yr" has the /ĭ/ + /r/ sounds as in the word pyramid	"yr" has the /ī/ + /r/ sounds as in the word gyro	"yr" has the /ə/ + /r/ sounds as in the word martyr
1. myrrh	✓			
2. Cyrus			✓	
3. myriad		✓		
4. syringe				✓

Learn To Read English With Directions In Spanish   239   Copyrighted Material

Classwork

Name: _____ Date: ___/___/_____ Score: _____

Lesson 25.6

Reading Letter "y" Words with the Schwa Vowel Sound

✓ Lesson Check Point

Directions: Read each target word. Circle the word in the column that has the same "y" sound as the target word.

Direcciones: Lee cada palabra objetivo. Encierra en un círculo la palabra en la columna que tenga el mismo sonido "y" que la palabra objetivo.

| Polynesian | (a. polyvinyl) |
| | b. pyramid |

| sibyl | a. mandatory |
| | (b. vinyl) |

| nicely | (a. vacancy) |
| | b. polymerize |

| Pennsylvania | (a. polymer) |
| | b. younger |

Directions: Read each target word. Put a check (✓) under the correct column heading.

Direcciones: Lee cada palabra objetivo. Coloca un signo de verificación (✓) bajo el encabezado de la columna correcta.

Target Words	"y" has the /ə/ sound as in the word <u>syringe</u>	"y" does not have the /ə/ sound
1. Polynesian	✓	
2. sibyl	✓	
3. nicely		✓
4. Pennsylvania	✓	

Answer Key

 Name: _____ Date: ___/___/_____ Score: _____

Lesson 25.7

Reading Words with a Silent Letter "y"

✓ **Lesson Check Point**

 Directions: Read the target words in the word box. Write the words that have a silent letter "y" in the first column. Write the words that do not have a silent letter "y" in the second column.

Direcciones: Lee las palabras objetivo en el cuadro de texto. Escribe las palabras que tengan una letra muda "y" en la primera columna. Escribe las palabras que no tengan una letra muda "y" en la segunda columna.

Target Word Box				
prey	mayor	yes	payday	playing
yeast	jeopardy	donkey	midday	yellow
abundantly	yogurt	friendly	safely	always
layer	chewy	youth	prayer	today

Letter "y" is silent

- prey
- mayor
- payday
- playing
- donkey
- midday
- always
- layer
- prayer
- today

Letter "y" has the /y/ or /ē/ sound

- yes
- yeast
- chewy
- yellow
- youth
- yogurt
- friendly
- safely
- jeopardy
- abundantly

Learn To Read English With Directions In Spanish

Classwork

 Name: _____ Date: ___/___/_____ Score: _____

The Reading Challenge

Lesson 25.8

Reading Multisyllable Words

✓ **Lesson Check Point**

Directions: Read and divide each target word into syllables. Write each word and place a hyphen (-) between the syllables in the second column. Write the number of syllables in the third column. Use a dictionary or the Internet to check your answers.

Direcciones: Lee y separa en sílabas cada palabra objetivo. Escribe cada palabra y coloca un guión (-) entre las sílabas en la segunda columna. Escribe el número de sílabas en la tercera columna. Usa un diccionario o Internet para verificar tus respuestas.

Target Words	Words Divided into Syllables	Number of Syllables
1. yourself	your-self	2
2. Yemenite	Yem-en-ite	3
3. Yorktown	York-town	2
4. yoga	yo-ga	2
5. yonder	yon-der	2
6. Yankee	Yan-kee	2
7. yardstick	yard-stick	2
8. yearly	year-ly	2
9. yodeling	yo-del-ing	3
10. youthfulness	youth-ful-ness	3

Answer Key

 Name: _____ Date: ____/ ____/ _____ Score: _____

The Reading Challenge

Lesson 25.8

Reading Multisyllable Words

✓ **Lesson Check Point**

 Directions: Read each target word. Circle the word in the row that is divided correctly into syllables. Use a dictionary or the Internet to check your answers.

Direcciones: Lee cada palabra objetivo. Encierra en un círculo la palabra en la fila que esté correctamente separada en sílabas. Usa un diccionario o Internet para verificar tus respuestas.

Model

| yesterday | a. ye-ster-day | b. yest-er-day | c. yes-ter-day ⭕ |

| 1. Yucatán | a. Yuc-a-tán | b. Yu-ca-tán ⭕ | c. Yu-cat-án |

| 2. yarmulke | a. yar-mul-ke ⭕ | b. yar-mulk-e | c. yarm-u-lke |

| 3. yodeling | a. yod-e-ling | b. yo-de-ling | c. yo-del-ing ⭕ |

| 4. youthful | a. youthf-ul | b. youth-ful ⭕ | c. you-thful |

| 5. Yoruba | a. Yo-ru-ba ⭕ | b. Yor-u-ba | c. Yo-rub-a |

| 6. Yankee | a. Yank-ee | b. Ya-nk-ee | c. Yan-kee ⭕ |

| 7. yielding | a. yield-ing ⭕ | b. yiel-di-ng | c. yieldi-ng |

| 8. younger | a. you-nger | b. youn-ger | c. young-er ⭕ |

Classwork

Name: _____ Date: ___/___/_____ Score: _____

Lesson 25.9

Reading and Writing

Proper and Common Nouns and Adjectives

Directions: Read the words in the word box. Put an (X) on the line next to each word that is written incorrectly. Remember that all proper nouns and proper adjectives are capitalized. Use a dictionary or the Internet to check your answers.

Direcciones: Lee las palabras en el cuadro de texto. Coloca una (X) en la línea próxima a las palabras que estén escritas de forma incorrecta. Recuerda que todos los nombres propios y adjetivos propios empiezan con mayúscula. Usa un diccionario o Internet para verificar tus respuestas.

Word Box					
__	Yemen	X	yokosuka	__	yachting
__	yellow	__	Yankees	X	Yogurt
X	Young	__	yardage	__	yesterday
X	yoruba	X	Yourself	X	yorktown

Directions: Read each unedited sentence and underline the word that is written incorrectly. Write each sentence correctly on the line.

Direcciones: Lee cada oración sin editar y subraya la palabra que está escrita de forma incorrecta. Escribe cada oración correctamente en la línea.

Model
Is the New York <u>yankees</u> your favorite baseball team?
<u>Is the New York Yankees your favorite baseball team?</u>

1. Yolanda's friend loves to eat <u>yoplait</u> yogurt.
<u>Yolanda's friend loves to eat Yoplait yogurt.</u>

2. All the signs in <u>yorktown</u> are painted yellow.
<u>All the signs in Yorktown are painted yellow.</u>

3. Last year, the <u>young</u> family visited Yosemite National Park.
<u>Last year, the Young family visited Yosemite National Park.</u>

4. <u>yesterday</u>, Yusef plotted the y-axis and the x-axis on graph paper.
<u>Yesterday, Yusef plotted the y-axis and the x-axis on graph paper.</u>

 Name: _____ Date: ___/___/_____ Score: _____

Answer Key

Lesson 26.1

Reading Words with the Letter Z/z

✓ Lesson Check Point

 Directions: Read each target word. Find the letter "z" and put a check (✓) in the column that identifies its position: beginning, within or end.
Direcciones: Lee cada palabra objetivo. Encuentra la letra "z" y coloca un signo de verificación (✓) en la columna que identifique su posición: inicio, interior o final.

Target Words	Beginning (First Letter)	Within	End (Last Letter)
1. blizzard		✓	
2. topaz			✓
3. Tanzania		✓	
4. zebra	✓		
5. zookeeper	✓		

 Directions: Read each sentence and underline the words that begin with the letter "z." Write all the underlined words in alphabetical order on the lines below.
Direcciones: Lee cada oración y subraya las palabras que empiecen con la letra "z." Escribe todas las letras subrayadas en orden alfabético en las líneas que siguen.

6. Samira <u>zipped</u> up her <u>zebra</u> costume.

7. Danny wants to work at the <u>zoo</u> as a trained <u>zoologist</u>.

8. The two <u>zoom</u> lenses on <u>Zianna's</u> camera are very expensive.

9. In New <u>Zealand</u>, Abdulla wore his shirt with a <u>zigzag</u> design.

10. Valeria is studying the rich cultures of <u>Zambia</u> and <u>Zimbabwe</u>.

Zambia	Zealand	zebra
Zianna's	zigzag	Zimbabwe
zipped	zoo	zoologist
	zoom	

Learn To Read English With Directions In Spanish

Classwork

 Name: _____ Date: ___/___/_____ Score: _____

Lesson 26.1

Reading Words with the Letter Z/z

✓ **Lesson Check Point**

  Directions: Read each target word. Circle the word in the column that has the same "z" sound as the target word.
Direcciones: Lee cada palabra objetivo. Encierra en un círculo la palabra en la columna que tenga el mismo sonido "z" que la palabra objetivo.

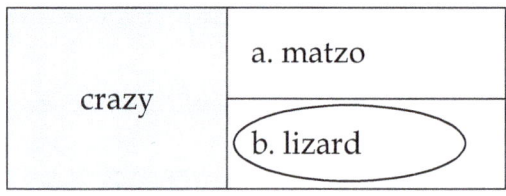

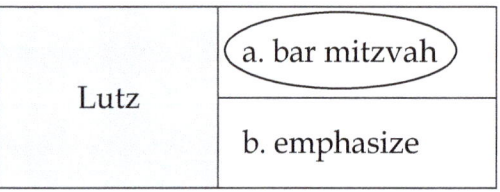 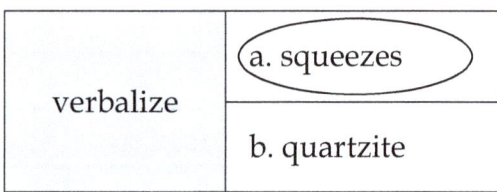

  Directions: Read each target word. Put a check (✓) under the correct column heading.
Direcciones: Lee cada palabra objetivo. Coloca un signo de verificación (✓) bajo el encabezado de la columna correcta.

Target Words	"z" has the /z/ sound as in the word <u>zipper</u>	"z" has the /s/ sound as in the word <u>quartz</u>
1. crazy	✓	
2. normalize	✓	
3. Lutz		✓
4. verbalize	✓	

Unit Z
Lesson 26.1

Learn To Read English With Directions In Spanish

Answer Key

Name: _____ Date: ___/___/____ Score: _____

Lesson 26.2

Reading Words with a Silent Letter "z"

✓ Lesson Check Point

Directions: Read the target words in the word box. Write the words that have a silent letter "z" in the first column. Write the words that do not have a silent letter "z" in the second column.

Direcciones: Lee las palabras objetivo en el cuadro de texto. Escribe las palabras que tengan una letra muda "z" en la primera columna. Escribe las palabras que no tengan una letra muda "z" en la segunda columna.

Target Word Box				
fizzle	sizzler	Brazil	analyze	capitalize
agonize	dozen	dizziness	amazing	gizzard
cadenza	blazing	puzzling	economize	blizzard
sizzles	fuzz	centralize	drizzling	puzzle

Letter "z" is silent
- fuzz
- sizzler
- puzzle
- gizzard
- fizzle
- blizzard
- sizzles
- puzzling
- dizziness
- drizzling

Letter "z" has the /z/ or /s/ sound
- Brazil
- analyze
- capitalize
- agonize
- dozen
- amazing
- cadenza
- blazing
- economize
- centralize

Classwork

 Name: _____ Date: ___/___/_____ Score: _____

The Reading Challenge

Lesson 26.3

Reading Multisyllable Words

✓ **Lesson Check Point**

 Directions: Read and divide each target word into syllables. Write each word and place a hyphen (-) between the syllables in the second column. Write the number of syllables in the third column. Use a dictionary or the Internet to check your answers.

Direcciones: Lee y separa en sílabas cada palabra objetivo. Escribe cada palabra y coloca un guión (-) entre las sílabas en la segunda columna. Escribe el número de sílabas en la tercera columna. Usa un diccionario o Internet para verificar tus respuestas.

Target Words	Words Divided into Syllables	Number of Syllables
1. Zaire	Za-ire	2
2. zealot	zeal-ot	2
3. zodiac	zo-di-ac	3
4. zigzag	zig-zag	2
5. Zulu	Zu-lu	2
6. zeniths	ze-niths	2
7. zany	za-ny	2
8. zinger	zing-er	2
9. zestfulness	zest-ful-ness	3
10. Zambia	Zam-bi-a	3

Answer Key

Name: _____ Date: ___/___/_____ Score: _____

The Reading Challenge

Lesson 26.3

Reading Multisyllable Words

✓ **Lesson Check Point**

Directions: Read each target word. Circle the word in the row that is divided correctly into syllables. Use a dictionary or the Internet to check your answers.

Direcciones: Lee cada palabra objetivo. Encierra en un círculo la palabra en la fila que esté correctamente separada en sílabas. Usa un diccionario o Internet para verificar tus respuestas.

Model

| zoology | a. zo-ol-o-gy *(circled)* | b. zoo-lo-gy | c. zool-o-gy |

1. Zealand	a. Zea-land *(circled)*	b. Zeal-an-d	c. Zeal-and
2. Zimbabwe	a. Zimb-ab-we	b. Zim-bab-we *(circled)*	c. Zim-ba-bwe
3. zodiac	a. zo-di-a-c	b. zod-ia-c	c. zo-di-ac *(circled)*
4. zoologist	a. zo-ol-o-gist *(circled)*	b. zoo-log-ist	c. zoo-lo-gist
5. zeroing	a. ze-roi-ng	b. zer-o-ing	c. ze-ro-ing *(circled)*
6. zonal	a. zo-nal	b. zon-al *(circled)*	c. zo-n-al
7. Zambia	a. Za-mbi-a	b. Zam-bi-a *(circled)*	c. Zamb-i-a
8. zestful	a. ze-stf-ul	b. ze-stful	c. zest-ful *(circled)*

Unit Z Lesson 26.3

Classwork

Name: _____ Date: ___/___/_____ Score: _____

Lesson 26.4

Reading and Writing

Proper and Common Nouns and Adjectives

Directions: Read the words in the word box. Put an (X) on the line next to each word that is written incorrectly. Remember that all proper nouns and proper adjectives are capitalized. Use a dictionary or the Internet to check your answers.

Direcciones: Lee las palabras en el cuadro de texto. Coloca una (X) en la línea próxima a las palabras que estén escritas de forma incorrecta. Recuerda que todos los nombres propios y adjetivos propios empiezan con mayúscula. Usa un diccionario o Internet para verificar tus respuestas.

Word Box					
X	Zillion	__	zippers	__	Zealand
__	Zambia	X	Zookeeper	__	Zululand
X	zurich	__	zealous	X	Zoom lens
__	Zeus	X	zanzibar	X	Zoology

Directions: Read each unedited sentence and underline the word that is written incorrectly. Write each sentence correctly on the line.

Direcciones: Lee cada oración sin editar y subraya la palabra que está escrita de forma incorrecta. Escribe cada oración correctamente en la línea.

Model
The steep path zigzags through the <u>zagros</u> Mountains.
<u>The steep path zigzags through the Zagros Mountains.</u>

1. Zoey lives in the Eastern Time <u>zone</u>.
<u>Zoey lives in the Eastern Time Zone.</u>

2. At noon, the <u>Zebras</u> at the Bronx Zoo were sleeping.
<u>At noon, the zebras at the Bronx Zoo were sleeping.</u>

3. My school, Zesty Academy, has <u>Zero</u> tolerance for bullying.
<u>My school, Zesty Academy, has zero tolerance for bullying.</u>

4. Mr. Zinger's new movie is a <u>Zillion</u> times better than his first one.
<u>Mr. Zinger's new movie is a zillion times better than his first one.</u>

Answer Key

Appendix 1.0

Introduction of the Letter A/a

 Lesson Check Point

 Directions: Circle the correct letter "a" pair: uppercase and lowercase letters.

Direcciones: Encierra en un círculo el par correcto de letras "a": letras mayúsculas y minúsculas.

    Ao   (Aa)   aE   Au   iA

 Directions: The uppercase letter "A" is in the first column. Look at the four letters in the row and circle the lowercase letter that matches the uppercase letter "A."

Direcciones: La letra mayúscula "A" está en la primera columna. Mire las cuatro letras en la fila y encierre en un círculo la letra minúscula que coincida con la letra mayúscula "A".

A	o	e	u	(a)
A	(a)	c	z	x
A	e	w	(a)	c
A	o	(a)	c	u

 Directions: The lowercase letter "a" is in the first column. Look at the four letters in the row and circle the uppercase letter that matches the lowercase letter "a."

Direcciones: La letra minúscula "a" está en la primera columna. Mire las cuatro letras en la fila y encierre en un círculo la letra mayúscula que coincida con la letra minúscula "a".

a	Z	(A)	V	W
a	V	C	(A)	Z
a	D	O	W	(A)
a	(A)	H	V	Q

Classwork

 Name: _____ Date: ___/___/_____ Score: _____

Appendix 2.0

Introduction of the Letter B/b

✓ **Lesson Check Point**

 Directions: Circle the correct letter "b" pair: uppercase and lowercase letters.

Direcciones: Encierra en un círculo el par correcto de letras "b": letras mayúsculas y minúsculas.

    Bd   (Bb)   bF   Db   Bk

 Directions: The uppercase letter "B" is in the first column. Look at the four letters in the row and circle the lowercase letter that matches the uppercase letter "B."

Direcciones: La letra mayúscula "B" está en la primera columna. Mire las cuatro letras en la fila y encierre en un círculo la letra minúscula que coincida con la letra mayúscula "B".

B	(b)	f	q	d
B	g	(b)	d	h
B	f	p	d	(b)
B	h	(b)	p	k

 Directions: The lowercase letter "b" is in the first column. Look at the four letters in the row and circle the uppercase letter that matches the lowercase letter "b."

Direcciones: La letra minúscula "b" está en la primera columna. Mire las cuatro letras en la fila y encierre en un círculo la letra mayúscula que coincida con la letra minúscula "b".

b	F	D	(B)	G
b	Q	P	D	(B)
b	P	(B)	F	M
b	H	R	Q	(B)

Unit B Appendix 2.0

Learn To Read English With Directions In Spanish

Answer Key

Name: _____ Date: ___/___/_____ Score: _____

Appendix 2.0

Letter Recognition B/b

Uppercase and Lowercase Letter

✓ **Lesson Check Point**

Directions: Read each target word. Read the words in the row and circle the word that begins with a different letter.

Direcciones: Lee cada palabra objetivo. Lee las palabras en la fila y encierre en un círculo la palabra que comienza con una letra diferente.

Target Words				
1. boy	bin	bean	(fat)	buns
2. buzz	balloon	(house)	bandit	blood
3. both	bandage	brick	(queen)	bang
4. bubbles	(drip)	bank	bag	break
5. because	(puppet)	ballot	baggage	black

Directions: Read the words in the four boxes. Circle two words that start with the uppercase and lowercase letter "b."

Direcciones: Lee las palabras en los cuatro recuadros. Encierra en un círculo dos palabras que comiencen con la letra "b" mayúscula y minúscula.

(bin)	win		(Bit)	sit		(Bake)	Make
tin	(Bin)		Hit	(bit)		(bake)	dare

(bat)	(Bat)		Float	oat		Wet	(Best)
hat	Sat		(Boat)	(boat)		date	(best)

Unit B
Appendix 2.0

Classwork

 Name: _____ Date:___/___/_____ Score:_____

Appendix 3.0

Introduction of the Letter C/c

✓ Lesson Check Point

 Directions: Circle the correct letter "c" pair: uppercase and lowercase letters.

Direcciones: Encierra en un círculo el par correcto de letras "c": letras mayúsculas y minúsculas.

(Cc)   Kc   Co   Oc   cS

 **Directions:** The uppercase letter "C" is in the first column. Look at the four letters in the row and circle the lowercase letter that matches the uppercase letter "C."

Direcciones: La letra mayúscula "C" está en la primera columna. Mire las cuatro letras en la fila y encierre en un círculo la letra minúscula que coincida con la letra mayúscula "C".

C	o	(c)	u	g
C	v	a	r	(c)
C	(c)	g	d	o
C	q	(c)	p	k

 Directions: The lowercase letter "c" is in the first column. Look at the four letters in the row and circle the uppercase letter that matches the lowercase letter "c."

Direcciones: La letra minúscula "c" está en la primera columna. Mire las cuatro letras en la fila y encierre en un círculo la letra mayúscula que coincida con la letra minúscula "c".

c	Q	O	(C)	G
c	(C)	T	Q	M
c	D	B	H	(C)
c	(C)	K	J	D

Answer Key

Name: _____ Date: ___/___/_____ Score: _____

Appendix 3.0

Letter Recognition C/c

Uppercase and Lowercase Letter

✓ Lesson Check Point

Directions: Read each target word. Read the words in the row and circle the word that begins with a different letter.

Direcciones: Lee cada palabra objetivo. Lee las palabras en la fila y encierre en un círculo la palabra que comienza con una letra diferente.

Target Words				
1. clip	cool	came	(poll)	color
2. cart	caramel	(open)	capture	clump
3. cent	cell	(queen)	choice	chap
4. curtain	chat	center	(goat)	city
5. church	chocolate	(engage)	chair	civic

Directions: Read the words in the four boxes. Circle two words that start with the uppercase and lowercase letter "c."

Direcciones: Lee las palabras en los cuatro recuadros. Encierra en un círculo dos palabras que comiencen con la letra "c" mayúscula y minúscula.

book	(Camel)
Brook	(clue)

(comb)	Octopus
(Cook)	Kite

(Cake)	keep
Goat	(capital)

(Cat)	Queen
(cow)	open

Grow	(cute)
(Cab)	float

(come)	home
Tom	(Candy)

Learn To Read English With Directions In Spanish

Classwork

 Name: _____ Date: ___/___/_____ Score: _____

Appendix 4.0

Introduction of the Letter D/d

✓ **Lesson Check Point**

 Directions: Circle the correct letter "d" pair: uppercase and lowercase letters.

Direcciones: Encierra en un círculo el par correcto de letras "d": letras mayúsculas y minúsculas.

Db   Df   (Dd)   Bd   Op

 Directions: The uppercase letter "D" is in the first column. Look at the four letters in the row and circle the lowercase letter that matches the uppercase letter "D."

Direcciones: La letra mayúscula "D" está en la primera columna. Mire las cuatro letras en la fila y encierre en un círculo la letra minúscula que coincida con la letra mayúscula "D".

D	p	(d)	t	b
D	h	y	(d)	t
D	l	t	b	(d)
D	t	(d)	k	f

 Directions: The lowercase letter "d" is in the first column. Look at the four letters in the row and circle the uppercase letter that matches the lowercase letter "d."

Direcciones: La letra minúscula "d" está en la primera columna. Mire las cuatro letras en la fila y encierre en un círculo la letra mayúscula que coincida con la letra minúscula "d".

d	B	Q	(D)	F
d	K	(D)	P	B
d	B	T	(D)	K
d	(D)	F	B	P

Answer Key

Name: _____ Date: ___/___/_____ Score: _____

Appendix 4.0

Letter Recognition D/d

Uppercase and Lowercase Letter

✓ Lesson Check Point

Directions: Read each target word. Read the words in the row and circle the word that begins with a different letter.

Direcciones: Lee cada palabra objetivo. Lee las palabras en la fila y encierre en un círculo la palabra que comienza con una letra diferente.

Target Words				
1. dad	day	(box)	drive	duck
2. deep	(pull)	drum	dove	dull
3. dwell	doll	dawn	dock	(peace)
4. dryer	do	dense	(queen)	dash
5. drink	(both)	den	down	deer

Directions: Read the words in the four boxes. Circle two words that start with the uppercase and lowercase letter "d."

Direcciones: Lee las palabras en los cuatro recuadros. Encierra en un círculo dos palabras que comiencen con la letra "d" mayúscula y minúscula.

(date)	late		(Ditch)	Queen		Bell	Quite
open	(Draw)		(dock)	boat		(Deal)	(doll)

Quick	(dream)		Back	(dome)		Race	(drive)
quack	(Dawn)		belt	(Drip)		(Dog)	Quill

Learn To Read English With Directions In Spanish   257   Copyrighted Material

Classwork

 Name: _____   Date: ___/___/_____   Score: _____

Appendix 5.0

Introduction of the Letter E/e

✓ **Lesson Check Point**

 Directions: Circle the correct letter "e" pair: uppercase and lowercase letters.
Direcciones: Encierra en un círculo el par correcto de letras "e": letras mayúsculas y minúsculas.

| eF | Ex | fE | (eE) | Ae |

 Directions: The uppercase letter "E" is in the first column. Look at the four letters in the row and circle the lowercase letter that matches the uppercase letter "E."
Direcciones: La letra mayúscula "E" está en la primera columna. Mire las cuatro letras en la fila y encierre en un círculo la letra minúscula que coincida con la letra mayúscula "E".

E	r	(e)	f	a
E	c	a	w	(e)
E	(e)	c	x	r
E	z	s	(e)	a

 Directions: The lowercase letter "e" is in the first column. Look at the four letters in the row and circle the uppercase letter that matches the lowercase letter "e."
Direcciones: La letra minúscula "e" está en la primera columna. Mire las cuatro letras en la fila y encierre en un círculo la letra mayúscula que coincida con la letra minúscula "e".

e	D	(E)	R	F
e	G	H	T	(E)
e	(E)	F	V	D
e	F	(E)	S	X

Name: _____ Date: ___/___/_____ Score: _____

Answer Key

Appendix 6.0

Introduction of the Letter F/f

✓ **Lesson Check Point**

 Directions: Circle the correct letter "f" pair: uppercase and lowercase letters.

Direcciones: Encierra en un círculo el par correcto de letras "f": letras mayúsculas y minúsculas.

    fE   Fh   (fF)   Ef   Tf

 Directions: The uppercase letter "F" is in the first column. Look at the four letters in the row and circle the lowercase letter that matches the uppercase letter "F."

Direcciones: La letra mayúscula "F" está en la primera columna. Mire las cuatro letras en la fila y encierre en un círculo la letra minúscula que coincida con la letra mayúscula "F".

F	l	t	k	(f)
F	j	l	(f)	m
F	t	(f)	b	h
F	(f)	l	t	h

 Directions: The lowercase letter "f" is in the first column. Look at the four letters in the row and circle the uppercase letter that matches the lowercase letter "f."

Direcciones: La letra minúscula "f" está en la primera columna. Mire las cuatro letras en la fila y encierre en un círculo la letra mayúscula que coincida con la letra minúscula "f".

f	(F)	E	K	H
f	L	(F)	J	E
f	E	K	H	(F)
f	H	(F)	D	B

Classwork

 Name: _____ Date: ___/___/_____ Score: _____

Appendix 6.0

Letter Recognition F/f

Uppercase and Lowercase Letter

✓ Lesson Check Point

 Directions: Read each target word. Read the words in the row and circle the word that begins with a different letter.

Direcciones: Lee cada palabra objetivo. Lee las palabras en la fila y encierre en un círculo la palabra que comienza con una letra diferente.

Target Words				
1. face	force	fault	(house)	form
2. fire	(pizza)	fizz	friend	flow
3. fork	frisk	(quiet)	fourth	fall
4. flirt	(love)	from	fast	fur
5. full	fright	flash	firm	(boys)

 Directions: Read the words in the four boxes. Circle two words that start with the uppercase and lowercase letter "f."

Direcciones: Lee las palabras en los cuatro recuadros. Encierra en un círculo dos palabras que comiencen con la letra "f" mayúscula y minúscula.

(Field)	(flake)
Years	take

both	(Fig)
(fond)	Hours

(fame)	teach
(Fist)	Laugh

book	Drip
(fight)	(Few)

(Flank)	tea
Pup	(fair)

happens	(fee)
Dreams	(Float)

Learn To Read English With Directions In Spanish

Answer Key

 Name: _____ Date: ___/___/_____ Score: _____

Appendix 7.0

Introduction of the Letter G/g

✓ **Lesson Check Point**

 Directions: Circle the correct letter "g" pair: uppercase and lowercase letters.
Direcciones: Encierra en un círculo el par correcto de letras "g": letras mayúsculas y minúsculas.

yG   Gj   gJ   (Gg)   gO

 Directions: The uppercase letter "G" is in the first column. Look at the four letters in the row and circle the lowercase letter that matches the uppercase letter "G."
Direcciones: La letra mayúscula "G" está en la primera columna. Mire las cuatro letras en la fila y encierre en un círculo la letra minúscula que coincida con la letra mayúscula "G".

G	p	q	y	(g)
G	j	y	(g)	p
G	(g)	j	y	q
G	j	(g)	q	y

 Directions: The lowercase letter "g" is in the first column. Look at the four letters in the row and circle the uppercase letter that matches the lowercase letter "g."
Direcciones: La letra minúscula "g" está en la primera columna. Mire las cuatro letras en la fila y encierre en un círculo la letra mayúscula que coincida con la letra minúscula "g".

g	Q	O	J	(G)
g	U	(G)	O	J
g	Q	K	C	(G)
g	(G)	Q	P	O

Classwork

Name: _____ Date: ___/___/_____ Score: _____

Appendix 7.0

Letter Recognition G/g

Uppercase and Lowercase Letter

✓ Lesson Check Point

Directions: Read each target word. Read the words in the row and circle the word that begins with a different letter.

Direcciones: Lee cada palabra objetivo. Lee las palabras en la fila y encierre en un círculo la palabra que comienza con una letra diferente.

Target Words				
1. gel	guest	garb	(jeep)	gown
2. grant	(pet)	goal	guard	gulp
3. game	grief	grant	(queen)	go
4. goat	glove	(ball)	glaze	grown
5. gold	(jump)	glide	gray	ghost

Directions: Read the words in the four boxes. Circle two words that start with the uppercase and lowercase letter "g."

Direcciones: Lee las palabras en los cuatro recuadros. Encierra en un círculo dos palabras que comiencen con la letra "g" mayúscula y minúscula.

(gold)	open		(ground)	Down		Once	June
Queen	(Greece)		(Gulf)	jump		(Graph)	(game)

Ooze	(Gone)		year	(Grub)		(Glee)	(gram)
(greed)	jeep		Dock	(glare)		joke	Day

Learn To Read English With Directions In Spanish

Answer Key

Name: _____ Date: ___/___/_____ Score: _____

Appendix 8.0

Introduction of the Letter H/h

✓ Lesson Check Point

Directions: Circle the correct letter "h" pair: uppercase and lowercase letters.
Direcciones: Encierra en un círculo el par correcto de letras "h": letras mayúsculas y minúsculas.

Hf   (hH)   Ht   hB   Hb

Directions: The uppercase letter "H" is in the first column. Look at the four letters in the row and circle the lowercase letter that matches the uppercase letter "H."
Direcciones: La letra mayúscula "H" está en la primera columna. Mire las cuatro letras en la fila y encierre en un círculo la letra minúscula que coincida con la letra mayúscula "H".

H	(h)	f	t	b
H	m	(h)	f	t
H	l	k	(h)	f
H	b	t	d	(h)

Directions: The lowercase letter "h" is in the first column. Look at the four letters in the row and circle the uppercase letter that matches the lowercase letter "h."
Direcciones: La letra minúscula "h" está en la primera columna. Mire las cuatro letras en la fila y encierre en un círculo la letra mayúscula que coincida con la letra minúscula "h".

h	T	F	U	(H)
h	(H)	J	F	M
h	E	M	C	(H)
h	D	(H)	B	T

Learn To Read English With Directions In Spanish

Classwork

Name: _____ Date: ___/___/_____ Score: _____

Appendix 8.0

Letter Recognition H/h

Uppercase and Lowercase Letter

✓ Lesson Check Point

Directions: Read each target word. Read the words in the row and circle the word that begins with a different letter.

Direcciones: Lee cada palabra objetivo. Lee las palabras en la fila y encierre en un círculo la palabra que comienza con una letra diferente.

Target Words				
1. home	hat	(land)	heart	hill
2. head	horse	heat	hulk	(boat)
3. hatch	heel	(down)	harm	here
4. heir	hold	high	host	(love)
5. hint	half	hitch	(team)	hemp

Directions: Read the words in the four boxes. Circle two words that start with the uppercase and lowercase letter "h."

Direcciones: Lee las palabras en los cuatro recuadros. Encierra en un círculo dos palabras que comiencen con la letra "h" mayúscula y minúscula.

tune	love
(help)	(Hold)

(Hole)	bless
pole	(hiss)

flame	(Hint)
blink	(hence)

(hook)	(Heel)
trees	peel

(Hit)	kind
(hood)	look

dress	(hope)
(Here)	from

Name: _____ Date: ___/___/_____ Score: _____

Appendix 9.0

Introduction of the Letter I/i

✓ **Lesson Check Point**

 Directions: Circle the correct letter "i" pair: uppercase and lowercase letters.
Direcciones: Encierra en un círculo el par correcto de letras "i": letras mayúsculas y minúsculas.

    Ji   Ti   (Ii)   jI   Il

 Directions: The uppercase letter "I" is in the first column. Look at the four letters in the row and circle the lowercase letter that matches the uppercase letter "I."
Direcciones: La letra mayúscula "I" está en la primera columna. Mire las cuatro letras en la fila y encierre en un círculo la letra minúscula que coincida con la letra mayúscula "I".

I	j	(i)	t	u
I	q	g	j	(i)
I	(i)	t	g	l
I	l	t	(i)	h

 Directions: The lowercase letter "i" is in the first column. Look at the four letters in the row and circle the uppercase letter that matches the lowercase letter "i."
Direcciones: La letra minúscula "i" está en la primera columna. Mire las cuatro letras en la fila y encierre en un círculo la letra mayúscula que coincida con la letra minúscula "i".

i	(I)	T	J	L
i	K	G	H	(I)
i	Y	L	(I)	T
i	J	(I)	Y	K

Classwork

 Name: _____ Date:___/___/_____ Score:_____

Appendix 10.0

Introduction of the Letter J/j

✓ **Lesson Check Point**

 Directions: Circle the correct letter "j" pair: uppercase and lowercase letters.
Direcciones: Encierra en un círculo el par correcto de letras "j": letras mayúsculas y minúsculas.

    Gj   Ji   (jJ)   Jl   Pj

 Directions: The uppercase letter "J" is in the first column. Look at the four letters in the row and circle the lowercase letter that matches the uppercase letter "J."
Direcciones: La letra mayúscula "J" está en la primera columna. Mire las cuatro letras en la fila y encierre en un círculo la letra minúscula que coincida con la letra mayúscula "J".

J	p	(j)	n	q
J	(j)	q	y	k
J	b	c	(j)	v
J	y	h	c	(j)

 Directions: The lowercase letter "j" is in the first column. Look at the four letters in the row and circle the uppercase letter that matches the lowercase letter "j."
Direcciones: La letra minúscula "j" está en la primera columna. Mire las cuatro letras en la fila y encierre en un círculo la letra mayúscula que coincida con la letra minúscula "j".

j	B	Q	(J)	G
j	G	V	F	(J)
j	(J)	U	C	O
j	Q	H	(J)	T

Answer Key

 Name: _____ Date: ___/___/_____ Score: _____

Appendix 10.0

Letter Recognition J/j

Uppercase and Lowercase Letter

✓ Lesson Check Point

 Directions: Read each target word. Read the words in the row and circle the word that begins with a different letter.

Direcciones: Lee cada palabra objetivo. Lee las palabras en la fila y encierre en un círculo la palabra que comienza con una letra diferente.

Target Words					
1. jaw	just	(house)	Jim	jumbo	
2. jolt	(bunny)	jelly	juice	joy	
3. junk	job	jam	(yearly)	jump	
4. jet	(giggles)	joke	June	joint	
5. just	jigsaw	(puppy)	journal	Jack	

 Directions: Read the words in the four boxes. Circle two words that start with the uppercase and lowercase letter "j."

Direcciones: Lee las palabras en los cuatro recuadros. Encierra en un círculo dos palabras que comiencen con la letra "j" mayúscula y minúscula.

quest	(journey)
yarn	(Join)

(Jacket)	boat
gold	(just)

pie	you
(juicy)	(Jelly)

(Jumbo)	(jail)
good	yes

(junk)	great
(Job)	queen

youth	(Jungle)
(jealous)	guest

Learn To Read English With Directions In Spanish

Classwork

 Name: _____ Date:___/___/_____ Score:_____

Appendix 11.0

Introduction of the Letter K/k

✓ Lesson Check Point

 Directions: Circle the correct letter "k" pair: uppercase and lowercase letters.
Direcciones: Encierra en un círculo el par correcto de letras "k": letras mayúsculas y minúsculas.

Bk   (Kk)   kL   Mk   Kl

 Directions: The uppercase letter "K" is in the first column. Look at the four letters in the row and circle the lowercase letter that matches the uppercase letter "K."
Direcciones: La letra mayúscula "K" está en la primera columna. Mire las cuatro letras en la fila y encierre en un círculo la letra minúscula que coincida con la letra mayúscula "K".

K	p	h	(k)	q
K	(k)	f	b	l
K	f	b	d	(k)
K	h	(k)	p	l

 Directions: The lowercase letter "k" is in the first column. Look at the four letters in the row and circle the uppercase letter that matches the lowercase letter "k."
Direcciones: La letra minúscula "k" está en la primera columna. Mire las cuatro letras en la fila y encierre en un círculo la letra mayúscula que coincida con la letra minúscula "k".

k	B	(K)	N	L
k	(K)	P	L	B
k	B	X	(K)	C
k	P	G	L	(K)

Learn To Read English With Directions In Spanish   Copyrighted Material

Answer Key

 Name: _____ Date:___/__/____ Score:_____

Appendix 11.0

Letter Recognition K/k

Uppercase and Lowercase Letter

✓ **Lesson Check Point**

 Directions: Read each target word. Read the words in the row and circle the word that begins with a different letter.

Direcciones: Lee cada palabra objetivo. Lee las palabras en la fila y encierre en un círculo la palabra que comienza con una letra diferente.

Target Words				
1. keep	kale	kedge	(heal)	knoll
2. kick	(laugh)	knot	kid	ketch
3. knight	karts	(home)	kept	kick
4. know	kill	(bald)	kind	keel
5. keys	(down)	knock	keg	knob

 Directions: Read the words in the four boxes. Circle two words that start with the uppercase and lowercase letter "k."

Direcciones: Lee las palabras en los cuatro recuadros. Encierra en un círculo dos palabras que comiencen con la letra "k" mayúscula y minúscula.

light	house
(Kale)	(keep)

From	(Keen)
Right	(kick)

(key)	blue
low	(Kept)

(Knock)	Bold
(kid)	laugh

Rose	(kind)
(Knit)	bay

(know)	(Karts)
West	team

Unit K
Appendix 11.0

Classwork

 Name: _____ Date: ___/___/_____ Score: _____

Appendix 12.0

Introduction of the Letter L/l

✓ **Lesson Check Point**

 Directions: Circle the correct letter "l" pair: uppercase and lowercase letters.
Direcciones: Encierra en un círculo el par correcto de letras "l": letras mayúsculas y minúsculas.

    Lb   Kl   (lL)   lH   lJ

 Directions: The uppercase letter "L" is in the first column. Look at the four letters in the row and circle the lowercase letter that matches the uppercase letter "L."
Direcciones: La letra mayúscula "L" está en la primera columna. Mire las cuatro letras en la fila y encierre en un círculo la letra minúscula que coincida con la letra mayúscula "L".

L	h	(l)	f	b
L	(l)	k	y	p
L	f	b	(l)	d
L	h	b	k	(l)

 Directions: The lowercase letter "l" is in the first column. Look at the four letters in the row and circle the uppercase letter that matches the lowercase letter "l."
Direcciones: La letra minúscula "l" está en la primera columna. Mire las cuatro letras en la fila y encierre en un círculo la letra mayúscula que coincida con la letra minúscula "l".

l	B	K	(L)	D
l	H	F	K	(L)
l	(L)	H	C	P
l	D	(L)	V	H

Answer Key

 Name: _____ Date: ___/___/_____ Score: _____

Appendix 12.0

Letter Recognition L/l

Uppercase and Lowercase Letter

✓ Lesson Check Point

 Directions: Read each target word. Read the words in the row and circle the word that begins with a different letter.

Direcciones: Lee cada palabra objetivo. Lee las palabras en la fila y encierre en un círculo la palabra que comienza con una letra diferente.

Target Words				
1. love	lace	(home)	low	lent
2. load	(tree)	laugh	lid	loaf
3. last	lip	lease	lapse	(mail)
4. learn	(hope)	lark	least	lungs
5. large	limbs	life	lamps	(boats)

 Directions: Read the words in the four boxes. Circle two words that start with the uppercase and lowercase letter "l."

Direcciones: Lee las palabras en los cuatro recuadros. Encierra en un círculo dos palabras que comiencen con la letra "l" mayúscula y minúscula.

teach	found
(lake)	(Leave)

branch	(League)
touch	(loud)

(leech)	Trees
dreams	(Lamb)

(Lounge)	leash
Bold	keeps

Young	(Lean)
(lame)	drawn

lime	Friends
(Lawn)	deep

Learn To Read English With Directions In Spanish

Classwork

 Name: _____ Date:___/___/_____ Score:_____

Appendix 13.0

Introduction of the Letter M/m

✓ **Lesson Check Point**

 Directions: Circle the correct letter "m" pair: uppercase and lowercase letters.
Direcciones: Encierra en un círculo el par correcto de letras "m": letras mayúsculas y minúsculas.

| Mn | Nm | Um | (Mm) | Mw |

 Directions: The uppercase letter "M" is in the first column. Look at the four letters in the row and circle the lowercase letter that matches the uppercase letter "M."
Direcciones: La letra mayúscula "M" está en la primera columna. Mire las cuatro letras en la fila y encierre en un círculo la letra minúscula que coincida con la letra mayúscula "M".

M	(m)	n	v	w
M	v	(m)	w	s
M	n	x	p	(m)
M	(m)	v	n	j

 Directions: The lowercase letter "m" is in the first column. Look at the four letters in the row and circle the uppercase letter that matches the lowercase letter "m."
Direcciones: La letra minúscula "m" está en la primera columna. Mire las cuatro letras en la fila y encierre en un círculo la letra mayúscula que coincida con la letra minúscula "m".

m	N	V	Z	(M)
m	K	(M)	N	U
m	W	V	(M)	X
m	N	(M)	V	W

Answer Key

Name: _____ Date: ___/___/_____ Score: _____

Appendix 13.0

Letter Recognition M/m

Uppercase and Lowercase Letter

✓ Lesson Check Point

Directions: Read each target word. Read the words in the row and circle the word that begins with a different letter.

Direcciones: Lee cada palabra objetivo. Lee las palabras en la fila y encierre en un círculo la palabra que comienza con una letra diferente.

Target Words				
1. maid	(nose)	mud	mock	mince
2. moon	make	mixed	(used)	mouth
3. mint	(went)	moist	map	musk
4. meal	meat	(need)	mole	Maine
5. must	mix	mail	moan	(under)

Directions: Read the words in the four boxes. Circle two words that start with the uppercase and lowercase letter "m."

Direcciones: Lee las palabras en los cuatro recuadros. Encierra en un círculo dos palabras que comiencen con la letra "m" mayúscula y minúscula.

none	(Made)		nod	vase		night	(Mouse)
wind	(mood)		(Miss)	(mean)		(might)	wage

(mold)	Much		(mild)	noise		(mumps)	voice
Whose	Noun		watch	(Mane)		(Moat)	nail

Learn To Read English With Directions In Spanish

Classwork

 Name: _____ Date: ___/___/_____ Score: _____

Appendix 14.0

Introduction of the Letter N/n

✓ **Lesson Check Point**

 Directions: Circle the correct letter "n" pair: uppercase and lowercase letters.
Direcciones: Encierra en un círculo el par correcto de letras "n": letras mayúsculas y minúsculas.

nM   (nN)   wN   Nu   Wn

 Directions: The uppercase letter "N" is in the first column. Look at the four letters in the row and circle the lowercase letter that matches the uppercase letter "N."
Direcciones: La letra mayúscula "N" está en la primera columna. Mire las cuatro letras en la fila y encierre en un círculo la letra minúscula que coincida con la letra mayúscula "N".

N	w	m	(n)	v
N	(n)	v	w	x
N	m	b	(n)	w
N	v	(n)	c	x

 Directions: The lowercase letter "n" is in the first column. Look at the four letters in the row and circle the uppercase letter that matches the lowercase letter "n."
Direcciones: La letra minúscula "n" está en la primera columna. Mire las cuatro letras en la fila y encierre en un círculo la letra mayúscula que coincida con la letra minúscula "n".

n	S	M	(N)	X
n	C	V	M	(N)
n	(N)	M	Z	V
n	M	(N)	X	W

Answer Key

 Name: _____ Date:__/__/_____ Score: _____

Appendix 14.0

Letter Recognition N/n

Uppercase and Lowercase Letter

✓ Lesson Check Point

 Directions: Read each target word. Read the words in the row and circle the word that begins with a different letter.

Direcciones: Lee cada palabra objetivo. Lee las palabras en la fila y encierre en un círculo la palabra que comienza con una letra diferente.

Target Words				
1. neck	nine	news	(milk)	next
2. noon	(used)	neat	notch	niche
3. name	nice	note	(wrong)	nip
4. numb	none	new	nod	(male)
5. notice	nerve	(unto)	nuke	Nile

 Directions: Read the words in the four boxes. Circle two words that start with the uppercase and lowercase letter "n."

Direcciones: Lee las palabras en los cuatro recuadros. Encierra en un círculo dos palabras que comiencen con la letra "n" mayúscula y minúscula.

Mail	van
(Nile)	(nail)

(Noise)	under
wine	(noon)

flag	(Nine)
miss	(nice)

(Noun)	(note)
word	Mouth

night	mind
(Next)	set

(news)	win
united	(Nod)

Learn To Read English With Directions In Spanish

Classwork

 Name: _____ Date:___/___/_____ Score: _____

Appendix 15.0

Introduction of the Letter O/o

✓ **Lesson Check Point**

 Directions: Circle the correct letter "o" pair: uppercase and lowercase letters.
Direcciones: Encierra en un círculo el par correcto de letras "o": letras mayúsculas y minúsculas.

    Oc   (oO)   uO   pO   qO

 Directions: The uppercase letter "O" is in the first column. Look at the four letters in the row and circle the lowercase letter that matches the uppercase letter "O."
Direcciones: La letra mayúscula "O" está en la primera columna. Mire las cuatro letras en la fila y encierre en un círculo la letra minúscula que coincida con la letra mayúscula "O".

O	s	p	g	(o)
O	c	(o)	b	j
O	q	d	c	(o)
O	(o)	g	q	h

 Directions: The lowercase letter "o" is in the first column. Look at the four letters in the row and circle the uppercase letter that matches the lowercase letter "o."
Direcciones: La letra minúscula "o" está en la primera columna. Mire las cuatro letras en la fila y encierre en un círculo la letra mayúscula que coincida con la letra minúscula "o".

o	Q	C	G	(O)
o	(O)	D	U	R
o	C	B	(O)	D
o	G	(O)	C	E

Name: _____ Date: ___/___/_____ Score: _____

Answer Key

Appendix 16.0

Introduction of the Letter P/p

✓ **Lesson Check Point**

 Directions: Circle the correct letter "p" pair: uppercase and lowercase letters.
Direcciones: Encierra en un círculo el par correcto de letras "p": letras mayúsculas y minúsculas.

    Bp   Dp   Pg   Fp

 Directions: The uppercase letter "P" is in the first column. Look at the four letters in the row and circle the lowercase letter that matches the uppercase letter "P."
Direcciones: La letra mayúscula "P" está en la primera columna. Mire las cuatro letras en la fila y encierre en un círculo la letra minúscula que coincida con la letra mayúscula "P".

P	(p)	q	b	d
P	b	f	(p)	q
P	h	(p)	b	f
P	q	d	s	(p)

 Directions: The lowercase letter "p" is in the first column. Look at the four letters in the row and circle the uppercase letter that matches the lowercase letter "p."
Direcciones: La letra minúscula "p" está en la primera columna. Mire las cuatro letras en la fila y encierre en un círculo la letra mayúscula que coincida con la letra minúscula "p".

p	Q	(P)	B	F
p	H	B	D	(P)
p	F	(P)	S	D
p	(P)	F	D	B

Learn To Read English With Directions In Spanish

Classwork

 Name: _____ Date: ___/___/_____ Score: _____

Appendix 16.0

Letter Recognition P/p

Uppercase and Lowercase Letter

✓ **Lesson Check Point**

 Directions: Read each target word. Read the words in the row and circle the word that begins with a different letter.

Direcciones: Lee cada palabra objetivo. Lee las palabras en la fila y encierre en un círculo la palabra que comienza con una letra diferente.

Target Words				
1. pitch	pack	(grow)	pound	purse
2. plots	(bind)	plush	proud	plight
3. peace	plate	page	(quest)	prowl
4. pale	(good)	plant	poor	pull
5. punch	prude	(quick)	pike	pool

 Directions: Read the words in the four boxes. Circle two words that start with the uppercase and lowercase letter "p."

Direcciones: Lee las palabras en los cuatro recuadros. Encierra en un círculo dos palabras que comiencen con la letra "p" mayúscula y minúscula.

(Praise)	quaint
youth	(phase)

(point)	(Prince)
quart	group

grew	(purse)
(Prime)	quiet

(Pink)	quick
(place)	jam

jump	quite
(Paid)	(peace)

young	(peach)
guess	(Port)

Name: _____ Date: ___/___/_____ Score: _____

Answer Key

Appendix 17.0

Introduction of the Letter Q/q

✓ **Lesson Check Point**

 Directions: Circle the correct letter "q" pair: uppercase and lowercase letters.
Direcciones: Encierra en un círculo el par correcto de letras "q": letras mayúsculas y minúsculas.

    Qd   Gq   Oq   (qQ)   Qp

 Directions: The uppercase letter "Q" is in the first column. Look at the four letters in the row and circle the lowercase letter that matches the uppercase letter "Q."
Direcciones: La letra mayúscula "Q" está en la primera columna. Mire las cuatro letras en la fila y encierre en un círculo la letra minúscula que coincida con la letra mayúscula "Q".

Q	g	h	p	**(q)**
Q	**(q)**	j	y	b
Q	p	**(q)**	b	d
Q	y	p	**(q)**	b

 Directions: The lowercase letter "q" is in the first column. Look at the four letters in the row and circle the uppercase letter that matches the lowercase letter "q."
Direcciones: La letra minúscula "q" está en la primera columna. Mire las cuatro letras en la fila y encierre en un círculo la letra mayúscula que coincida con la letra minúscula "q".

q	D	O	**(Q)**	P
q	**(Q)**	A	D	O
q	O	C	G	**(Q)**
q	G	**(Q)**	C	O

Learn To Read English With Directions In Spanish

Classwork

Name: _____ Date: ___/___/_____ Score: _____

Appendix 17.0

Letter Recognition Q/q

Uppercase and Lowercase Letter

✓ **Lesson Check Point**

Directions: Read each target word. Read the words in the row and circle the word that begins with a different letter.

Direcciones: Lee cada palabra objetivo. Lee las palabras en la fila y encierre en un círculo la palabra que comienza con una letra diferente.

Target Words				
1. quack	quaint	quick	(please)	quiz
2. quilt	(guess)	quip	quire	quote
3. quirt	quirk	(young)	quit	quartz
4. quench	quite	quiet	(jump)	quince
5. quake	quota	quail	quest	(guest)

Directions: Read the words in the four boxes. Circle two words that start with the uppercase and lowercase letter "q."

Direcciones: Lee las palabras en los cuatro recuadros. Encierra en un círculo dos palabras que comiencen con la letra "q" mayúscula y minúscula.

pajamas	(Qualm)
(quality)	Orchid

jacket	peanut
(quarrel)	(Quarter)

joint	(quicken)
oxygen	(Quartz)

(quest)	jumper
(Quiver)	yours

(quote)	(Quotient)
picture	Ocean

(quick)	painter
young	(Quebec)

Answer Key

 Name: _____ Date: ___/___/_____ Score: _____

Appendix 18.0

Introduction of the Letter R/r

✓ Lesson Check Point

 Directions: Circle the correct letter "r" pair: uppercase and lowercase letters.
Direcciones: Encierra en un círculo el par correcto de letras "r": letras mayúsculas y minúsculas.

Rz   (rR)   jR   rE   Fr

 Directions: The uppercase letter "R" is in the first column. Look at the four letters in the row and circle the lowercase letter that matches the uppercase letter "R."
Direcciones: La letra mayúscula "R" está en la primera columna. Mire las cuatro letras en la fila y encierre en un círculo la letra minúscula que coincida con la letra mayúscula "R".

R	x	(r)	v	u
R	(r)	x	z	c
R	b	h	c	(r)
R	n	z	(r)	s

 Directions: The lowercase letter "r" is in the first column. Look at the four letters in the row and circle the uppercase letter that matches the lowercase letter "r."
Direcciones: La letra minúscula "r" está en la primera columna. Mire las cuatro letras en la fila y encierre en un círculo la letra mayúscula que coincida con la letra minúscula "r".

r	Y	U	(R)	Z
r	(R)	H	C	M
r	U	N	F	(R)
r	M	(R)	D	O

Learn To Read English With Directions In Spanish

Classwork

Name: _____ Date: ___/___/_____ Score: _____

Appendix 18.0

Letter Recognition R/r

Uppercase and Lowercase Letter

✓ Lesson Check Point

Directions: Read each target word. Read the words in the row and circle the word that begins with a different letter.

Direcciones: Lee cada palabra objetivo. Lee las palabras en la fila y encierre en un círculo la palabra que comienza con una letra diferente.

Target Words				
1. race	roach	reel	(match)	rains
2. rode	(nurse)	range	roam	rule
3. rinse	ranch	(mouse)	robe	reed
4. raise	rend	rock	rank	(cease)
5. ripping	(cards)	read	rack	rope

Directions: Read the words in the four boxes. Circle two words that start with the uppercase and lowercase letter "r."

Direcciones: Lee las palabras en los cuatro recuadros. Encierra en un círculo dos palabras que comiencen con la letra "r" mayúscula y minúscula.

(rate)	moose
Piece	(Rice)

(rob)	(Rave)
nose	mother

Part	(Roar)
mouse	(rhythm)

Pat	maple
(roost)	(Rat)

team	Price
(rope)	(Rich)

dream	(Room)
(ramp)	neck

Answer Key

 Name: _____ Date: ___/___/_____ Score: _____

Appendix 19.0

Introduction of the Letter S/s

✓ **Lesson Check Point**

 Directions: Circle the correct letter "s" pair: uppercase and lowercase letters.
Direcciones: Encierra en un círculo el par correcto de letras "s": letras mayúsculas y minúsculas.

    sA   sB   Zs   Cs   (sS)

 Directions: The uppercase letter "S" is in the first column. Look at the four letters in the row and circle the lowercase letter that matches the uppercase letter "S."
Direcciones: La letra mayúscula "S" está en la primera columna. Mire las cuatro letras en la fila y encierre en un círculo la letra minúscula que coincida con la letra mayúscula "S".

S	c	o	d	(s)
S	(s)	c	u	o
S	o	a	(s)	c
S	u	(s)	c	o

 Directions: The lowercase letter "s" is in the first column. Look at the four letters in the row and circle the uppercase letter that matches the lowercase letter "s."
Direcciones: La letra minúscula "s" está en la primera columna. Mire las cuatro letras en la fila y encierre en un círculo la letra mayúscula que coincida con la letra minúscula "s".

s	G	(S)	O	C
s	Q	C	U	(S)
s	(S)	U	O	C
s	Z	Q	(S)	V

Classwork

J. Name: _____ Date: ___/___/_____ Score: _____

Appendix 19.0

Letter Recognition S/s

Uppercase and Lowercase Letter

✓ **Lesson Check Point**

Directions: Read each target word. Read the words in the row and circle the word that begins with a different letter.

Direcciones: Lee cada palabra objetivo. Lee las palabras en la fila y encierre en un círculo la palabra que comienza con una letra diferente.

Target Words				
1. smart	soft	(chart)	smith	shop
2. sail	(opens)	saw	skit	soil
3. skill	smooth	shoot	seat	(van)
4. source	soup	side	(zero)	sight
5. sky	snooze	(cake)	short	smell

Directions: Read the words in the four boxes. Circle two words that start with the uppercase and lowercase letter "s."

Direcciones: Lee las palabras en los cuatro recuadros. Encierra en un círculo dos palabras que comiencen con la letra "s" mayúscula y minúscula.

zero	(Six)
(shore)	cone

(Shield)	cup
(sink)	zoo

(shame)	(Said)
zap	clean

Cross	(slurp)
(Shine)	win

none	child
(soap)	(Snail)

camp	(song)
zebra	(Shake)

Answer Key

 Name: _____ Date: ___/___/_____ Score: _____

Appendix 20.0

Introduction of the Letter T/t

✓ **Lesson Check Point**

 Directions: Circle the correct letter "t" pair: uppercase and lowercase letters.
Direcciones: Encierra en un círculo el par correcto de letras "t": letras mayúsculas y minúsculas.

    Tf   tE   (Tt)   tF   iT

 Directions: The uppercase letter "T" is in the first column. Look at the four letters in the row and circle the lowercase letter that matches the uppercase letter "T."
Direcciones: La letra mayúscula "T" está en la primera columna. Mire las cuatro letras en la fila y encierre en un círculo la letra minúscula que coincida con la letra mayúscula "T".

T	(t)	h	f	d
T	b	f	(t)	h
T	l	(t)	b	f
T	h	d	b	(t)

 Directions: The lowercase letter "t" is in the first column. Look at the four letters in the row and circle the uppercase letter that matches the lowercase letter "t."
Direcciones: La letra minúscula "t" está en la primera columna. Mire las cuatro letras en la fila y encierre en un círculo la letra mayúscula que coincida con la letra minúscula "t".

t	F	(T)	H	E
t	(T)	B	E	F
t	H	B	(T)	Y
t	R	F	S	(T)

Learn To Read English With Directions In Spanish

Classwork

 Name: _____ Date: ___/___/_____ Score: _____

Appendix 20.0

Letter Recognition T/t

Uppercase and Lowercase Letter

✓ **Lesson Check Point**

 Directions: Read each target word. Read the words in the row and circle the word that begins with a different letter.

Direcciones: Lee cada palabra objetivo. Lee las palabras en la fila y encierre en un círculo la palabra que comienza con una letra diferente.

Target Words				
1. twin	that	(day)	trust	talk
2. tooth	tight	team	top	(face)
3. tempt	(key)	time	trash	tweed
4. torch	though	their	temp	(live)
5. treat	thick	twice	(herd)	thief

 Directions: Read the words in the four boxes. Circle two words that start with the uppercase and lowercase letter "t."

Direcciones: Lee las palabras en los cuatro recuadros. Encierra en un círculo dos palabras que comiencen con la letra "t" mayúscula y minúscula.

Floor	(Trade)
(tear)	draw

horses	(toil)
lunch	(Track)

(tease)	keep
(Toll)	load

(Text)	Pie
(troop)	Joy

Egg	lone
(theme)	(Trip)

(taste)	pants
beach	(Think)

 Name: _____ Date: ___/___/_____ Score: _____

Answer Key

Appendix 21.0

Introduction of the Letter U/u

✓ **Lesson Check Point**

 Directions: Circle the correct letter "u" pair: uppercase and lowercase letters.
Direcciones: Encierra en un círculo el par correcto de letras "u": letras mayúsculas y minúsculas.

(uU)   Yu   Gu   Uv   Au

 Directions: The uppercase letter "U" is in the first column. Look at the four letters in the row and circle the lowercase letter that matches the uppercase letter "U."
Direcciones: La letra mayúscula "U" está en la primera columna. Mire las cuatro letras en la fila y encierre en un círculo la letra minúscula que coincida con la letra mayúscula "U".

U	(u)	v	c	y
U	h	x	(u)	z
U	j	b	v	(u)
U	s	(u)	g	a

 Directions: The lowercase letter "u" is in the first column. Look at the four letters in the row and circle the uppercase letter that matches the lowercase letter "u."
Direcciones: La letra minúscula "u" está en la primera columna. Mire las cuatro letras en la fila y encierre en un círculo la letra mayúscula que coincida con la letra minúscula "u".

u	Y	T	(U)	Z
u	(U)	B	N	Y
u	C	Q	(U)	D
u	J	V	G	(U)

Learn To Read English With Directions In Spanish

Classwork

 Name: _____ Date: ___/___/_____ Score: _____

Appendix 22.0

Introduction of the Letter V/v

✓ **Lesson Check Point**

 Directions: Circle the correct letter "v" pair: uppercase and lowercase letters.
Direcciones: Encierra en un círculo el par correcto de letras "v": letras mayúsculas y minúsculas.

    vW   Vu   Cv   (Vv)   Wv

 Directions: The uppercase letter "V" is in the first column. Look at the four letters in the row and circle the lowercase letter that matches the uppercase letter "V."
Direcciones: La letra mayúscula "V" está en la primera columna. Mire las cuatro letras en la fila y encierre en un círculo la letra minúscula que coincida con la letra mayúscula "V".

V	w	(v)	x	y
V	y	w	n	(v)
V	(v)	x	y	u
V	x	z	(v)	w

 Directions: The lowercase letter "v" is in the first column. Look at the four letters in the row and circle the uppercase letter that matches the lowercase letter "v."
Direcciones: La letra minúscula "v" está en la primera columna. Mire las cuatro letras en la fila y encierre en un círculo la letra mayúscula que coincida con la letra minúscula "v".

v	X	Z	(V)	Y
v	Y	W	X	(V)
v	(V)	Y	N	M
v	W	(V)	X	C

Answer Key

Name: _____ Date: ___/___/_____ Score: _____

Appendix 22.0

Letter Recognition V/v

Uppercase and Lowercase Letter

✓ **Lesson Check Point**

Directions: Read each target word. Read the words in the row and circle the word that begins with a different letter.

Direcciones: Lee cada palabra objetivo. Lee las palabras en la fila y encierre en un círculo la palabra que comienza con una letra diferente.

Target Words				
1. voice	volt	(wool)	vase	verse
2. verb	vest	vow	vogue	(used)
3. vain	(west)	veil	vault	vine
4. view	void	(mouse)	versed	vile
5. vote	vex	voiced	(wig)	vein

Directions: Read the words in the four boxes. Circle two words that start with the uppercase and lowercase letter "v."

Direcciones: Lee las palabras en los cuatro recuadros. Encierra en un círculo dos palabras que comiencen con la letra "v" mayúscula y minúscula.

skill	(vouch)
(Vamp)	Wrote

(vague)	(Van)
rose	name

whiz	(valve)
mail	(Vice)

(Vent)	cove
Weep	(verge)

(vane)	(Very)
must	goat

(Visit)	card
(vet)	West

Classwork

 Name: _____ Date: ___/___/_____ Score: _____

Appendix 23.0

Introduction of the Letter W/w

✓ Lesson Check Point

 Directions: Circle the correct letter "w" pair: uppercase and lowercase letters.
Direcciones: Encierra en un círculo el par correcto de letras "w": letras mayúsculas y minúsculas.

wU　　　(Ww)　　　Xw　　　Vw　　　Wv

 Directions: The uppercase letter "W" is in the first column. Look at the four letters in the row and circle the lowercase letter that matches the uppercase letter "W."
Direcciones: La letra mayúscula "W" está en la primera columna. Mire las cuatro letras en la fila y encierre en un círculo la letra minúscula que coincida con la letra mayúscula "W".

W	x	(w)	v	z
W	v	z	(w)	y
W	(w)	y	v	m
W	n	v	y	(w)

 Directions: The lowercase letter "w" is in the first column. Look at the four letters in the row and circle the uppercase letter that matches the lowercase letter "w."
Direcciones: La letra minúscula "w" está en la primera columna. Mire las cuatro letras en la fila y encierre en un círculo la letra mayúscula que coincida con la letra minúscula "w".

w	V	(W)	Y	M
w	X	Y	V	(W)
w	(W)	V	X	M
w	Y	F	(W)	X

Learn To Read English With Directions In Spanish

Answer Key

 Name: _____ Date:___/___/_____ Score:_____

Appendix 23.0

Letter Recognition W/w

Uppercase and Lowercase Letter

✓ Lesson Check Point

 Directions: Read each target word. Read the words in the row and circle the word that begins with a different letter.
Direcciones: Lee cada palabra objetivo. Lee las palabras en la fila y encierre en un círculo la palabra que comienza con una letra diferente.

Target Words				
1. wind	west	(vacuum)	whole	waste
2. wrote	(night)	wink	wolf	wish
3. which	wrap	whom	were	(vessel)
4. wept	whale	(card)	whose	wide
5. wash	wrench	watch	word	(zebra)

 Directions: Read the words in the four boxes. Circle two words that start with the uppercase and lowercase letter "w."
Direcciones: Lee las palabras en los cuatro recuadros. Encierra en un círculo dos palabras que comiencen con la letra "w" mayúscula y minúscula.

crow	(Work)	(wheat)	nerve	Village	cars
visitor	(wave)	zoom	(Wax)	(wild)	(Wheel)

(will)	x-rays	(Worth)	when	corn	(ways)
(Would)	Nile	violet	Never	(Wine)	vintage

Learn To Read English With Directions In Spanish   291   Copyrighted Material

Classwork

 Name: _____ Date: ___/___/_____ Score: _____

Appendix 24.0

Introduction of the Letter X/x

✓ Lesson Check Point

 Directions: Circle the correct letter "x" pair: uppercase and lowercase letters.
Direcciones: Encierra en un círculo el par correcto de letras "x": letras mayúsculas y minúsculas.

    Xw   xY   (xX)   Sx   Kx

 Directions: The uppercase letter "X" is in the first column. Look at the four letters in the row and circle the lowercase letter that matches the uppercase letter "X."
Direcciones: La letra mayúscula "X" está en la primera columna. Mire las cuatro letras en la fila y encierre en un círculo la letra minúscula que coincida con la letra mayúscula "X".

X	k	(x)	y	z
X	v	w	(x)	m
X	(x)	z	e	s
X	v	z	h	(x)

 Directions: The lowercase letter "x" is in the first column. Look at the four letters in the row and circle the uppercase letter that matches the lowercase letter "x."
Direcciones: La letra minúscula "x" está en la primera columna. Mire las cuatro letras en la fila y encierre en un círculo la letra mayúscula que coincida con la letra minúscula "x".

x	K	(X)	Z	M
x	W	K	V	(X)
x	(X)	M	K	Y
x	V	Y	(X)	Z

Answer Key

Name: _____ Date: ___/___/_____ Score: _____

Appendix 24.0

Letter Recognition X/x

Uppercase and Lowercase Letter

✓ Lesson Check Point

Directions: Read each target word. Read the words in the row and circle the word that does not contain a letter "x."

Direcciones: Lee cada palabra objetivo. Lee las palabras en la fila y encierre en un círculo la palabra que no contiene una letra "x".

Target Words				
1. fix	wax	excite	(sing)	flax
2. box	taxes	expo	foxes	(cold)
3. flex	ox	(night)	taxi	exalt
4. exam	toxin	axle	sixty	(loving)
5. text	vex	(young)	next	coax

Directions: Read the words in the four boxes. Circle two words that start with the uppercase and lowercase letter "x."

Direcciones: Lee las palabras en los cuatro recuadros. Encierra en un círculo dos palabras que comiencen con la letra "x" mayúscula y minúscula.

vogue	(xylems)
(Xanthine)	kid

youth	voiced
(xanthone)	(Xenograft)

kept	(Xanthous)
one	(x-axis)

(xylem)	voiced
(Xerox)	keys

(Xyster)	know
yes	(xylan)

(Xylene)	xylose
moose	view

Learn To Read English With Directions In Spanish

Classwork

 Name: _____ Date: ___/___/_____ Score: _____

Appendix 25.0

Introduction of the Letter Y/y

✓ **Lesson Check Point**

 Directions: Circle the correct letter "y" pair: uppercase and lowercase letters.
Direcciones: Encierra en un círculo el par correcto de letras "y": letras mayúsculas y minúsculas.

    Yx   (yY)   Yz   Ky   Vy

 Directions: The uppercase letter "Y" is in the first column. Look at the four letters in the row and circle the lowercase letter that matches the uppercase letter "Y."
Direcciones: La letra mayúscula "Y" está en la primera columna. Mire las cuatro letras en la fila y encierre en un círculo la letra minúscula que coincida con la letra mayúscula "Y".

Y	v	(y)	b	x
Y	x	z	(y)	u
Y	(y)	x	z	w
Y	x	z	v	(y)

 Directions: The lowercase letter "y" is in the first column. Look at the four letters in the row and circle the uppercase letter that matches the lowercase letter "y."
Direcciones: La letra minúscula "y" está en la primera columna. Mire las cuatro letras en la fila y encierre en un círculo la letra mayúscula que coincida con la letra minúscula "y".

y	V	X	Z	(Y)
y	(Y)	V	X	Z
y	W	(Y)	X	M
y	U	M	(Y)	X

Learn To Read English With Directions In Spanish

Answer Key

Name: _____ Date: ___/___/_____ Score: _____

Appendix 25.0

Letter Recognition Y/y

Uppercase and Lowercase Letter

✓ Lesson Check Point

Directions: Read each target word. Read the words in the row and circle the word that begins with a different letter.
Direcciones: Lee cada palabra objetivo. Lee las palabras en la fila y encierre en un círculo la palabra que comienza con una letra diferente.

Target Words				
1. yield	(grown)	yogurt	yam	yeast
2. yacht	(jeep)	yolk	yucca	yawn
3. yuppie	yodel	young	(quick)	your
4. yellow	yelp	(please)	yummy	yoga
5. yourself	yank	yes	yo-yo	(game)

Directions: Read the words in the four boxes. Circle two words that start with the uppercase and lowercase letter "y."
Direcciones: Lee las palabras en los cuatro recuadros. Encierra en un círculo dos palabras que comiencen con la letra "y" mayúscula y minúscula.

gum	jump
(yelp)	(Youth)

(Yarn)	quill
paint	(yells)

jet	(You)
globe	(yaw)

jog	(yak)
(Year)	grace

(Yet)	(yams)
judge	glow

(yawn)	June
(Yeast)	peach

Learn To Read English With Directions In Spanish   295   Copyrighted Material

Classwork

 Name: _____ Date: ___/___/_____ Score: _____

Appendix 26.0

Introduction of the Letter Z/z

✓ **Lesson Check Point**

 Directions: Circle the correct letter "z" pair: uppercase and lowercase letters.
Direcciones: Encierra en un círculo el par correcto de letras "z": letras mayúsculas y minúsculas.

(zZ)   Nz   Zn   zM   zA

 Directions: The uppercase letter "Z" is in the first column. Look at the four letters in the row and circle the lowercase letter that matches the uppercase letter "Z."
Direcciones: La letra mayúscula "Z" está en la primera columna. Mire las cuatro letras en la fila y encierre en un círculo la letra minúscula que coincida con la letra mayúscula "Z".

Z	n	x	(z)	t
Z	v	(z)	x	w
Z	m	w	s	(z)
Z	(z)	v	w	n

 Directions: The lowercase letter "z" is in the first column. Look at the four letters in the row and circle the uppercase letter that matches the lowercase letter "z."
Direcciones: La letra minúscula "z" está en la primera columna. Mire las cuatro letras en la fila y encierre en un círculo la letra mayúscula que coincida con la letra minúscula "z".

z	B	V	(Z)	N
z	W	(Z)	X	U
z	(Z)	S	W	V
z	A	N	X	(Z)

Answer Key

 Name: _____   Date: ___/___/_____   Score: _____

Appendix 26.0

Letter Recognition Z/z

Uppercase and Lowercase Letter

✓ Lesson Check Point

 Directions: Read each target word. Read the words in the row and circle the word that begins with a different letter.
Direcciones: Lee cada palabra objetivo. Lee las palabras en la fila y encierre en un círculo la palabra que comienza con una letra diferente.

Target Words				
1. zebu	zap	zebra	(cage)	zoo
2. zones	(seals)	zany	zeal	zest
3. zip	zing	zero	zinc	(flesh)
4. Zhan	zoom	(moon)	ziti	zonal
5. zest	(sung)	zone	zoos	zebra

 Directions: Read the words in the four boxes. Circle two words that start with the uppercase and lowercase letter "z."
Direcciones: Lee las palabras en los cuatro recuadros. Encierra en un círculo dos palabras que comiencen con la letra "z" mayúscula y minúscula.

cents	(Zeta)
(zing)	sea

mix	(zap)
(Zip)	sick

(Zoom)	(zit)
index	wind

(zinc)	remix
(Zipper)	cents

nice	Plant
(ziti)	(Zone)

rest	(Zoo)
eggs	(zoom)

Learn To Read English With Directions In Spanish

Classwork

**Your Next Step:
Learn To Read English Vowels With Directions In Spanish**

www.ingramcontent.com/pod-product-compliance
Lightning Source LLC
Chambersburg PA
CBHW080800300426
44114CB00020B/2777